The Vézelay tympanum

BLUE GUIDE

Burgundy

Ian Ousby

Maps and plans by John Flower

A & C Black
London

WW Norton
New York

First edition 1992

Published by A & C Black (Publishers) Limited
35 Bedford Row, London WC1R 4JH

A CIP catalogue record of this book
is available from the British Library.

ISBN 0–7136–3384–0

Published in the United States of America by
WW Norton and Company, Inc
500 Fifth Avenue, New York, NY 10110

Published simultaneously in Canada by
Penguin Books Canada Limited
2801 John Street, Markham, Ontario, LR3 1B4

ISBN 0–393–30886–3 USA

The author and the publishers have done their best to ensure the accuracy of all the information in Blue Guide Burgundy; they can accept no responsibility for any loss, injury or inconvenience sustained by any traveller as a result of information or advice contained in the guide.

Ian Ousby was educated at Cambridge and Harvard and has taught at universities in both England and America. His publications include *Bloodhounds of Heaven: The Detective in English Fiction from Godwin to Doyle*; with John L. Bradley, *The Correspondence of John Ruskin and Charles Eliot Norton*; *The Cambridge Guide to Literature in English* (editor); *The Englishman's England: Taste, Travel and the Rise of Tourism*; *James Plumptre's Britain: The Journals of a Tourist in the 1790s* (editor); *Blue Guide England* and *Blue Guide Literary Britain and Ireland*.

Printed and bound in Great Britain by
Butler & Tanner Ltd, Frome and London

CONTENTS

Maps and Plans

Building plans

BURGUNDY PAST AND PRESENT

If you head for Marseille and the south coast of France down the Autoroute du Soleil from Paris, roughly the middle third of your journey will take you through what the French know as Bourgogne and the English for centuries have called Burgundy. Or rather, the middle third of your journey will take you through Burgundy as it is now defined by the system of regional administration de Gaulle launched in 1960 to counter the domination of Paris over the rest of France and its economy. The modern region consists of four departments: Côte d'Or with its *préfecture*, or 'county town', at Dijon; Nièvre with its *préfecture* at Nevers; Saône-et-Loire with its *préfecture* at Mâcon; and Yonne with its *préfecture* at Auxerre. At about 31,600 square kilometres (12,200 square miles) their combined area is one and a half times as big as Wales or London and the Home Counties. Dijon, whose population of just under 150,000 makes it by far the largest city, has again assumed its historic role as capital.

Even a brief look at the relief map shows that the region is not a unit of nature. The terrain gives little clue to its outline. True, it lies in that part of France where the headwaters of many rivers make what one historian has called 'a little Mesopotamia'. And true, most of the region is enclosed by the Seine and its tributary the Yonne in the north and north-west, the Loire in the south and the Saône in the east. Yet none of these rivers marks a natural boundary, and not even the Saône has proved a stable political frontier. Instead, they have always been arteries linking Burgundy with the rest of France, Paris and Lyon in particular, and emphasising its rôle as a *lieu de transition* between north and south. So have the hills that punctuate its map as prominently as the rivers, the gentle vineyard-covered slope of the Côte d'Or running northwards towards the Plateau de Langres and the chalky desert of Champagne, the peaks of the Mâconnais and the Charolais anticipating the Beaujolais mountains just over the southern border. Even the Morvan, the great chunk of granite that stands near the centre of Burgundy, proves to be an outlier of the Massif Central beyond its south-western boundary.

Internally, both rivers and hills help divide Burgundy into smaller units. France itself, of course, has never been 'one and indivisible' as the Jacobin slogan would have it, but rather a collection of different provinces which are themselves collections of different little *pays*, often no more than 20 or 30 kilometres across, each with its own distinctive landscape, economy, building style and cheeses and its own pride of place in native hearts. Yet even by French standards of diversity, Burgundy is a remarkable patchwork quilt. Bewildering though it may well be to the stranger, the list of the *pays* that give their names to most of the routes in this book is still not long enough to satisfy the local eye which distinguishes the Haut-Auxois from the Bas-Auxois, and both from the Terre Plaine, or observes the inflections that divide the Mâconnais proper from the Tournugeois, round Tournus, and the Clunisois, round Cluny.

That is not to deny the common features, of course. Though Burgundy's median position between north and south meant that both the *langue d'oc* and the *langue d'oïl* were once spoken, there is now (at least to the foreign ear) a Burgundian accent general to the region, rolling the r's and softening to a double s the x that crops up so frequently in the middle of its placenames (Auxois, Auxerre, Aloxe-Corton). Yet the landscape among which these speakers live ranges from the rolling prairies and woods of the Châtillonnais to the green English-looking field patterns of the Brionnais. It embraces extremes as different as the forested hills of the Morvan and the flat expanses of the Bresse. Wine may be the most famous product of Burgundy's rural economy, but it would be a dull palate that did not register the difference between the reds of the Côte d'Or and those of the Mâconnais, or between the whites of Chablis and Pouilly-sur-Loire. And, besides, you do not need to drive far from any vineyard to enter another *pays* whose soil makes cereals or chickens or Charolais cattle the local staple. The most car-bound tourist still notices how the changes in geology provide building materials as different as the limestone of the Auxois and the brick and timber of the Bresse, and even create roofing styles as different as the polychrome tile patterns which spread like Oriental carpets over the roofs of Dijon and the Côte d' Or and the pantiles which, not so many kilometres further south, announce that Burgundy is getting nearer the Midi.

By and large this guidebook accepts the modern definition of Burgundy and stays inside the boundaries of the present administrative region. Yet the fact that it is not a geographical unit demands a preliminary look at the history which first brought Burgundy into being and then preserved its sense of identity even while territory fluctuated and boundaries expanded or contracted.† Such change has been the very stuff of its history. Dijon and the Côte d'Or have almost always been its heartland, but otherwise Burgundy has sometimes seemed not so much a fixed place as an idea, elusive and portable, travelling across the map of France—and indeed of Europe—in search of realisation.

To find the origin of its name requires a particularly long jump to the Baltic Sea off the south coast of Sweden and to the island of Bornholm, originally Burgundarholm, from *borg*, 'high place', and *holm*, 'island'. It was home of the Burgundiones or Burgundii (whom the French now call Burgondes), or at least their jumping-off point from Scandinavia when climate changes and the decline of the Roman Empire in the West encouraged them to migrate south. A tall people (hence also called the Septipedes) with green eyes and blond hair which they bleached with lime and perfumed with butter, they otherwise bore little resemblance to the popular stereotype of the barbarian hordes then emerging as heirs to Imperial power. Early converts to Arian Christianity, the Burgundiones were eager to reach an accommodation with the Romans. Following the Vandals, they had got as far as the middle Rhine by the early 5C and made their capital at Worms, where their leader was recognised as king by the Roman authorities. The attempt to move westwards in disobedience to Imperial wishes provoked the Romans to unleash Attila the Hun, who inflicted a crushing defeat on the Burgundiones in about 436. Fused with the Frankish story of Siegfried, Brunhild (Brunehaut) and the Ring, the battle passed permanently into the northern European memory via the Icelandic Volsung saga, the Bavarian Nibelungenlied and, eventually, Wagner. In 443 the Romans settled the Burgundiones in Sapaudia (roughly the Savoie and the Vaud) with their capital at Geneva. From here they continued their migration south and west peaceably and without further disaster, acquiring Sequania (Franche-Comté) in 458 and reaching Lyon in 470. By the end of the century they had spread down the Rhône to Arles and Avignon and moved west of the

†For quick reference the chronology of Burgundian history on pages 169–170 lists the main events, with names and dates of the Capetian and Valois dukes.

Saône as far as Dijon. They had established what contemporaries came to call Burgundia—the name first appears in a letter by Theodoric the Ostrogoth in 507—and historians remember as the first kingdom of Burgundy.

Of course, the land west of the Saône already had its own long history. The cave system at Azé and the rock which now overlooks the Pouilly-Fuissé vineyards at Solutré show significant evidence of human use from the Upper Palaeolithic era onwards. By about 30,000 BC the contemporaries of Cro-Magnon man in the Dordogne were using the Solutré rock as a centre for slaughtering the horses which passed its base on their annual migration. The penetration of Greeks into the western Mediterranean and the rise of the Etruscans made Burgundy a *lieu de passage* during the first Iron Age. It became a region of hill settlements commanding trade routes like those which brought tin from Britain over the Alps via the Brenner Pass or down the Saône and the Rhône to Marseille. The Hallstatt Celts who were flourishing about 500 BC on Mont Lassois, a crucial staging post close to the navigable limit of the Seine, have left a vivid relic of their culture in the grave goods known as the Vix treasure, now in the museum at nearby Châtillon. The cosmopolitan origins of the treasure already point to Burgundy's future role as a place where goods, styles and ideas from the different corners of Europe met, mingled and were distributed.

Though the Romans developed this role, their first interest in Burgundy was military. *Lieux de passage* and *lieux de transition* are also commonly battlegrounds, so it was fitting that the Roman conquest of Gaul should have been a Burgundian affair. Caesar set the seal on it by defeating Vercingetorix, chieftain of the resisting Gallic tribes, at Alesia (Mont Auxois) in 52 BC and celebrated it by beginning his 'Commentaries' at his winter camp on another Burgundian hilltop, the capital of the Aedui at Bibracte (Mont Beuvray). Imperial rule increased the trade in salt, amber, copper and tin, giving the region a road network that hints at the outlines of its modern highway system and making the Saône a major commercial artery. Gallo-Roman Alesia flourished as a metalworking centre and Augustodunum, the modern Autun, as a centre of learning which became the third largest city in Gaul.

Such was the territory which the Burgundiones inherited in the 5C. From the start it put them in conflict with the Frankish kingdom which the heirs of Merovius were building up in north-western Gaul. The marriage of the Burgundian princess Clotilda (Clothilde) to Clovis brought about the Frankish king's conversion to Christianity but did not end the rivalry. The Frankish defeat of the Burgundiones at Autun in 534 is commonly taken to mark the end of Burgundia. It had proved only a brief epilogue to Imperial rule and had left no monuments to compare with the Gallo-Roman remains that still distinguish the city of Autun. Yet for all its brevity, it had given the map a name that would survive the changes of the following centuries. And with the name Burgundia went the stubbornly enduring memory of a kingdom.

Assimilated into Frankish territory, Burgundia suffered with it the wave of foreign invasions that lasted almost to the end of the millennium, only briefly interrupted by the victories of Charles Martel and the rise of Charlemagne's empire. In the 8C the Saracens—or Moors from Spain—razed Autun, ravaged Langres and reached the gates of Sens. Near the end of the 9C Norse invaders sacked Bèze, Flavigny, Vézelay and Auxerre. The Magyars devastated Tournus in 937.

By this time the idea of the kingdom had resurfaced, though in a different form, with the disintegration of the Carolingian empire. When the Treaty of Verdun divided Charlemagne's territory between his three squabbling grandsons in 843, Charles le Chauve (the Bald) became ruler of Western Francia, the future France, and Louis ruler of Eastern Francia, the future Germany. Between them lay the portion which fell to the defeated brother Lothair and so was called Lotharingia. Better known as the Middle Kingdom, it formed a long central corridor running from Friesland to south of Rome and including Charlemagne's capital at Aix-la-Chapelle in Lorraine. The river Saône marked the border between Western Francia and the Middle Kingdom in the old Burgundia, dividing it into a north-western part, nucleus of the future duchy and the modern region, and an eastern part, which included the future county of Burgundy or Franche-Comté.

The Middle Kingdom proved no more stable or enduring than Burgundia had been, quickly splitting into northern and southern kingdoms and being progressively swallowed up by its neighbours. During its brief life it supplied the *chansons de geste* and the folk memory of Burgundy with a hero in Girart de Roussillon, count of Lyon and Vienne, who ruled the southern kingdom of Arles and Provence in 853–870 as regent for Lothair's son. On the larger European stage the Middle Kingdom left a troublesome ghost, its former territories still disputed and its map increasingly cluttered with the crossed swords that mark battlefields. In 1914, the historian Fernand Braudel has reminded fellow Europeans, 'we French and Germans were still fighting for possession of Lotharingia'. And more than a thousand years after the Middle Kingdom had disappeared, the Nazis were proposing to revive it in their eventual reorganisation of Europe's frontiers.

The history of French Burgundy ran a smoother course. In 1031 Henri I, third of the Capetian kings of France, assigned it to his brother Robert sans Terre (Lackland) and thus created a dynasty which would control Burgundy for more than three hundred years. Yet the Capetian dukes have been long since overshadowed by the fame of their Valois successors. The Valois dukes at least had the popular advantage of colourful surnames, while the Capetians remain a confusing roster of Hugues and Eudues (Hughs and Odos) who scarcely emerge from the anonymity of early history. This slights their achievement in helping to lay the foundations of Burgundy's future greatness. Reasonably loyal to their kings and their Church, at least by the loose standards of medieval vassalage, the Capetians protected their duchy from external conflict. They dutifully took part in crusades against the infidel in Spain, Palestine and Egypt and against Albigensian heretics in southern France. Closer to home they consolidated their power against rivals like the neighbouring counts of Champagne and internally they quelled disloyal vassals like the powerful house of Vergy and the counts of Nevers.

One result was to confirm Burgundy as a great religious centre. Its early history had already made it particularly fertile soil for the flowering of Christian culture which followed the end of the so-called Dark Ages in Europe. The trading routes had attracted early missionaries from the Christian East, and by the mid 5C Auxerre had produced Germanus (Germain), the most prestigious of all Burgundian saints. In later centuries Burgundy's inland position had protected it from some of the worst foreign invasions and made it an obvious refuge for saints' relics, even briefly those of the great St Martin of Tours himself. Mâcon, for example, had acquired the relics of St Vincent of Saragossa in the 6C and so guaranteed the patron saint of *vignerons* a strong local following and many church dedications.

Religious communities had been attracted to Burgundy for the same reason. The monks of Tournus may have suffered at the hands of the Magyars but they would certainly have fared worse had they stayed in their original place off the exposed west coast of France near Nantes.

Tournus was only one, and not the most important, of the communities founded before the creation of the Capetian duchy: most notably, at Bèze in about 630, at Vézelay (by Girart de Roussillon and his wife) between 855 and 859, and at Cluny in 910. During the Capetian period Cluny developed into an ecclesiastical empire which at the height of its power controlled more than a thousand houses in Europe through its firmly centralised system of administration. In about 1085 Hugues de Semur (St Hugh of Cluny) began Cluny III, so known to scholars because it was the third abbey church on the site. Also the greatest, it was pioneer and inspiration for the other churches which spread over the surrounding landscape—like a white mantle, said a contemporary—and left Burgundy so rich in Romanesque architecture.

In this regard Burgundy's achievement was neither isolated nor unique, as any visitor to (say) Poitou or Provence can testify. Far from being a local style, Romanesque was international, as its historian Kenneth Conant has insisted. Yet as an established and secure centre of communications, Burgundy was ideally placed to become the crucible where the elements of the style were forged into unity. Its position put it comfortably in touch with western France by the Loire, with Lombardy by the Rhône and with the Holy Roman Empire by the Saône, while its monasteries and shrines stood on a rapidly extending network of pilgrimage routes.

The leading characteristics of the Romanesque style established by Cluny III were the tunnel-vaulted nave, often already pointed; the three-storey elevation with a pointed arcade below a round-arched triforium (usually false) and clerestory; and fluted pilasters rather than engaged columns, plainly announcing the Roman origins of Romanesque. The Cluniac atelier of masons dispersed the style throughout Burgundy so that today, with Cluny III itself all but destroyed by Revolutionary hammers, we can still see its cousins at La Charité, Paray-le-Monial and Autun. When it reached the villages and monasteries of the Brionnais and the great basilica of La Madeleine at Vézelay, the Cluniac form was already adapting and developing, for as Kenneth Conant has again insisted Romanesque always tended toward experiment and variety. Yet even at Vézelay the line of descent is still proclaimed by the sculpture which makes the tympanum over the west door an epic design and ornaments the capitals with biblical scenes, saints' legends and monsters whose fantastic shapes still harbour memories of paganism.

To the modern eye the rich and vital heterodoxy of its sculpture is perhaps the most immediately appealing aspect of Romanesque. St Bernard took a different view:

> What are these fantastic monsters doing in the cloisters under the very eyes of the brothers as they read?... What is the meaning of these unclean monkeys, these savage lions, and monstrous centaurs? To what purpose are here placed these creatures, half-beast, half-man, or these spotted tigers? I see several bodies with one head and several heads with one body. Here is a quadruped with a serpent's head, there a fish with a quadruped's head, there again an animal half-horse, half-goat... Surely if we do not blush for such for absurdities we should at least regret what we have spent on them!

His attack on Cluniac ornament, of course, was merely one aspect of the Cistercian reaction against Cluny, and that reaction in turn was merely one of the successive waves of purification, reform and decay by which monasticism developed in the Middle Ages. Its appeal made St Bernard the most powerful preacher and the leading voice in the Church of his day, advocating the Second Crusade, hounding Abélard and counselling the Pope.

St Bernard's career belongs to the wider history of the medieval church, but it was rooted in Burgundy, where he was born at Fontaine-lès-Dijon in 1090 and joined the infant community at Cîteaux in 1113. Fontenay abbey and the church at Pontigny still stand as local testimony to the purifying drive of the Cistercians, borrowing the structural features of Vézelien Romanesque but stripping its ornament to produce a building that is no longer a microcosm of the world's variety but simply a workshop for prayer. It says a great deal about the restless paradoxes not just of the medieval character but specifically of the medieval Burgundian character that in scarcely more than half a century its masons should have pioneered Cistercian severity as naturally as they pioneered Cluniac richness.

Whatever the source of that energy, it had its conservative limit. 'Burgundian half-Gothic', to use Conant's term for the Cistercian style, led quickly on to Gothic itself. But that experiment took place largely outside Burgundy while Burgundian masons remained attached to the forms they had already evolved. When Gothic came to the duchy, it came from outside and its achievements—like the cathedral at Auxerre—echoed the Île de France and Chartres. The local variants Robert Branner has analysed never give Burgundian Gothic the distinctive, palpable force of Burgundian Romanesque or root it as deeply in the Burgundian soil. After the flowering of Romanesque in the time of the early Capetians, Burgundy's next period of greatness would come with the Valois dukes in the late Middle Ages.

When the last Capetian duke, Philippe de Rouvres, died of plague in 1361 the Capetian royal house was already extinct. The crown of France had passed to the house of Valois, then represented by Jean II (misleadingly surnamed le Bon, or the Good), whom the English had captured at Poitiers. Shortly before his death in 1364 Jean gave the duchy of Burgundy to his youngest son Philippe, surnamed le Hardi (the Bold) for flying to defend his father's honour from what he took to be insults by the victorious English at Poitiers. Styling themselves the 'Grands ducs de l'Occident', Philippe and his three Valois successors—Jean sans Peur (the Fearless), Philippe le Bon and Charles le Téméraire (the Bold or the Rash)—raised the duchy to new heights of power during the century that followed. They expanded its territories, made its court a splendid pattern for the royal courts of Europe and finally revived the ancient dream of Burgundy as a kingdom. The collapse of the Valois duchy with the death of Charles le Téméraire at Nancy in 1477 left contemporaries to reflect on the revolution of Fortune's Wheel and has tempted historians, even the subtle Jan Huizinga, to moralise from hindsight over 'an epic of overweening and heroic pride'.

Though centred on Dijon and the Côte d'Or, the duchy Philippe inherited was rather smaller than the modern region. He and his successors set about expanding it, usually by marriage, purchase, treaty or intrigue rather than open aggression. In this fashion they added the counties of Charolais, Tonnerre, Mâcon and Auxerre, together with Franche-Comté, the 'free county' east of the Saône which had once been part of the Middle Kingdom, and Nevers, which (with the county of Rethel) soon passed to a junior branch of the family but remained a friendly client state of its powerful neighbour.

Nevers, Rethel and Franche-Comté were part, and not the most significant part, of the inheritance brought by Marguerite de Flandre, 'laide et creuse' but still the most desirable heiress in Europe, whom Philippe le Hardi married in 1369. Her father's death in 1384 also made Philippe the possessor of Flanders, with its flourishing cities at Bruges, Ghent, Lille and Antwerp, and the neighbouring county of Artois, which included Hesdin and Arras. This northern annexe—'waterish Burgundy', Shakespeare called it, presumably to distinguish it from the winy Burgundy of the Côte—became the focus of Valois ambition. Jean sans Peur added the county of Boulogne. Philippe le Bon acquired the Somme towns in Picardy, the counties of Namur, Hainaut, Holland (where Amsterdam was already a powerful city) and Zeeland, the duchies of Brabant (which included Brussels), Limburg and Luxembourg. In the last years of the duchy Charles le Téméraire added the duchy of Guelders, the county of Zutphen and Alsace before trying to seize Lorraine, strategically important for helping to link his divided northern and southern territories and symbolically important for helping to resurrect the ghost of the old Middle Kingdom. Even in its stable extent under Philippe le Bon, Burgundy had grown to more than five times the size of the youngest son's portion which had fallen to the first duke. Though still smaller than France itself, the Valois empire was as large as some European kingdoms, England and Wales among them.

At Dijon, which they confirmed as capital of the duchy, and in the northern cities, castles and palaces which increasingly absorbed their attention the dukes could hold a court rivalling any in Europe. 'Le duc y fit éclater sa magnificence', wrote a contemporary chronicler of the welcome Philippe le Hardi gave his nephew Charles VI at Dijon in 1390. It was not the only occasion when he or his successors flaunted their splendour. Huizinga's 'The Waning of the Middle Ages' has described the Valois passion for etiquette and display which turned the doffing of a hat or even the dispatch of orders on the battlefield into a complex ceremony, and made elaborately staged spectacles of a duke's *joyeuse entrée* into his inheritance or his marriage or his funeral.

The dukes took particular delight in passages of arms, jousts, tournaments and chivalric orders, like the Toison d'Or (Order of the Golden Fleece) which Philippe le Bon founded on his marriage to Isabelle de Portugal in 1429. The culture of their court was everywhere deliberately archaizing, harking back to legends of Troy and *chansons de geste* even while its knights inhabited the harsh and volatile world of late medieval *realpolitik*. Philippe le Bon's banquet celebrating the Vow of the Pheasant at Lille in 1454 was supposed to launch a final crusade, never actually attempted, to recapture Constantinople from the Turks who had overrun it the previous year. Jacques de Lalaing, extravagant hero of several passages of arms patronised by Philippe, died from a rebel cannonball during the Ghent campaign in 1453.

In general, the Valois dream of chivalry did not prevent effective pursuit of political ambition. Yet it cut Burgundian culture off from the Renaissance humanism already emerging in Italy—to which the dukes turned mainly for the bankers who funded their ambitious policies. Of course, France itself hardly lacked traditions of art or princely patronage, as the example of Philippe le Hardi's own brothers showed. Charles V assembled the great manuscript library which became the nucleus of the Bibliothèque Nationale, Louis d'Anjou commissioned the Apocalypse tapestries still preserved in the castle at Angers, while Jean de Berry—the most tasteful or most acquisitive brother of them all—was the age's greatest patron of illuminated manuscripts, notably the 'Très Riches Heures' by the Limburg brothers.

The work commissioned by Philippe le Hardi showed him turning to the Low Countries as soon as he had acquired his territories there. The French court may have supplied an architect like Drouet de Dammartin for the Chartreuse de Champmol, the ducal mausoleum Philippe founded on the outskirts of Dijon, but Flanders and the Netherlands were the chief source for the sculpture and painting of the Valois court. Claus Sluter of Haarlem, the greatest sculptor of late Gothic, arrived in Dijon about 1385 and was within a few years at work on the Chartreuse. The base of his Calvary survives on the site, while Philippe's tomb, essentially the work of Sluter and his nephew Claus de Werve, is preserved in Dijon's Musée des Beaux-Arts with Jean sans Peur's tomb and several altarpieces presented to the Chartreuse. Sluter's style left its mark throughout Burgundy, though its monumental clarity is progressively diluted as it becomes sweeter and eventually, with the Flamboyant fashion, fussy. Its influence can be felt in the work of Juan de la Huerta and Antoine Le Moiturier, who made Jean sans Peur's tomb, and in the Burgundian school that gave many churches the delicate, human Madonnas and female saints whose hair falls in cascades of ringlets and the vigorously realistic figures of the Entombments.

Produced in the flourishing cities of the Low Countries, much of the Flemish and Netherlandish art of the Valois court was never exported to the Burgundy of Dijon and the Côte. The collapse of the duchy meant that works which were brought south have since been dispersed. Jan van Eyck, for example, joined Philippe le Bon's household in 1425 and may also have been entrusted with diplomatic missions, yet he worked mainly in Lille and Bruges. The 'Annunciation' he contributed to the Chartreuse is now in the National Gallery of Art in Washington DC, while his painting of the Virgin and Child with Philippe's chancellor, Nicolas Rolin, hangs in the Louvre. Visitors to London's National Gallery can see his 'Arnolfini Marriage', the Arnolfini family being the Italian bankers with whom the dukes dealt. Van Eyck's more shadowy contemporary Roger van der Weyden did not apparently hold an appointment at court, though its leading members employed him. Art historians attribute to him the lost original of a portrait of Charles le Téméraire, now represented by an early copy in the Dahlen Museum at Berlin, and they identify Philippe le Bon's illegitimate son Antoine, the splendidly named Grand Bâtard de Bourgogne, as the subject of a striking portrait in the Beaux-Arts at Brussels. But Burgundy keeps at least one great, and definitely attributed, treasure in the 'Last Judgement' van der Weyden painted for the Hôtel-Dieu which Nicolas Rolin and his wife founded at Beaune.

The steadily enlarging size of their territory and the growing splendour of their court announced that the Valois dukes meant to play a powerful role on the French and European stage. The turbulence of the Hundred Years War guaranteed that their role would prove divisive. To start with, Burgundy was 'carried into history on the broad shoulders of France', in Richard Vaughan's phrase. Charles V, for example, was eager to smooth the path for Marguerite de Flandre's marriage to his younger brother Philippe, if only to prevent her marrying Edward III's son Edmund and so forging an Anglo-Flemish alliance. First the minority and then the intermittent lunacy of Charles VI made Philippe a leading figure in the council of regency, indeed the virtual ruler of France. Yet this convenient arrangement did not outlive him, and Jean sans Peur quickly found himself locked in power struggles at the royal court. His rivalry with Louis d'Orléans finally prompted him to arrange Louis' murder on the streets of Paris in 1407. Some contemporaries suggested that Jean won his surname, the Fearless, by his leadership of the Nicopolis crusade or his victory at Othée, but others claimed it was an ironic comment on the almost obsessive anxiety he showed for his own safety in the aftermath of Louis' murder, as France sank into civil war between Burgundians and Armagnacs, inheritors of the Orléanist cause. Events proved that the Fearless was right to be scared. When Jean went to treat with the Dauphin, the future Charles VII, on the bridge at Montereau in 1419 he was cut down by the Armagnacs. It was said that the Dauphin himself gave the signal for the killing.

A hundred and fifty years after Jean's death, when a Carthusian monk was showing François I round the Valois mausoleum at the Chartreuse de Champmol, he pointed to Jean sans Peur's broken skull and said: 'This is the hole through which the English entered France'. Even before the murder Henry V had reaped ample profit from France's weakness during the Burgundian and Armagnac rivalry—on the field of Agincourt, for example. Jean's death pushed the Burgundians decisively into the English camp. His successor Philippe le Bon signed the Treaty of Troyes in 1420, excluding the Dauphin and recognising Henry as regent and future king of France. One result of the alliance was that the Burgundians handed the Dauphin's champion Jeanne d'Arc over to the English at Compiègne in 1430. Another was that its geographical position no longer protected Burgundy from the horrors of a war that had already devastated exposed regions like the Pas de Calais, Normandy, Brittany and Guyenne. Charles VII had every reason to encourage the 'free companies' of knights ravaging the countryside—known as *routiers* ('rutters' in the English of the day) or *écorcheurs* ('fleecers' or 'flayers')—to pay attention to Burgundy.

No treaty, alliance or political grouping lasted long during the Hundred Years War, and the Anglo-Burgundian alliance proved almost as unstable as earlier Burgundian relations with the French crown. Yet it is a mistake to see it merely as an act of personal revenge by Philippe le Bon for his father's death, just as it is a mistake to surrender to the temptation of reading Valois history in terms of the personalities of its dukes. In fact, the shift in Burgundian loyalty marked a deliberate and largely successful change in policy. Philippe le Bon no longer aimed, as the first Philippe had, at internal domination of France but cultivated his territories outside France. Some degree of rapprochement with England, however unstable, was useful both because of England's ability to reduce the power of the French monarchy even further and because of English interests in the Low Countries through the wool trade.

Philippe le Bon achieved his goal in the build-up of territory and power in the Low Countries he left to the last duke, Charles le Téméraire, in 1467. The inheritance encouraged Charles to hint at the goal of reviving the Middle Kingdom, an ambition historians have often called foolish and unrealistic. But we should remember that it was nineteenth-century scholars who dubbed Charles 'le Téméraire', not his contemporaries, who knew him as 'le Travailleur' (the Industrious) or, like his great-grandfather, 'le Hardi'. In fact, the dream lay both tantalisingly close and irritatingly remote. For all its size Valois Burgundy still lacked the unity of a kingdom: its northern and southern territories were still inconveniently split in two. And for all their power the dukes still lacked the unifying title of a king. Technically they still ruled here as a vassal of the king of France and there as a vassal of the Holy Roman Emperor, here as a duke and there as a count.

The pursuit of the title led Charles into fruitless attempts to bully or bribe the Holy Roman Emperor into crowning him King of the Romans. The pursuit of the kingdom itself led him to seize Lorraine, part of the buffer zone between waterish and winy Burgundy, in 1475. This venture and his troubled interests in Alsace brought him into conflict with the Eidgenossen or 'Great League of Upper Germany', the confederation of cantons led by Berne which was emerging from the tangle of the Holy Roman Empire as a powerful force in its own right. The armies of the Eidgenossen defeated Charles in the Vaud at Grandson and Morat, where curious travellers were several centuries later still being shown the skulls of the 8000 Burgundian dead. The Eidgenossen then supplied mercenaries to René de Lorraine in his vigorous campaign to regain his territory. Charles le Téméraire died outside the gates of Nancy on 5 January 1477, the Grand duc de l'Occident and would-be King of the Romans toppled by the halberdiers of the future Swiss republic. His body was found in a frozen pond two days later, stripped of its armour and half-eaten by wolves.

Charles le Téméraire left no son. Louis XI of France, an adroit politician who had already forestalled a Burgundian attempt to embroil his kingdom in war with England, cited the Salic law to exclude Charles' daughter Marie de Bourgogne from inheriting and laid his hands on as much of the duke's territory as he could: the duchy itself, Franche-Comté, Artois and the Somme towns of Picardy. With the support of her husband, Maximilian of Habsburg, Marie managed to hold on to Flanders and the non-French territories of Burgundy, and after her death he recovered Franche-Comté and Artois from Louis' successor Charles VIII. The relics of Valois ambition continued in the Habsburg line. Marie's daughter, the formidable Marguerite d'Autriche, backed the German, Swiss and Franc-Comtois expedition which ended unsuccessfully before the gates of Dijon in 1513 and Marie's grandson, the Holy Roman Emperor Charles V, did not formally give up his claim to Burgundy until some thirty years later.

The duchy itself, heartland of Burgundy in all its expanding and contracting definitions, passed into the charge of royally appointed governors, notably the Condé family which served from 1631 until the Revolution. The history of Burgundy joined the history of France, and its participation in the Wars of Religion, the Fronde rebellion and the Revolution itself were local aspects of the larger life of the nation. Yet Burgundy was not absorbed into France without trace. Just as the Valois dukes had nourished their separatist ambitions by looking back to the old Middle Kingdom, so the memory of their own opposition to the French crown was still strong enough some three centuries afterwards to make the first Revolutionaries in Dijon preserve, not demolish, the tombs of Philippe le Hardi and Jean sans Peur. In 'The Identity of France' Fernand Braudel has written eloquently of Burgundy still 'imperious and aloof', a dazzling example of how a province could resist the centralising tendency of the *ancien régime* and maintain its privileges, traditions and inconsistencies. The *parlement*, or supreme court, established at Dijon by Louis XII epitomised Burgundy's historic identity, as well as producing the *noblesse de robe* which gave the city so brilliant a career during the Enlightenment and left it with so rich an architectural heritage.

Nor could political change alter Burgundy's essential character as a nerve centre of communications and trade routes. Its towns flourished as staging posts on the coaching roads and its rivers shipped wine from Chablis and the Côte, or timber from the Morvan forests, to Paris. Traffic increased with the opening of Emiland Gauthey's Canal du Centre, linking the Saône and the Loire, in 1791 and the choice of Dijon as a major junction on the Paris–Lyon railway line in 1851. Such changes further encouraged the industries which had a long history in Burgundy, notably the iron foundries of the Châtillonnais, the Loire valley and the coal-rich Blanzy basin, now conveniently penetrated by Gauthey's canal. The Schneider brothers' purchase of the foundries at Le Creusot in 1836 signalled the beginning of an industrial empire.

Yet even today Burgundy is no more industrialised than most regions in a country whose slowness of development in this regard can leave observers from Britain or Germany wondering whether they are seeing backwardness or a different, more humane model of change. Even when glimpsed all too fleetingly by tourists speeding down the autoroutes, it still presents a landscape largely rural and agricultural. The woodland which occupies a generous 30 per cent of its surface (the national average for France is 25 per cent) runs to ancient oaks and beeches, not just serried ranks of Corsican pine, and it can still support deer, wild boars and buzzards. Agriculture still employs about 11 per cent of the workforce. The vineyards which make the most famous and immediately attractive aspect of the rural economy account for only a small fraction of this figure, but even elsewhere the fields remain small, busy workplaces and have not yet become the lifeless expanses familiar in England or, for that matter, in Champagne on the way down to Burgundy from the north.

This is not to deny that Burgundy's rural status has brought problems, particularly the steady shrinking of a population which was never numerous. The region may be about the same size as Wales but, with about 1.6 million people, it has only about half the inhabitants. Its average population density of 50 people per square kilometre (and of course the figure is much lower in some *pays*) is only half the French average and less than a quarter of the British average. The very efficiency of the modern communications network—the autoroutes and the TGV—has strengthened the drawing power of Paris and Lyon, leaving many villages with a dwindling, ageing population. You will hear the remaining inhabitants talk with concern of the *désert bourguignon* or lament the empty houses and the shuttered *maisons secondaires* which their Parisian owners visit only at weekends.

But you will not hear Burgundians speak less proudly or less eloquently of their rivers and their forests, their Romanesque churches and their wine. It is surely no accident that the same years which saw the population draining away also produced local classics in the novels of Henri Vincenot. Works like 'Les Étoiles de Compostelle' ('The Stars of Compostela', 1982) and particularly 'Le Pape des escargots' ('The King of the Snails', 1972) expressed the blend of earthy practicality and romantic absorption with the past that can still bind Burgundians to their native soil. Like so much else you will find in the life of modern Burgundy, they reaffirmed that all the changes to its status and its shape on the map did not destroy an underlying sense of identity, even if they made it more elusive. The first thing Burgundians have always liked to say about their native region is that Burgundy has a centre—or, as some put it, a heart—but no frontiers.

TOURING BURGUNDY WITH THIS GUIDE

This book follows the usual Blue Guide method of dividing the territory it covers into routes designed chiefly for motorists. It defines Burgundy as the modern region consisting of the departments of the Côte d'Or, Nièvre, Saône-et-Loire and Yonne but also includes a few places in neighbouring departments strongly connected with historic Burgundy: Langres is briefly noticed in Route 1, while Bourg-en-Bresse is described in Route 9 and Charlieu in Route 20.

The routes are not selected excursions from major centres or, except in one case, circuits returning to their point of departure. They cover Burgundy in a series of linked journeys, each concentrating on a distinctive stretch of country or *pays* and beginning with a general description of its main features. Wherever possible they avoid motorways (*autoroutes*) for N-roads and D-roads (*routes nationales* and *routes départementales*), and sometimes smaller local roads, which take in points of historic interest and give a better flavour of the countryside. The itineraries are not meant to be hard and fast: all suggest alternatives, detours and diversions. If you want to follow your own plan, there is a detailed index of places (with a separate index of people) to encourage you.

The headnote to each route gives a brief summary of road directions, with cumulative distances for the main places, and a brief summary of the main links with other routes. The text itself gives detailed road directions and distances between each of the landmarks passed. Population figures, taken from the 1990 census and rounded off to the nearest ten, are noted for towns and villages with more than 500 inhabitants, and for smaller places with Tourist Information Centres. The descriptions of places concentrate unashamedly on their art, architecture and history, though without assuming that these belong in some special category apart from contemporary life. As in other Blue Guides, asterisks mark points of special interest: one asterisk means something is worth stopping to see and two asterisks mean it is worth travelling a great distance to see.

To help planning, the asterisked items are listed under 'Highlights' on pages 24–26. The rest of this section deals with practical matters: ways of getting to Burgundy and travelling round it; maps; accommodation, restaurants and food; and access to châteaux, museums and churches. Addresses and phone numbers of the tourist organisations mentioned, and of local Tourist Information Centres (*Syndicats d'Initiative* and *Maisons de Tourisme*), are listed on pages 175–179.

Getting to Burgundy

By car and ferry. The following car ferry services are the most convenient: P & O European Ferries: Dover to Boulogne in 1 hour 40 minutes; Dover to Calais in 1 hour 15 minutes; Dover to Ostend in 4 hours; Dover to Zeebrugge in 4 hours 30 minutes; Felixstowe to Zeebrugge in 5 hours 45 minutes. (Address: Channel House, Channel View Road, Dover CT17 9TJ; for reservations phone 081 5758555 or 0304 203388.) Sally Ferries: Ramsgate to Dunkerque in 2 hours 30 minutes. (Travel shop at 81 Piccadilly, London W1; for reservations phone 081 858 1127 or 081 5758555.) Sealink Stena

Line: Dover to Calais in 1 hour 30 minutes. (Address: Charter House, Park Street, Ashford, Kent TN24 8EX; for reservations phone 0233 647047.) Seacat: Dover to Calais in 45 minutes; Dover to Boulogne in 50 minutes. (Phone 081 554 7061.)

Boulogne, Calais, Dunkerque, Ostend and Zeebrugge offer a wide choice of routes to Burgundy. You can avoid Paris and head for Reims and Châlons-sur-Marne, continuing via Chaumont to Langres or via Troyes to Châtillon-sur-Seine. **Langres**, 215km (135 miles) from Reims, is the starting point of Route 1. **Châtillon**, 190km (118 miles) from Reims, is the starting point of Route 2. If you go via Paris, you can leave the city by A6, the Autoroute du Soleil and Burgundy's main motorway, or by N6 via Fontainebleau for **Sens**, 116km (72 miles) from Paris and the starting point of Route 3.

By train. The rail journey from London (Victoria) to Paris (Gare du Nord) takes anything from 5 hours 30 minutes to 10 hours, depending on the route and whether the crossing is made by ferry or Hovercraft. Motorail services carry cars, motorbikes and passengers overnight on the same train. TGV services run from Paris (Gare de Lyon) to Montbard in 1 hour 5 minutes, Dijon in 1 hour 36 minutes, Beaune in 1 hour 58 minutes and Mâcon in 1 hour 40 minutes. Further information from International British Rail Enquiries at Victoria Station (phone 071 834 2345) and the UK office of SNCF (French railways) at 179 Piccadilly, London W1V OBA (phone 071 409 3518).

By coach. For details of the London–Paris service contact Euroways/Eurolines, 52 Grosvenor Gardens, Victoria, London SW1W OAU (phone 071 730 8235).

By air. Proteus Air (phone 0279 680641) runs a weekday service from London (Stansted) to Dijon in 1 hour 40 minutes. Air France handles reservations (158 New Bond Street, London W1Y OAY; phone 081 742 6600). Otherwise you have to fly to Paris and then take the TGV: Air France and SNCF offer a combined ticket.

Travelling round Burgundy

Driving is almost essential if you want to tour a sizeable area conveniently or in any detail. If you arrive in Dijon by train or plane you can choose from a number of car-hire firms, including Avis, Europcar and Hertz.

In budgeting for driving expenses, remember that petrol prices are higher in France than in the UK. The garages attached to supermarket chains usually offer the best prices. Unleaded petrol (*sans plomb* or, colloquially, *le vert*), a bit less expensive than *essence* or *super*, can still be hard to find away from the larger towns and autoroutes. If you want to get across country quickly, remember that the roads are usually clearest during the lunch hour, when all good French people are at table.

Cycling is also popular in a region with a varied landscape that only occasionally proves strenuous. Bicycles can be hired from some Syndicats d'Initiative and railway stations as well as independent firms. Further information and advice about routes can be obtained from the Ligue Régionale de Bourgogne de Cyclotourisme, 45 bis, rue du Tire-Pesseau, 21000 Dijon (phone 80 45 04 87).

Walking is particularly popular in the Morvan and the Puisaye, which abound in local walks and are crossed by the long-distance Sentiers de Grande Randonnée known as GRs. These are described in the excellent series of 'Topoguides' published by the Fédération Française de Randonnée Pédestre, 8, avenue Marceau, 75008 Paris. Information can also be obtained from the four Comités Départementaux de la Randonnée Pédestre. For Côte d'Or: BP 1601, 21035 Dijon Cédex (phone 80 73 81 81). For Nièvre: 3, rue du Sort, 58000 Nevers (phone 86 36 37 01). For Saône-et-Loire: Mairie, 71460 St-Gengoux-le-National (phone 85 92 61 67). For Yonne: Maison des Sports, 12, boulevard Gallieni, 89000 Auxerre.

Boating has its obvious attraction in a region whose role as a centre of communications has given it about 1200km (746 miles) of navigable canals and rivers. The Comité Régional du Tourisme publishes a useful introductory brochure ('Boating Holidays in Burgundy') which includes details of the many boat-hire companies.

Maps

Michelin and the Institut Géographique National (IGN) both produce good maps. If you find the handy size of a bound atlas makes up for the awkward page breaks, the hardback 'Michelin Road Atlas of France', published by Paul Hamlyn, is adequate to most driving needs in Burgundy. Its scale is 1:200,000 (1cm to 2km or 3.15 miles to 1 inch). The paperback edition published each year is now spiral-bound, much better than the flimsy glued version which did not survive even a short tour. If you prefer sheet maps, the IGN Série Rouge number 108 (Nivernais, Bourgogne) is to be recommended, though it does chop off the bottom tip of the Brionnais and is too generous in its definition of significant ruins and monuments. Its scale is 1:250,000 (1cm to 2.5km or 3.94 miles to 1 inch). Michelin's yellow regional maps at 1:200,000 (1cm to 2km or 3.15 miles to 1 inch) are less convenient, dividing modern Burgundy between numbers 238 (Centre, Berry, Nivernais) and 243 (Bourgogne, Franche-Comté) in the large sheet size and five maps in the smaller sheet size.

If you are walking, cycling or making an intensive tour of a particular *pays*, you will need one of the following series of IGN maps: the Série Verte at 1:100,000 (1cm to 1km or 1.57 miles to 1 inch), the smallest scale to mark contours; the Série Orange at 1:50,000 (1cm to 0.5km or 0.78 miles to 1 inch); the Série Bleue at 1:25,000 (1cm to 250m or 0.39 miles to 1 inch). See also the remarks about the 'Topoguides' series above.

Accommodation

Hotels in France are officially classified by a system of one to four stars, indicating the range of amenities provided. There are also many unstarred hotels which, particularly away from large towns, can still prove perfectly comfortable, though modest. The star system is not a guide to prices, which vary considerably in each category (and even each hotel). Prices are quoted per room, usually for two people, not per person. Hotels often list them outside or in the window, and are required by law to post the price of each room in the room itself. The figure rarely includes breakfast and in city hotels may not include a charge for offstreet or covered parking. Overnight guests at smaller establishments are expected to eat dinner in the hotel so, if you are watching your budget, check the combined cost of room, breakfast and dinner before booking. Hotels have been known to offset low room prices with high restaurant bills.

Burgundy's long history as a *lieu de passage* has ensured that it can offer a good range of hotels to suit most tastes and purses. The Comité Régional du Tourisme publishes a full brochure listing them. It also recommends advance booking during the May–October tourist season but, unless your needs are particularly exacting, you are not likely to come to grief taking pot-luck on an unplanned tour, except in July and August. The big hotel chains tend to be represented only in large cities like Dijon and Auxerre. Prices here and in popular tourist areas like the Côte d'Or are noticeably higher than in less publicised areas like the Nivernais. Hotels of any sort are much thinner on the ground in the Morvan and the Puisaye, where you should consider the alternatives described below.

It is worth looking out for hotels belonging to Logis de France, a network of small independent establishments in the one- or two-star categories. There are more than 170 in Burgundy and their distinctive emblem of a yellow and green chimney makes them easy to spot. Prices cover a wide spectrum but there are many rooms available between 150F and 300F (1991 rates). Full details are given in the annual brochure published by the Union Régionale des Logis de Bourgogne, 68, rue Chevreuil, BP 309, 21006 Dijon Cédex (phone 80 63 52 51). The national handbook is published annually by the Féderation Nationale des Logis de France, 83, avenue d'Italie, 75013 Paris (phone 16 1 45 84 70 00); copies are available for the cost of postage from the French Government Tourist Office in London.

Other useful sources of information are the 'Michelin Red Guide' and the 'Routiers Guide to France' (available by post from Routiers, 354 Fulham Road, London SW10 9UH). Personal callers at the French Government Tourist Office in London can consult its computerised register of hotels.

Gîtes, or self-catering accommodation rented by the week, make a convenient and sometimes picturesque base in rural areas. They are particularly useful for families or groups of more than two people. Typical weekly prices for a *gîte* accommodating four people are 1000–1200F in season and 800–1000F out of season (1991 rates). You can join the official booking service, Gîtes de France, for a small annual fee and receive its handbook of listings by contacting the French Government Tourist Office in London. Each of the four departments of Burgundy also has a branch of Gîtes de France which issues listings and handles bookings. For Côte d'Or: Relais des Gîtes de France, 14, rue de la Préfecture, 21000 Dijon (phone 80 50 15 60; fax 80 30 48 74). For Nièvre: Service Réservation Loisirs Acceuil, 3, rue du Sort, 58000 Nevers (phone 86 59 14 22). For Saône-et-Loire: Relais des Gîtes de France, Chambre d'Agriculture, Esplanade du Breuil, BP 522, 71000 Mâcon (phone 85 29 55 60). For Yonne: Relais des Gîtes de France, Chambre d'Agriculture, 14 bis, rue Guynemer, 89015 Auxerre Cédex (phone 86 46 47 48 or 86 46 01 39) and Service de Réservation Gîtes de France, 1–2, quai de la République, 89000 Auxerre (phone 86 52 86 59; fax 86 51 68 47; telex 351 860F). These services also cover *chambres d'hôte* (bed and breakfast), *fermes auberges* (farmhouse inns), *campings à la ferme* (farm camping) and *gîtes d'étape* (simple hostel accommodation near walkers' routes). The Comité Régional du Tourisme publishes a list of the many camping and caravan sites.

Restaurants and Food

Burgundy's cuisine and its top restaurants—at, for example, Joigny, Saulieu, Chagny and Vézelay—have a high reputation with gourmets. Prices at such places are correspondingly high, with set menus costing anything from 250F to 600F (1991 rates). Yet even if you are not willing to pay gourmet prices, there is no reason why you should not eat well for comparatively little money.

The set, or fixed price, menus are almost always a better bet than *à la carte* meals. All restaurants offer them and most offer at least three different ones ranging, in good but modest places, up to 150F with at least one menu under 100F. The more expensive the menu, the greater the choice it offers (though it still may not run to vegetarian dishes) and the more likely it is to include both cheese and dessert (eaten in that order) rather than cheese or dessert. You do not need to pay more than 150F for a decent meal, and you should not pay more without a special recommendation. Prices of set menus are prominently advertised outside restaurants, and the figures quoted exclude drinks of any sort but include a service charge. You should add a tip only if you are particularly pleased with the service.

The obvious sources of guidance are the 'Michelin Red Guide', the 'Routiers Guide to France' (particularly useful for cheaper restaurants) and, sometimes best of all, the local people themselves. The French are proud of their cuisine and take the business of judging restaurants seriously, so they will not simply point you to the nearest, largest, best-publicised or most expensive one.

Whether you are eating in restaurants or fending for yourself in a *gîte*, you will quickly realise that traditional Burgundian food extends far beyond *escargots*, *coq au vin* and *boeuf bourguignon* or the habit of making meat dishes *à la dijonnaise* (with mustard). Particular *pays* have their distinctive ingredients, products and dishes, like the yellow corn-fed chickens of the Bresse or the hams, wild honey and wild mushrooms of the Morvan. The list below identifies some of the items you are most likely to encounter and a few you may wish to seek out.

Eggs. *Oeufs en meurette* are poached eggs served with *croûtons* and red-wine sauce.

Fish. *Pôchouse* is speciality of Verdun-sur-le-Doubs, Seurre and St-Jean-de-Losne: freshwater *bouillabaisse* made with fish from the Saône (pike, perch, tench, carp and eel) in white wine. *Meurette de poissons* uses red wine.

Ham. *Jambon à la crème* is ham in a sharp sauce of wine and cream. Though associated particularly with the Morvan, it is served throughout Burgundy, like *jambon persillé*, an *hors d'oeuvre* of ham with chopped parsley preserved in a white-wine aspic.

Cheese. Burgundy makes at least one great cheese in Époisses, smooth and soft, given a distinctive flavour by being washed in the local *marc* and a distinctive look by its orange rind. Bleu de Bresse, Cîteaux, St-Florentin, Soumaintrain and Chaource are all known outside the region, though the last two are not strictly Burgundian, coming from just over the northern border. The Côte d'Or round Nuits-St-Georges produces Amours de Nuit, Nuits d'Or and Ami de Chambertin, rich and creamy cheeses that deserve to be better known, as does the cheese made by the monastery farm at La Pierre-qui-Vire. The Mâconnais *chèvretons* and Chavignol *crottins* (from the area round Pouilly-sur-Loire) are goat cheeses, also made in the Chalonnais and the Morvan. The Charolais and Brionnais produce a soft, mild *mi-chèvre* made with anything from one-fifth to one-half goats' milk, depending on the season. Despite their appearance, the little *cailloux* from the Morvan are made from cows' milk.

Pastries and sweets. The *gougère* is a puff pastry made with cheese and eaten cold as an *hors d'oeuvre* or snack. *Pain d'épice* (gingerbread) is a speciality of Dijon, *anis* (aniseed sweets) of Flavigny and *nougatines* of Nevers.

Visiting châteaux, museums and churches

Opening times for châteaux, museums, etc are not given in this guide since they can change too greatly from year to year for any details to be reliable for long. In the case of châteaux, where arrangements are particularly prone to change, the description merely notes whether or not a given property has in general been open to visitors during recent years. You should be careful to check in advance before making a special trip. Up-to-date information can easily be obtained from local Syndicats d'Initiative and from the annual brochures or broadsheets issued by each of the four Comités Départementaux du Tourisme: their addresses and phone numbers are listed on page 174.

A few general rules should be remembered. Most châteaux and many museums in smaller towns are closed outside the tourist season, which stretches roughly from Easter to October and reaches its peak in July and August. Even during the season they are unlikely to be open all day and every day. Tuesday is a closing day for municipal museums and other properties staffed by public employees, and for some privately owned properties as well. Sundays and public holidays (*jours fériés*) are uncertain in their effect. Smaller properties may open only in the afternoons, and those properties that also open in the mornings still observe the lunch hour, usually 12.00 to 14.00 or 14.30. Some town churches otherwise left open are locked at lunchtime. In villages where you need to get the key to the church, the key-keeper will not appreciate being bothered during his or her meal.

Some châteaux, abbeys and other historic properties host concerts during the summer: for further details see the 'Calendar of events' on pages 170–173 and the annual programme published by ASSECARM de Bourgogne (l'Association d'Étude pour la Coordination des Activités Régionales Musicales), 41, rue Vannerie, 21000 Dijon (phone 80 67 22 33).

The annual 'Portes Ouvertes' day, usually a Sunday in September, gives the public access to *Monuments Historiques* (listed buildings) not open at other times and organises special events at those that are usually open. Details are available in the brochure published annually by the Direction Régionale des Affaires Culturelles, Conservation Régionale des Monuments Historiques, 39, rue Vannerie, 21000 Dijon.

Châteaux open to the public do not cultivate the slick professionalism of the English country-house industry, except in the case of a handful of major properties. Visiting smaller or less well-known properties has its special charms and special frustrations.

Do not be misled by the white-on-brown 'Châteaux de Bourgogne' signposts, or the older black-on-white 'Monuments Historiques' ones, which point the way from major roads. They do not guarantee that the château is open, or even remotely friendly, to visitors. In at least one case a journey of several kilometres down backroads ends with a view of a firmly locked gate and a notice saying 'Chien Lunatique'. Nor, in the case of smaller châteaux, do advertised opening hours constitute a guarantee: rain, staff problems, the need for repairs or the chance of a week in Paris can cause owners to abandon visitors to their own devices. Even some of the best-publicised châteaux look much more impressive outside than inside, where only a few rooms may be shown and these in a poor state of repair. The guided tour (*visite accompagnée*) still prevails over the *visite libre*. The tour usually lasts about an hour and your guide may prove anything from bored and ill-informed to enthusiastic and knowledgeable. German is the most common second language, though a few guides bravely speak English and many properties have a pamphlet in English available. The guide expects to be tipped and will contrive to end the tour standing by a notice prominently reminding you of the fact.

Museums present a much more lively and diverse picture than châteaux. Some, like the Musée Archéologique du Châtillonnais, the Musée Alésia and the Musée Archéologique de la Porte du Croux in Nevers, still display first-class collections in a highly traditional manner, though the new 'museology' is represented by the Archéodrome near Beaune and the Musée Départemental de la Préhistoire at Solutré. Major reorganisation has recently been completed or is still underway at Sens, Auxerre (St-Germain) and Cluny, while the lovely little Musée Magnin in Dijon reopened in 1990 after refurbishment. Industrial museums, like the Grande Forge at Buffon, show a welcome interest in previously neglected aspects of Burgundy's past, as do the *Écomusées*—or 'museums of the environment'—headquartered in the château at Pierre-de-Bresse and the Château de la Verrerie at Le Creusot. Further information about the excellent network of such museums throughout the country can be obtained from Écomusées en France, Anciennes Salines, Tour du Reculoz, 39110 Salins-les-Bains.

Highlights

Pays. *Double asterisks*: the Auxois; the Brionnais; and the Mâconnais. *Single asterisks*: the Bresse; the eastern Charolais; the Côte d'Or; the Morvan; and the Puisaye.

    Cities and larger towns. *Double asterisk*: Dijon. *Single asterisks*: Autun; Auxerre; Beaune; and Nevers.

    Smaller towns and villages. *Single asterisks*: Avallon; Brancion; Châteauneuf-en-Auxois; Flavigny-sur-Ozerain; Joigny; Louhans; Mont-St-Jean; Mont-St-Vincent; Noyers-sur-Serein; St-Gengoux-le-National; and Semur-en-Auxois.

    Carolingian, Romanesque and Cistercian churches. *Double asterisks*: Autun (cathedral of St-Lazare); Auxerre (crypt of St-Germain); the Brionnais churches collectively; La Charité-sur-Loire (Notre-Dame); Fontenay abbey; Paray-le-Monial (Sacré-Coeur); Saulieu (St-Andoche); Tournus (St-Philibert); and best of all, Vézelay (La Madeleine). *Single asterisks*: Anzy-le-Duc; Avallon (St-Lazare); Beaune (Notre-Dame); Béard; Brancion; Chapaize; Charlieu abbey; Châtillon-sur-Seine (St-Vorles); Cluny abbey; Curgy; Dijon (crypt of St-Bénigne cathedral); Donzy-le-Pré; Gourdon; Montceaux-l'Étoile; Nevers (St-Étienne); Perrecy-les-Forges; Pontigny; St-Cydroine; St-Julien-de-Jonzy; St-Parize-le-Châtel (crypt); St-Pierre-le-Moûtier; St-Révérien; Semur-en-Brionnais; and Til-Châtel.

Gothic and later churches. *Double asterisks*: Bourg-en-Bresse (Brou) and Dijon (Chartreuse de Champmol). *Single asterisks*: Auxerre (cathedral of St-Étienne); Clamecy (St-Martin); Dijon (Notre-Dame); Givry; Joigny (St-Jean); Nevers (Chapelle Ste-Marie); Prémery; St-Florentin; St-Père-sous-Vézelay; St-Thibault; Semur-en-Auxois (Notre-Dame); and Sens (cathedral of St-Étienne).

Church furnishings. *Double asterisk*: Berzé-la-Ville (wall paintings). *Single asterisks*: Bard-le-Regulier (choir stalls); Bourg-en-Bresse (Notre-Dame, choir stalls); La Ferté-Loupière (wall paintings); Flavigny-sur-Ozerain (St-Genès, choir stalls); Montréal (choir stalls); Moutiers (wall paintings); St-Julien-du-Sault (stained glass); St-Saulge (stained glass); and Ste-Magnance (saint's tomb).

Châteaux. *Single asterisks*: Beaumont-sur-Vingeanne; Bussy-Rabutin; Cormatin; Druyes-les-Belles-Fontaines; Époisses; Pierre-de-Bresse (see also Écomusées); St-Fargeau; Ratilly; Sully; Tanlay; and Clos de Vougeot.

Civic buildings. *Double asterisks*: Beaune (Hôtel-Dieu) and Dijon (Palais des Ducs et des États de Bourgogne and the *hôtels particuliers* collectively). *Single asterisks*: Tonnerre (Vieil Hôpital and Fosse Dionne); and Louhans (Grande Rue and Hôtel-Dieu).

Archaeological finds, sites and museums. *Double asterisks*: Châtillon-sur-Seine (Vix treasure in Musée Archéologique du Châtillonnais) and Dijon (Musée Archéologique). *Single asterisks*: Alise Ste-Reine and Mont Auxois (Musée Alésia and site of Gallo-Roman town); Autun (Gallo-Roman remains and the collection in Musée Rolin); Auxerre (Gallo-Roman collection in St-Germain); Azé (cave); Beaune (Archéodrome); Mont Beuvray (site of Bibracte); Chalon-sur-Saône (Volgu flints in Musée Denon); Compierre (site of Gallo-Roman vicus); Sens (Gallo-Roman collection in museum); and Solutré (rock and Musée Départemental de la Préhistoire).

Collections of medieval sculpture. *Double asterisks*: Autun (Musée Rolin); Cluny (Musée Ochier and the capitals in the Farinier); and Dijon (Valois tombs in Musée des Beaux-Arts and items in Musée Archéologique). *Single asterisk*: Nevers (Musée Archéologique de la Porte du Croux).

Paintings and collections of paintings. *Double asterisks*: Beaune (Roger van der Weyden's polyptych in Hôtel-Dieu) and Dijon (Musée des Beaux-Arts). *Single asterisks*: Autun (Master of Moulin's Nativity in Musée Rolin); Bourg-en-Bresse (Musée de Brou); Chalon-sur-Saône (Musée Denon); Cormatin (château); Dijon (Musée Magnin); and Mâcon (Musée des Ursulines).

Industrial sites and museums, and Écomusées. *Single asterisks*: Buffon (Grande Forge); Le Creusot (Château de la Verrerie, which includes the Écomusée de la Communauté Urbaine Le Creusot–Montceau-les-Mines); and Pierre-de-Bresse (Écomusée de la Bresse bourguignonne in château).

Faïence collections. *Single asterisks*: Auxerre (Musée Leblanc-Duvernoy); Digoin (Centre de Documentation sur la Céramique); Marcigny (Musée de la Tour du Moulin); Nevers (Musée Municipal); Paray-le-Monial

(Musée de la Faïence charolaise); and Villiers-sur-Benoît (Musée de l'Art Régional).

Special interest museums. *Single asterisks*: Chalon-sur-Saône (Musée Nicéphore-Niepce for photography) and St-Brisson (Musée de la Résistance).

Grotto at the source of the Douix, Châtillon-sur-Seine (see Route 2)

1   Langres to Dijon via the Vingeanne Valley

Directions and distances. Total distance 123km (76 miles). N74 from **Langres** to (20km) **Vaux-sous-Aubigny**. D140 to (26km) Cusey. D128, (31km) D30, (38.5km) D690 to (42km) St-Seine-sur-Vingeanne. D30, (49km) D27 to (51km) Beaumont-sur-Vingeanne. D27c, (54.5km) D30 to (68km) Talmay. D976 to (74km) **Pontailler-sur-Saône**. D959 to (87km) **Mirebeau** and (96km) **Bèze**. D960 to (115km) Varois. D70 to (123km) **Dijon**.

Connections with other routes. For the way to Langres see the section called 'Getting to Burgundy' in 'Touring Burgundy with this guide'. Route 5 describes Dijon.

Langres (11,400 Langrois; Tourist Information), a hill town overlooking the Marne and its tributary the Bonnelle, stands amidst the wide limestone plateaux that link Champagne with Burgundy and form the northern approach to Dijon. There are fine views from the old walls which preserve the town's character as a medieval fortress. Now outside the boundaries of Burgundy, Langres developed from the tribal capital of the Lingones into one of the three capitals of the ancient kingdom of Burgundy and then into the stronghold of a powerful bishopric. Feudal barons whose surrender of Dijon to the French crown in 1016 paved the way for the creation of the Capetian duchy, the bishops of Langres kept ecclesiastical control of Dijon until the 18C. Their cathedral hardly lives up to the dignity of their position, though its 18C façade conceals a sober, well-proportioned Romanesque interior. Both the town's museums, the Musée Didier and the Musée du Breuil-de-St-Germain, have paintings by Richard and Jean Tassel, the 17C father and son from Langres whose work also hangs in the Musée des Beaux-Arts at Dijon. The Musée du Breuil-de-St-Germain devotes a room to the town's most famous native, the philosopher and encyclopaedist Diderot.

N74 ploughs a straight line across the **Plateau de Langres** towards Dijon, following the course of the Roman road that linked Metz and Lyon. Like its western neighbour, the Châtillonnais (explored in Route 2), the plateau keeps some of its original forest as it nears the city. And like those of the Châtillonnais, its uplands are the nursing ground of rivers and Vauclusian springs, locally called *douix*. At 5km N74 passes near the source of the Marne; the canal linking the river with Saône continues to Pontailler. Otherwise, there is little to note before (28km) **Til-Châtel** (770 people; Tourist Information at Is-sur-Tille to the W and Selongey to the N). The Romanesque *church has a W tympanum showing Christ surrounded by the emblems of the Evangelists; the smaller, less well-preserved tympanum of Christ in Majesty above the S doorway is signed by 'Pierre de Dijon'. The very pure interior contains a good 12C wooden figure of Christ in the S choir aisle.

A more interesting but also more roundabout route, a good 56km longer than the direct way by N74, leaves the main road before Til-Châtel at (20km) **Vaux-sous-Aubigny**, on the little river Badin, and heads E to the *Vingeanne Valley**. A tributary of the Saône, quiet, slow-moving and fringed with willows, the Vingeanne flows alongside the Marne–Saône canal on a course that defines the north-eastern tip of the department of Côte d'Or and hence of the modern region of Burgundy. With the Saône (see Route 9) it traditionally marked the division between the duchy and Franche-Comté, the 'free county' of Burgundy, alternately allied and severed in their early history. Philippe le Hardi, first of the Valois dukes, made their union secure by his marriage to Marguerite de Flandre in 1369 but after the downfall of Charles le Téméraire in 1477 Franche-Comté passed to the Austrian Habsburgs and then to the Spanish Habsburgs. France finally acquired it by the Treaty of Nijmegen which ended the Dutch War in 1678. Its history as an unstable border explains why the Vingeanne should have been lined with medieval fortresses, just as its calm and peaceful landscape makes it appropriate that many of them should have developed into handsome country houses.

D140 from Vaux-sous-Aubigny passes (2km) **Isômes**, with its Romanesque church, before meeting the river and the canal at (4km) **Cusey**, with its castle ruins. **Sacquenay**, 5km S, stands on the ridge of a little hill that breaks the otherwise flat and undramatic countryside. From Cusey D128, D30 and D960 follow the river to (16km) **St-Seine-sur-Vingeanne**, where the 17–18C château (not open) incorporates towers of the medieval castle destroyed by the Spanish. **Fontaine-Française** (800 people; Tourist Information), 5km W, was French in the sense of being a royal fief inside the duchy. It was the scene of Henri IV's victory over the Spanish army and the Catholic supporters of La Ligue in 1595. The fortress where he stayed after the battle was transformed in the 1750s by the Parisian architect Souhard into the superb château (not open) that still dominates the centre of the little town. Here Madame de St-Julien held the literary salons which attracted Voltaire, Rousseau, Madame de Staël and Madame Récamier.

D30 continues to (4km) **Rosières**, where the commanding 14–15C keep of the border stronghold built by the St-Seine family, refurbished as a château in the 17–18C, is being rescued from near ruin (open). At **Beaumont-sur-Vingeanne**, on the other side of the water 5km further S, the *château (open) is one of the loveliest surprises in all Burgundy. The king's chaplain, Claude Jolyot, built it as a summer residence in the 1720s, reproducing all the urban and urbane sophistication of the age in miniature: his château effectively has only three rooms on each of its three storeys. Its only concession to rural Burgundy is the polychrome tile roof, and even this is concealed behind the balustrade. D27c and D30 go on to (9km) **Renève**, which tradition identifies as the place where the notorious Merovingian queen Brunehaut, or Brunhild, was put to death in 612 (see also Montréal and Époisses in Route 10).

D70 offers a quick way from Renève to Dijon via Mirebeau, but it is worth continuing S on D30 to (8km) **Talmay** (520 people) where the château (open), between two arms of the Vingeanne, combines handsome mid 18C work by Jacques-Louis Daviler with the tall keep of the 13C fortress. Its rooms contain 17–18C woodwork and the view from the top stretches from the Côte d'Or to the Jura. E of Talmay the Vingeanne flows into the Saône. The canal joins the river to the S, on the way to the little riverside town of (6km) **Pontailler-sur-Saône** (1320 people; Tourist Information). Mont Ardoux makes a good viewpoint over the Saône plain, explored in Route 9.

The present route heads N on D959, passing (11km) **Bezouotte**, with its 13C church and early 17C manor house (open). **Mirebeau**, on D70 2km beyond, is a pleasant little town (1460 people; Tourist Information) which grew up near the site of a Roman military camp. The early 13C church is simple and heavily buttressed outside, but made impressive inside by the height of its nave. Note the 17C pulpit. D70 again offers a quick way into Dijon, but it is still worth taking a more devious route, continuing N on D959 to (9km) **Bèze** (570 Bèzois). Some of its old houses in, for example, the Place de Verdun preserve fragments of the powerful abbey which owned and gave its name to the Clos de Bèze vineyard at Gevrey-Chambertin on the Côte d'Or. Félix Kir, the future mayor of Dijon, was *curé* of the 18C parish church in the years during and after World War I. On the outskirts of the village the river Bèze gushes to the surface as a Vauclusian spring; part of its underground course can be seen in the nearby caves (open). At **Lux**, 5.5km NW on the way to Til-Châtel and N74, the 18C château (not open) was developed from the castle owned by the Malain family, who had grown rich as bankers to the Valois dukes.

The final leg of the journey follows D960 SW from Bèze through Beire-le-Châtel and Arceau to (14km) the 18C château of **Arcelot** (open), handsome pioneer of the neo-classical style in the Côte d'Or. D960 joins D70 at (5km) Varois. **Dijon**, 7km W, is described in Route 5.

2   The Châtillonnais: Châtillon-sur-Seine to Dijon

Directions and distances. Total distance 84km (52 miles). N71 all the way from **Châtillon-sur-Seine** to (22km) **St-Marc-sur-Seine**, (57km) **St-Seine-l'Abbaye** and (84km) **Dijon**.

Connections with other routes. For the way to Châtillon see the section called 'Getting to Burgundy' in 'Touring Burgundy with this guide'. Route 5 describes Dijon.

CHÂTILLON-SUR-SEINE (6860 Châtillonnais; Tourist Information), in the limestone country of northern Burgundy, has made depressingly regular appearances in military history since the early days of the Capetian duchy. Napoléon met representatives of the Fourth Coalition here in February 1814 as their armies advanced on Paris; his rejection of their terms paved the way for his abdication and exile on Elba. In September 1914, when a foreign army again threatened Paris, Joffre made Châtillon his headquarters in preparing for the Battle of the Marne. Bombing in 1940 has given much of the town its post-war look.

The old quarter on the loop of the Seine to the S of the modern centre keeps some charm and several points of considerable interest. The handsome 16C Maison Philandrier houses the **Musée Archéologique du Châtillonnais** whose centrepiece, the **··**Vix treasure, is by far the most striking archaeological find in Burgundy. Excavated in 1953 at the village of Vix, just N of the town in the shadow of Mont Lassois, it is vivid witness to the region's Iron Age culture. Commanding the Seine near its navigable limit, the hill was a crucial staging post on the trade routes bringing tin from Britain: the Etruscan route continued overland through Switzerland and over the Alps by the Brenner Pass, while the Phoenician and Phocaean route crossed the watershed to the Saône at Chalon and followed the Rhône to the Mediterranean, where Massilia (Marseille) was founded in 600 BC. The treasure consists of the grave goods buried with a Celtic princess or priestess in about 500 BC, towards the end of the Hallstatt culture. Its central item is a huge bronze krater or vase 1.64m (about 5½ feet) tall, apparently used for storing wine. The frieze of charioteers running around the rim and the lions, serpents and Gorgon's heads on the handles identify it as Greek or Etruscan work. Other objects illustrate the range of Mediterranean goods available to the Celts of Mont Lassois: among the jewellery the lovely gold diadem (perhaps Graeco-Scythian) is outstanding. The bronze parts of the burial chariot also survive, and there is a useful miniature reconstruction of the chariot itself. The Vix treasure overshadows the rest of the collection, though other items on the same floor broaden the picture of Hallstatt culture: painted pottery (5C BC) from Mont Lassois, a bronze alms basin (Greek 6C BC) from the chariot burial at Ste-Colombe-sur-Seine and finds from other tumuli. On the floor above, the collection from the Gallo-Roman site of Vertillum (the modern Vertault) is rich in small objects, like the 1C bronze Bacchus and the three stone fertility goddesses, but extends to kitchen utensils and tools for farming, metalworking and stonemasonry. The ground floor has fragments of Roman statuary and a 13C angel, perhaps from Fontenay.

High on a terrace overlooking the town and its river stand the castle ruins and the very early Romanesque church of *St-Vorles, more interesting for the Lombardic work outside than for its interior, though it does contain a lively Entombment of 1527. The chapel beneath the N transept has been renamed after St Bernard, a pupil of the canons of St-Vorles, who is said to have prayed here. Further E the Seine is joined by the Douix, which rises to the surface nearby as a Vauclusian spring, making a delightful little *grotto overhung with woods that would have gladdened the heart of any 18C gentleman.

The **Châtillonnais**, like the neighbouring region round Langres (Route 1), consists of wide limestone plateaux punctuated by valleys and the occasional outcropping hill. The Seine is the most important of many rivers that have their source here; the Vauclusian springs, where rivers surface or resurface fully grown after making their way through the porous limestone, are known locally as *douix*, after the one at Châtillon. Though some fine woodland survives, much of the heavy forest that once almost entirely covered the Châtillonnais was cleared in the Middle Ages by, among others, the monks of Fontenay on the southern edge of the region. The timber fuelled an ironworking industry that greatly expanded with the Industrial Revolution and has left its traces around Châtillon (compare Buffon, Route 3). Too dry to support cows or crops, the bare, rather dull landscape that resulted from forest clearance was largely given over to sheep pasture, making Châtillon a centre of the medieval wool trade for Burgundy and Champagne. Modern agricultural techniques have changed the picture, without making it any more cheering to the eye: arable farming has joined forestry and quarrying as a main source of livelihood. But the region is still poor and its sparse population continues to decline: it has less than 30 people per square kilometre, with only 5 people per square kilometre in some communes, and unemployment was running above 10 per cent in the mid 1980s.

D965, heading W from Châtillon to Tonnerre (Route 3), shows the bleaker side of the Châtillonnais. **Ste-Colombe-sur-Seine** (1150 people), to its N at 3km, was developed in the early 19C as an ironworking centre by Marmont, a former marshal to Napoléon, born and buried at Châtillon. Its factories now make cables, but the dam which originally generated water power survives and there is a small exhibition about the history of the site. **Marcenay**, N of D965 9.5km further W, keeps the tower of a blast furnace built in 1742; an exhibition of industrial history and also of the flora and fauna of the nearby lake is planned. The little town of **Laignes** (900 people; Tourist Information), 4.5km beyond, has a 13–15C church with double transepts. To its N D953 follows the Laignes river, passing (at 9km) near **Vertault**, site of the Gallo-Roman Vertillum. 3km beyond, **Molesmes** has the inexpressive remains of the Benedictine abbey originally established by St Robert in 1095, from which the experiment at Cîteaux and the Cistercian Order sprang.

The **Forêt de Châtillon**, spreading over about 25,000 acres SE of the town, shows the other, more attractive aspect of the region at its best. The little Route Forestière (D16) that cuts through its heart reaches (about 10km) a monument to the 37 members of the local Resistance who died fighting the Nazis in these woods in June 1944. Further on, side-roads lead to (10km) the lovely *Val-des-Choux (or Choues: Owlsdale), with the remains of a Cistercian abbey, founded in 1193, which became a favourite retreat of Louis XIII and Louis XIV. The buildings, which belong largely to the abbey's later history, are being restored to make a centre for rural accommodation, temporary exhibitions and a curious little hunting museum. They are overshadowed by their setting, the most beautifully chosen monastic site in Burgundy.

The monument and abbey can also be reached from the D928, which follows the picturesque valley of the Ource along the northern edge of the forest. **Voulaines-les-Templiers**, at 19.5km, has the 15C tower from a commandery of the Knights Templar. From **Leuglay**, 1.5km beyond, a little signposted circuit follows the ridges of the hills bounding the valley to the N. It offers an alternative way to **Recey-sur-Ource** (460 people; Tourist Information), 7km along D928, with its much altered and restored Romanesque church, now overstuffed with devotional objects. Memorials remind the visitor that Recey was the birthplace of Henri Lacordaire (1802–1861), champion of traditional Catholicism against the threat of rationalism, who revived the Dominican Order in France (see also Flavigny, Route 4). E of Recey D928, continued by D28, heads over to join N74 S of Langres (Route 1). D959 runs a splendid course S from Recey to join the Tille valley on its way to Til-Châtel on N74 (Route 1). At 7km it passes another Templar stronghold, **Bure-les-Templiers**, where the 13C church has a double nave. **Grancey-le-Château**, 15.5km beyond, was a fief of the bishops of Langres which passed to the dukes of Burgundy in the 13C. Tradition claims that St Bernard first discovered his vocation while visiting his brothers during a siege of Grancey by Hugues II, the Capetian duke, in 1113. Remnants of the fortress survive near the 18C château (not open) that replaced it.

The main route from Châtillon follows N71, flanked by the forest and the infant Seine. Near (7.5km) **Ampilly-le-Sec** the restored 19C blast furnace (open) and old wire mill are reminders that this stretch of the valley was once an ironworking centre. The little village of (6km) **Nod-sur-Seine** proudly remembers that the two Free French armies which took part in the Liberation of France met here on 12 September 1944, Leclerc's troops having fought their way from Normandy and Lattre de Tassigny's from Provence.

From (8.5km) **St-Marc-sur-Seine** D32 and D954 make a pleasant detour along the Seine and then the Coquille to (11km) Aignay-le-Duc. **Quemigny-sur-Seine**, S of the road at 6km, has an 18C château sandwiched between the keep and round towers of its predecessor (access to outside only). At **Aignay-le-Duc** (460 people; Tourist Information) the good early Gothic church contains a Renaissance altarpiece. The suffix remembers that the dukes of Burgundy held the lordship of its castle, long since destroyed. **Étalante**, to its SE, has the pretty *douix* where the Coquille rises to the surface. D16 and D6 extend the journey into the Ignon valley, from which Til-Châtel and N74 (Route 1) can easily be reached. **Courtivron**, by the Ignon about 30km from Aignay-le-Duç, has a medieval fortress much altered in later centuries (access to outside only).

Beyond St-Marc-sur-Seine N71 quits the Seine valley for the dry, wide landscape of the uplands. **Baigneux-les-Juifs** (250 people; Tourist Information), off the main road at 13km, became the home of a Jewish colony in the 13C. **Jours-lès-Baigneux**, 5km NW of the village, has a Renaissance château (not open) with a N façade which echoes Serlio's majestic courtyard at Ancy-le-Franc. For Frôlois, on the edge of the Auxois SW of Baigneux-les-Juifs, see Route 4.

N71 continues to (10km) **Chanceaux**, where the long main street recalls the days when the village was a staging post on the coach road. 3.5km beyond, a turning leads W to the **Source of the Seine**, still a pleasant spot despite the coy grotto and statue added by the city of Paris, which owns the land, at the behest of Napoléon III in 1865. Downstream stood the temples whose site yielded the remarkable collection of ex-votos displayed in the Musée Archéologique at Dijon. **Champagny**, 4km further S, preserves a 19C country school (open).

As it approaches Dijon and the Montagne the landscape grows more steeply enfolded, and N71 drops down from a dramatic view into (4.5km) **St-Seine-l'Abbaye** (330 people; Tourist Information) at the bottom of its valley. The little village takes its name from the powerful Benedictine abbey founded by St Seine, or Sequanus, in the 6C. The early Gothic church, refurbished in the 14C and 15C, contains 16C paintings of the saint's life and a fine set of 18C choir stalls. For the marvellous switchback journey W by D26 across the hills and valleys of the Auxois to Vitteaux, see Route 4. N71 also offers some striking scenery as it climbs out of the valley only to drop down again into (10.5km) *Val-Suzon, the name for a valley and its two little villages, Haut-Suzon and Bas-Suzon, E of the main road. The narrow, richly wooded course of the river, a little tributary of the Ouche, is well worth following in either direction: W towards its source near **Trouhaut** (about 11km) or E past the source of the Jouvence to (12km) **Messigny-et-Vantoux** (1070 people). The second of the two villages that make up this little commune has a château (not open) built in 1704 for the first president of the Burgundian *parlement*, so assured in its elegance that one accepts the attribution to Jules Hardouin-Mansart, the royal architect who converted the Palais in Dijon to its present appearance.

On the last leg of its journey from Val-Suzon into (16.5km) Dijon N71 passes several high-lying places, with good views, on the fringes of the city. **Hauteville-lès-Dijon** (960 people), to the left, has herringbone masonry (c 1000) on the outside of its church. **Fontaine-lès-Dijon** (7860 people), also to the left, was the birthplace of St Bernard in 1090. A square tower is the chief medieval fragment to survive from the castle originally belonging to his father, Tescelin le Roux. It stands near the late 14C church which contains a fine statue of the saint by Antoine Le Moiturier, one of the sculptors responsible for Jean sans Peur's tomb in the Musée des Beaux-Arts in the city. Amidst its engulfing suburban development **Talant** (12,860 people), right of N71, manages to preserves its old centre and early 13C church at the top of the hill. The village was founded by Eudes III and the castle he built here became, with Rouvres-en-Plaine, the main residence of the Capetian dukes. The centre of **Dijon** is described in Route 5.

3 The Yonne and the Armançon: Sens to Joigny, Montbard (Fontenay) and Semur-en-Auxois

Directions and distances. Total distance 147km (91 miles). N6 from **Sens** to (13km) Villeneuve-sur-Yonne and (30km) **Joigny**. D943, (52km) D905 to (56km) St-Florentin, (83km) **Tonnerre** and (129km) Montbard (**Fontenay** is 5.5km N). D980 to (147km) **Semur**.

Connections with other routes. For the way to Sens see the section called 'Getting to Burgundy' in 'Touring Burgundy with this guide'. Joigny is the starting point for Route 10 (along the Serein valley via Chablis to Semur or Avallon), Route 11 (to Auxerre, Avallon and Vézelay) and Route 16 (through the Puisaye to Cosne-sur-Loire). Semur is described at the beginning of Route 4, which continues through the Auxois to Dijon.

SENS (27,080 Sénonais; Tourist Information) is a little city on the N6 in the NW tip of the department of Yonne, a corner of land included in the modern but not the historical Burgundy. However, an edict of 1416 declared its bridge over the Yonne the northern limit for wine that could be called 'Burgundy' and, culturally if not administratively, the city marks the point where Burgundy met the Île de France and Champagne. It developed from the capital of the Senones (the tribe credited with sacking Rome in 390 BC, when geese saved the Capitol) into a Roman and medieval city whose walls followed the ring of boulevards that enclose the present centre. Henry V spent his honeymoon besieging it.

The cathedral of *St-Étienne, still the main landmark, gave Sens its importance in the Middle Ages, when the archbishop held sway over a roster of cities summed up in the acronymic device of the cathedral chapter, 'CAMPONT': Chartres, Auxerre, Meaux, Paris (which did not have an archbishopric of its own until 1627), Orléans, Nevers and Troyes. St Bernard finally succeeded in getting Abélard condemned for heresy at the council held here in 1140. Thomas à Becket was welcomed by the royal abbey of Ste-Colombe after Henry II had driven him from his first Burgundian refuge at Pontigny in 1166. Louis IX (St Louis) was married in the cathedral in 1234.

The building belongs to the height of the archbishopric's power. It was started in about 1130 in a Romanesque style that can still be seen in the St-Jean chapel off the N transept. But after about 1140 the work expressed a new Gothic spirit allying the cathedral with the Île de France and making it a contemporary and rival of Suger's great experiment at St-Denis. Its architect became known to the English as William of Sens when, in 1175–1184, he remodelled the E end of Canterbury cathedral in a manner closely akin to Sens, helping to spread the new style across the Channel.

At Sens his achievement survives best inside the cathedral. The outside tells a different and messier story. The grand design of the W façade, where work was several times interrupted, barely survives the unhappily matched towers and the mutilation of its doorways at the Revolution. The N doorway, at the foot of the unfinished late 12C Tour de Plomb, shows the life of John the Baptist. The original Tour de Pierre on the S side collapsed and was rebuilt in the late 13C–early 14C with a doorway showing the life of the Virgin. The tympanum of the central doorway (replaced when the Tour de Pierre was rebuilt) is devoted to St Stephen, who appears again on the central pier—a superb statue which alone escaped vandalism at the

Revolution. The transept doorways, the Porte d'Abraham to the N and the Porte de Moïse to the S, are Flamboyant work by Martin Chambiges of Troyes.

William of Sens' nave, in a sober grey stone, has a three-storey elevation divided into bays by alternating single and clustered columns, and roofed over with sexpartite vaulting. The superb rose windows in the Flamboyant transepts are not the only good examples of stained glass. Note the Renaissance windows attributed to the elder Jean Cousin in the third bay in the S aisle of the nave and in the chapel on the S side of the choir, and note particularly the *late 12C glass in the N ambulatory, showing Thomas à Becket, the legend of St Eustace (or St Hubert), the Prodigal Son and the Good Samaritan. The N arcade of the nave has monuments to Archbishop Salazar's parents (1515) and the brothers Perron (1637), both archbishops. The tomb of the Dauphin, Louis XVI's father (died 1765), by Guillaume Coustou is in the chapel on the N side of the choir.

The handsome 16C Archbishops' Palace and 13C Synodal Palace which form the courtyard on the S side of the cathedral now house a *Museum which brings together the cathedral treasury, one of the richest in France, with other collections from the town. A major campaign of rearrangement has resulted in a particularly imaginative Gallo-Roman display, with a striking reconstruction of the façade of the public baths as well as mosaics, funeral monuments and statuary. The first floor of the Henri II wing contains plaster models of the medallions which decorated Sens' 18C Porte Dauphine and fragments of the 18C choir screen from the cathedral. The treasury consists of ivories, enamels, plate, liturgical ornaments, tapestries, fabrics and robes, including Thomas à Becket's. An 11C Byzantine reliquary coffer, intricately carved in ivory, is outstanding. The Synodal Palace, currently used for temporary exhibitions, will display medieval sculpture from the cathedral when reorganisation of the museum is complete.

Though it has some interesting old streets and a pleasant circuit of boulevards marking the course of its walls, the little city centre does not demand a detailed walking tour. The 19C covered market faces the cathedral across the Place de la République; to the N rises the spire of the wonderfully vulgar neo-Renaissance **Hôtel de Ville** (1904). The Rue de la République leads S from the cathedral to the Rue Jean-Cousin, where the half-timbered 16C **Maison d'Abraham** with its carved corner post is one of several old houses. The 13–16C **St-Pierre-le-Rond**, on the Rue Rigault to the N, is now derelict and boarded up, like the neighbouring façade of the 13C **Hôtel-Dieu**, reconstructed here after it was demolished to make way for the covered market in the main square. The suburb of St-Savinien, linking the old centre with the modern town to the E, has two churches: **St-Jean**, a former abbey chapel, restored in the 17C, and **St-Savinien**, with a 13C bell-tower and a crypt from the older church built to shelter the saint's relics.

Like the city itself, the surrounding region of the **Sénonais** belongs as much to Burgundy's neighbours as to Burgundy. To the W is the tip of the **Gâtinais**, ideal country for fishing and hunting, criss-crossed by streams and ponds that feed into the Loing around Montargis. D26 passes **Nailly** (1010 people), **Brannay** and **Lixy**, all with interesting churches, on the way to (19km) **Vallery**, a village dominated by memories of the Condé family, leaders of the Protestant faction and governors of Burgundy in the 17–18C. They owned the Renaissance château (access to outside only) which stands by its ruined medieval predecessor. Henri (died 1646), father of the Grand Condé who led the Fronde rebellion, is buried in the church he built. E of

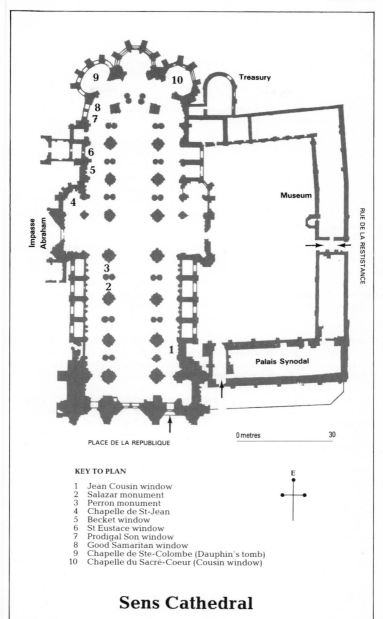

Treasury

Museum

Impasse Abraham

RUE DE LA RESTISTANCE

Palais Synodal

0 metres   30

PLACE DE LA REPUBLIQUE

KEY TO PLAN

1 Jean Cousin window
2 Salazar monument
3 Perron monument
4 Chapelle de St-Jean
5 Becket window
6 St Eustace window
7 Prodigal Son window
8 Good Samaritan window
9 Chapelle de Ste-Colombe (Dauphin's tomb)
10 Chapelle du Sacré-Coeur (Cousin window)

E

Sens Cathedral

Sens the river Vanne and the Forêt d'Othe, forming one of Burgundy's historical boundaries, lead towards Troyes and the Champagne. N60 follows the marshy course of the river to (24km) **Villeneuve-l'Archevêque**, a little town of 1140 people, founded by the archbishop of Sens in the 12C. Louis IX (St Louis) came here in 1239 to receive from the Venetians what purported to be Christ's crown of thorns, most highly prized of the relics he built the Ste-Chapelle in Paris to house. The church has a fine 13C N doorway dedicated to the Virgin Mary, who appears with Gabriel and St Anne on the left-hand columns, with the infant Christ on the central pillar, in Nativity scenes on the lintel and enthroned on the tympanum. Inside, the S aisle has an early 16C Entombment in the style of Champagne rather than Burgundy. **Fleurigny**, 18km NW of Villeneuve or 13km directly from Sens by D939, has a Renaissance château (open) with a chapel attributed to Jean Cousin the elder (born at Soucy, on the way from Sens).

The main route takes N6 along the wide valley of the Yonne, fringed with low hills, a course once followed by the Roman Via Agrippa linking Boulogne and Paris with Autun, Chalon and Lyon. **Villeneuve-sur-Yonne** (5050 Villeneuviens; Tourist Information), at 13km, was founded in 1163 as one of Louis VII's 'new towns' and marked the southern limit of royal territory on the river. It keeps a grid layout of streets between the two 13C gates that survive from the original five. Ditches and fragments of wall lead round from the Porte de Sens in the N to the Tour de Louis-le-Gros, an early 13C fragment of the royal château. When reorganisation of the town's museum system is complete, the Porte de Sens and its southern counterpart, the Porte de Joigny, will share the collections of local history and archaeology between them; paintings will be displayed nearby in the Rue Carnot, connecting the two gates. This wide main street makes a handsome effect, with tall brick chimneys, red-tiled roofs and the elaborate front of the 18C Maison des Sept Têtes. No. 56 was the home of the notorious Dr Marcel Petiot, who served as Villeneuve's mayor in the 1920s before leaving to pursue a career as a mass murderer in Paris during the Occupation; he was found guilty of 26 murders and guillotined in 1946. The Renaissance façade of Notre-Dame masks the 13C body of the church. Inside, the tall nave is continued, without transepts, by a choir of equal height. Note the capitals and the roof bosses, among which Louis IX (St Louis) and his queen, Marguerite de Provence, can be made out. A chapel on the N side of the nave contains an Entombment with a fine 14C Christ in limewood surrounded, inappropriately, by Renaissance plaster figures.

An alternative way S from Villeneuve, 28km in all, follows D15 up to (10km) **Dixmont** (660 people), where the church has a mutilated 13C doorway with statue-columns of Gabriel and the Virgin Mary, and angels above the tympanum. D20 continues S across a corner of the Forêt d'Othe and drops down into Joigny via the vineyards of the Côte St-Jacques.

The main route from Villeneuve follows N6 and the Yonne. At (8km) **St-Julien-du-Sault** (2160 people), on the opposite bank, the 16C choir of the church preserves nine roundels of 13C *glass, showing saints' legends and the life of Christ, quite as good as the glass in Sens cathedral. Just to the S, the hill at **Vauguillain** is crowned with a little late 12C chapel inside the ruined walls of the castle built by the archbishops of Sens; it gives a wide view over the curving river valley.

JOIGNY (9700 Joviniens; Tourist Information), 9km beyond, calls itself 'historique et gastronomique'. Its restaurants make it a favourite stopping place for travellers along the N6. Its historical character is much less apparent from the main road than it is on the way down from the Côte

St-Jacques to the 12C Porte du Bois. The old *centre, clinging to the steep hillside, is one of the best little townscapes in northern Burgundy. The fire of 1530 that destroyed many of its medieval streets also prompted some fine Renaissance rebuilding that testified to the prosperity and civic energy of its *vignerons*.

St-Thibault, which survived the fire, was built in 1490–1529 and spanned the transition from Gothic to Renaissance. It contains a fine Renaissance pulpit and a motley collection of paintings and statues (identified in detail on a notice by the door) among which the 14C Vierge au Sourire, on the fourth pillar on the S side of the nave, is outstanding. The **Maison du Pilori**, on the N side of the church, is the oldest half-timbered house in the town and the first of several on the Rue Montant-au-Palais as it heads E. Note the Tree of Jesse house and the corner house facing the 11C gate that leads up to **St-Jean** and the **Château des Gondi** (now being restored), both rebuilt after the fire. The church contains a wonderfully ornate Renaissance *vault over the nave and E end, and, in the S aisle, a 15C marble Entombment and the tomb of Adélaïs, comtesse de Joigny (died 1187). On the little Place de la République, further E, is another but more modest Renaissance church, **St-André**.

A major junction in north-western Burgundy, Joigny is the starting point for several journeys described later in this guide. The present route leaves N6 for D943 and D905, the St-Florentin road. At (5km) **St-Cydroine** the Romanesque *church, originally belonging to a priory controlled by the Benedictines of La Charité, has an octagonal tower, slightly later than the touchingly simple interior. Note the carved capitals at the crossing, particularly the elephant at the NE corner. At the ugly post-war sprawl of (3km) **Migennes** (8240 people; Tourist Information) the road quits the Yonne and follows its tributary the Armançon, though for most of the way it runs closer to the straight tree-lined **Canal de Bourgogne**, built in 1775–1834 to link the Yonne with the Saône at St-Jean-de-Losne beyond Dijon (a course of 242km with 189 locks). The undulating, fertile country of the Auxois stretches to its S, but historically the lower reaches of the Armançon valley have taken more of their character from Champagne and the bleaker, poorer Châtillonnais to the N. Their link with the Châtillonnais was strengthened by the growth of industries along the canal. Quarrying is now the most conspicuous.

The village of (14km) **Avrolles**, where the road changes from D943 to D905, has a church with a detached bell-tower begun in the 12C. **St-Florentin** (6430 Florentinois; Tourist Information), 4km further, stands on a hill overlooking the broad valley where the Armance joins the Armançon, site of a Gallo-Roman settlement renamed after a 5C martyr. The town itself is largely industrial: St-Florentin cheese comes from Beugnon and Soumaintrain in the Armance valley to the E (Soumaintrain also making a cheese under its own name). The hill is crowned by a terrace, marking the site of the abbey, with fragments of the ancient fortifications and a panoramic view. The *church was begun in the early 16C—perhaps by Martin Chambiges of Troyes, who built the transepts of Sens cathedral—in a mixed Gothic and Renaissance style. Note the elaborate façades of the transepts which, together with the big choir, dwarf the unfinished nave. Statues and glass, both from the school of Troyes, make the ambulatory and chapels of the choir particularly rich. St Florentin is one of several saints depicted in the glass; St James (dressed as a pilgrim) and St Roch or Rock (with his dog) are among the statues.

D905 continues uneventfully to (27km) **TONNERRE** (6010 Tonnerrois;

Tourist Information), at first glance no more attractive than the other towns on this reach of the canal and the river but with some pleasant surprises. The *Vieil Hôpital, currently being restored, is a remarkable survival. Founded in 1293 by Marguerite de Bourgogne, widow of St Louis' brother, Charles d'Anjou, it is 150 years older than the more famous Hôtel-Dieu at Beaune, whose arrangement of sick beds it anticipated. Behind the 18C W façade of the long, low building is the vast medieval Salle des Malades. It held 40 beds with a connecting gallery at window level above them. The panelled vault conceals a roof cavity with marvellous oak timbers. At the E end are the tomb of Louvois (see Ancy-le-Franc below) by Girardon and the 19C tomb of Marguerite de Bourgogne, replacing the original one destroyed at the Revolution. The neighbouring chapel contains a fine Entombment (1454) in the tradition of Claus Sluter. The **Hôtel d'Uzès**, a Renaissance house—now a bank—on the Rue des Fontenilles S of the hospital, was the birthplace of the Chevalier d'Éon (1728–1810), who spent much of his diplomatic career as a transvestite spy in Moscow and London. The little **Museum** on the neighbouring Rue Rougemont has mementoes and a collection of his papers. From the Place Charles-de-Gaulle picturesque streets climb up the old town to the Renaissance **St-Pierre** (note its S façade), with a view over the red-tiled roofs of the town to the surrounding country. The *Fosse Dionne, to the W, is an elegant 18C *lavoir* built over the Celtic Fons Divona, a large Vauclusian spring which attracted the first settlement of Tonnerre.

The **Tonnerrois** used to be famous for its wine—the invading English army drank 3000 butts at Tonnerre in 1360—but the vineyards that stretched across to join Chablis and the Auxerrois had largely died out by the beginning of this century. Wine production is now being revived on a smaller scale, notably by the reds of **Épineuil** (600 people), N of the town. *Lavoirs* often make a distinctive feature in the villages of the region: a useful pamphlet available from the Syndicat d'Initiative gives details and suggests tours.

At **Tanlay** (1110 people), 10km E, the *château (open) is one of the best in Burgundy. It was begun in 1559 by François d'Andelot, one of the three Coligny brothers who took a leading part in the Protestant faction during the Wars of Religion, and completed in the 1640s by its new owner, Mazarin's finance minister Particelli d'Émery. The century that lapsed is clearly marked in the difference between the cheerfully eclectic Petit Château and the main buildings inside the moat, where the Dijonnais architect Pierre Le Muet pulled together the earlier work into a restrained classical ensemble of central block, wings, towers and gatehouse around the main courtyard. The interior has good chimneypieces, wood panelling in the Salle de Compagnie and *trompe l'oeil* murals in the Grande Galerie. The top floor of the 16C Tour de la Ligue has a ceiling painted, by a pupil of Primaticcio, with a witty satire showing the participants in the religious wars as mythological characters: d'Andelot as Hercules, his brother Amiral de Coligny as Neptune, the Catholic Duc de Guise as Mars, Diane de Poitiers as Venus and Henri II as Janus.

Tanlay's southern neighbour is the château (open) at **Ancy-le-Franc** (1180 people; Tourist Information), 20km from Tonnerre by D905 but more pleasantly reached by side-roads leading from Tanlay through the canal scenery of Argentenay and Ancy-le-Libre. It was built in the 1540s by Antoine de Clermont, comte de Tonnerre and brother-in-law of Henri II's mistress, Diane de Poitiers. Sebastiano Serlio, whom François I had brought from Bologna to work on Fontainebleau, was his architect. Louvois, Louis

The château of Tanlay

XIV's minister of war, bought the château with the countship of Tonnerre in 1684. Serlio's *courtyard remains a masterpiece in combining severe design with rich detail, but the shabby state of the interior almost destroys the effect of the murals by Primaticcio, Niccolò dell'Abbate and other members of the Fontainebleau school in, for example, the Galerie de Pharsale. The little Chambre des Fleurs and Chambre des Arts keep some of their charm, and several rooms have interesting painted wooden ceilings. The outbuildings house a museum of carriages and vintage cars. Ancy-le-Franc also hosts a summer festival of music, opera and theatre.

Nuits and **Ravières**, on D905 8km beyond Ancy-le-Franc, are glum little towns (with a joint population of 1430) facing each other across the river and the canal. At Nuits the church contains a piscina by the local Rigolley brothers, who carved the splendid set of choir stalls at Montréal (see Route 10). The château (open) by the river is a Renaissance building of great charm. Ravières church has a Flamboyant W façade. At **Asnières-en-Montagne**, 4km E, stands the ruined castle of Rochefort. The 13C church of (9km) **Rougemont**, on a hill by the D905, has a mutilated tympanum.

The *Grande Forge** at (4km) **Buffon** has been restored as an impressive reminder of the long tradition of ironworking in the Châtillonnais, as well as the best local monument to the naturalist Georges-Louis Leclerc, comte de Buffon (1707–1788), keeper of the Jardin du Roi in Paris, author of the 'Histoire naturelle' and a native of nearby Montbard. He built the ironworks in 1768–1772 as both a scientific laboratory for his inquiries into heating and cooling and a business venture for exploiting charcoal from his forests. He chose a site near the course of the Canal de Bourgogne, projected but not yet built, and depended on a cut from the Armançon for water power. The up-to-date processes he used were partly inspired by the example of the Industrial Revolution in England. While employing a forgemaster, Buffon supervised work himself for the first ten years, the community finally growing to about 400 people, of whom 30 were directly involved in the foundry. Buffon's lodging, the workers' cottages and the forgemaster's house are laid out like a model farm. A staircase with an elegant wrought-iron balustrade leads down into the furnace room, where working copies of the original bellows and mill-wheel have been reconstructed; beyond are the refinery and the rolling and slitting mill, where the iron was cut into manageable rods.

Immediately beyond the forge the course of the Armançon swings S to Semur, avoiding Montbard and Fontenay, and passing at about 10km near the 17C buildings of the abbey at **Moutiers-St-Jean**, which dominate the village and the wide, rolling country. D905 and the canal follow a tributary river, the Brenne, to the knocked-about industrial town of (5km) **Montbard** (7110 Montbardois; Tourist Information). Napoléon's general Andoche Junot, duc d'Abrantès, born at Bussy-le-Grand, committed suicide here. There is not much of interest except for the mementoes of Buffon. His statue stands in the square bearing his name, opposite the house he built on the site of his birthplace. On the hill behind is the terraced park he created in the ruins of the castle he had inherited. The 15C Tour St-Louis houses a museum with mementoes including his chemical laboratory, and the Tour de l'Aubespin, also 15C, a museum of local archaeology. Near by is the outdoor study where Rousseau paid Buffon a visit of homage, now containing drawings of birds by his collaborator Martinet. Buffon is buried in the chapel next to the church of St-Urse. The Musée des Beaux-Arts, in a former chapel in the Rue Piron, has work by local artists.

None of this compares with the abbey of * ***Fontenay** in its little wooded valley 4km NE. The oldest ensemble of Cistercian buildings to survive, it embodies St Bernard's own vision of the Cistercian ideal in all its original severity. Even when that severity relaxed in later centuries, Fontenay's layout (like its name, Fountains) was still echoed in the Order's foundations throughout Europe.

In 1118, only three years after he had established Clairvaux, St Bernard sent twelve monks to found a community in the Montbard neighbourhood. The experiment proved successful enough by 1130 for them to move down from their original settlement into the valley, where wood, water and solitude ideally answered their needs. Étienne de Bâgé, the bishop of Autun who built St-Lazare, and St Bernard's uncle gave them the land, while his cousin, Godefroy de la Roche, served as the first abbot. The church—endowed by Everard, the former bishop of Norwich who took refuge here during the wars of Stephen and Matilda—was started in about 1139 and consecrated in 1147 by Pope Eugenius III, a former Clairvaux monk and protégé of St Bernard. The rest of the monastic buildings were complete by the end of the century. Fontenay grew into a community of about 300, survived the armies and marauders trampling through Burgundy during the Hundred Years War but declined with the Wars of Religion. After the Revolution it became a paper mill run by the Montgolfier family of pioneer ballooning fame. At the beginning of this century it passed into the hands of the Aynards, still the owners, who restored its monastic character. With its buildings reroofed in warm pink, red and brown tiles, its lawns neatly

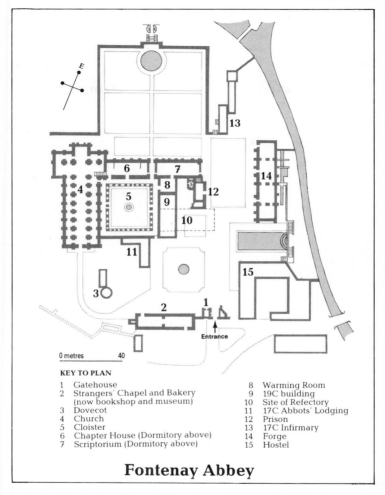

KEY TO PLAN

1   Gatehouse
2   Strangers' Chapel and Bakery
    (now bookshop and museum)
3   Dovecot
4   Church
5   Cloister
6   Chapter House (Dormitory above)
7   Scriptorium (Dormitory above)

8   Warming Room
9   19C building
10 Site of Refectory
11 17C Abbots' Lodging
12 Prison
13 17C Infirmary
14 Forge
15 Hostel

Fontenay Abbey

tended and only a few later additions to mar the ensemble, Fontenay today stands in striking contrast to the picturesque ruins at Fountains or Rievaulx that represent Cistercianism in England.

The low, simple mass of the church, unrelieved by any tower, proclaims its severity. The W façade, a surface the Cluniacs loved to enrich, has only seven simple, round-headed windows arranged in two rows above the doorway. They announce a building dedicated not to magnificence but to a demanding idea expressed through geometry and proportion. Inside, the nave is a pointed tunnel vault with transverse arches dividing it into eight bays. The deliberate avoidance of ornament (note the capitals) almost conceals the family resemblance to Vézelay, where the nave was being finished as Fontenay's was begun. The lack of a clerestory darkens it and

The cloister of Fontenay abbey

concentrates attention on the light entering through the windows in the transept ends, the crossing wall and the square-ended choir: holes punched into the heavy mass of the building in simple but subtly varied patterns. The effect would always have been sombre, for the monastic rule allowed only five candles to light the whole church. The few embellishments that survive mostly belong to the years when the Cistercians had abandoned the fervent austerity of St Bernard's time. The bare earth floor of the nave was originally paved, but the decorated 13C tiles in the chancel would have been prohibited by the builders. So would the late 14C altarpiece of the Nativity. The tombstones now grouped here include Bishop Everard's. A late 13C figure of the Virgin and Child stands near the N transept door, which led to the monks' cemetery.

From the S transept a staircase leads to the monk's dormitory, with a magnificent 15C chestnut roof. The cloister survives in the same original purity as the church: a big square with a round-arched arcade on double columns, the leaf patterns on the capitals simplified almost to the point of abstraction. Note how variations in the vaulting and columns, and the asymmetrical position of the entrances to the central square, relieve its regularity in the same way that the differing patterns of windows relieve the severity of the church. The loss of the refectory, demolished in 1745, creates the only major gap in the buildings around the cloister that indicate the different functions of the community: the vaulted rectangular chapter house, the scriptorium where the monks copied manuscripts, the warming room (the only heated part of the abbey except for the kitchens) and, beyond, the prison. Further S, in the pleasant grounds, is the vaulted forge built to exploit iron ore from the neighbouring hillside and powered by water from the canalised stream. It is powerful witness to the monks' part in the ironworking tradition of the Châtillonnais and, through their use of charcoal, in the destruction of its great forests—though the woods of Fontenay's own valley remain in all their beauty.

Beyond Montbard D905 follows the Brenne to Sombernon and the auto-route leading into Dijon. The present route heads S on D980 into the heartland of the Auxois, a hilly region the next route will explore on a more leisurely way into Dijon. At 10km a steep side-road leads 3km E to the village of **Lantilly**, where 23 members of the Resistance group Henri Bourgogne were killed during the last, chaotic months of Nazi occupation in 1944, a massacre that stands in the record with the atrocities in the Forêt de Châtillon and the luckless villages of the Morvan. The château (open), a pure neo-classical building of 1709 popularly known as the 'Château with a Hundred Windows', has a wide view over the Auxois and Alésia. So does **Grignon**, another hill village 3km beyond, with a largely 14C fortress (not open) which tradition claims as the spot where St Reine was imprisoned in the 3C (see Alise-Ste-Reine in the next route). **Semur-en-Auxois**, 18km beyond Montbard, is also described in the next route.

4 The Auxois: Semur to Dijon

Directions and distances. Total distance 111km (69 miles). D954 from **Semur** to (13km) Venarey-les-Laumes (for **Alise-Ste-Reine**, **Mont Auxois**, **Bussy-Rabutin** and **Flavigny-sur-Ozerain**). D905 to (32km) Vitteaux. D70, (35km) D26 to (39km) St-Thibault. D970 to (53km) Pouilly-en-Auxois. D18, (63km) D18a to (65km) Châteauneuf. D18 to (71km) Pont-d'Ouche. D33, (91km) A38 and (105km) N5 to (111km) **Dijon**.

Connections with other routes. Semur is reached at the end of the previous route and by an alternative way from Joigny, along the Serein valley, in Route 10. Dijon is described in Route 5.

Do not confuse the Auxois with the Auxerrois, the region round Auxerre. The Burgundian pronunciation of both names softens the x into a double s.

The relief map of Burgundy shows the ****Auxois** as a series of almost parallel ridges running in the same direction as the main roads that approach Dijon from Montbard and the NW. They mark the hills and valleys carved into the blue limestone plateau by the Armançon and its tributaries, the Brenne, the Ozerain and the Oze. In the depression separating it from the Morvan in the W the Auxois is popularly called the Terre Plaine. The more rugged landscape in the E, where the Auxois approaches the Châtil-lonnais and runs into the N–S barrier of the Hautes-Côtes, is known as the Montagne. The heart of the Auxois—its contours are too imprecise for it to have a strict geographical centre—is the area round Semur and Mont Auxois, overlooking the plain where the rivers meet.

Mont Auxois is the most famous of the hills that make far-reaching viewpoints. As Alesia, the fortress where Vercingetorix surrendered to Caesar, it is also the predecessor of the medieval fortified hill towns, like Flavigny and Châteauneuf, that later decayed into picturesque villages and now make popular tourist attractions. The countryside they survey is fertile agricultural land that earned the Auxois its reputation as the granary of Burgundy and linked it with the cereal-producing belt stretching beyond Burgundy up to the Beauce. The uplands are still largely arable but the valleys, with their compact limestone villages, are green pasture land for beef and dairy cattle—giving the region its cheeses and (as in so much of Burgundy) making the big, white Charolais one of its most typical sights.

The main roads that sweep through the Auxois were designed for the long-distance traveller, not the tourist trying to get the flavour of the country. The route below dodges between them on its way from Semur, takes long detours and, with some difficulty, avoids the autoroute until the last leg of the journey into Dijon.

*SEMUR-EN-AUXOIS (4550 Sémurois; Tourist Information), a centre and stronghold of the duchy from the beginning of the Capetian dynasty in the 11C, realises to the full the picturesque possibilities of its site where the narrowing valley of the Armançon loops round an outcrop of pink granite to create a naturally fortified position. Above the Pont Joly rise the four big drum towers of the 14C fortress that guarded the neck of the river and, among the red-tiled roofs of the medieval *bourg* that flourished next to its walls, the spire of Notre-Dame.

Near the **Maison du Tourisme** two medieval gates, the 15C Porte Sauvigny and the 13C Porte Guillier, are sandwiched together at the entrance to the *bourg*. Note the cheerfully obscene corbel on the left as you go under the second gate. The pedestrianised Rue Buffon, passing the 17C Logis du Roi on the little market place to the right, quickly leads up to ***Notre-Dame**. An abbey church built in the 1220s to replace the Romanesque church endowed by the first Capetian duke, it is often praised as the most perfect Gothic church in Burgundy. This is misleading: its original eclecticism, emphasised by later alterations and additions, makes Notre-Dame a treasure-house of details. At the W end two square towers rise behind the big, three-bayed Flamboyant porch. The Revolutionaries mutilated the sculpture of the main doorways but left an elephant at the base of the central door and a camel at the base of the south door to catch Henri Vincenot's attention in 'Le Pape des escargots'. The doorway to the N transept, the Porte des Bleds (Corn Door), is much better preserved. Its tympanum shows the legend of Doubting Thomas: note the boat taking him on his evangelical mission to India on the middle register and the acrobat on the lower register. The sitting man who takes the place of a conventional capital is one of several inventively witty details below. Inside Notre-Dame the effect of the narrow nave with its unusually tall clerestory is complicated by the Flamboyant and Renaissance side-chapels. Note, on the N side: the fine late 15C Entombment in the tradition of Claus Sluter in the second chapel; the 16C glass showing the legend of St Barbara in the third chapel; and the very different glass with butchers and drapers at work in the two 15C guild chapels that follow. An ornate 15C ciborium stands at the corner of the nearby transept. The last chapel on the S side of the nave has Renaissance gates. The choir is every bit as eclectic as the nave, with chubby pillars below a row of sculptured heads running round the triforium. The apse has a boss showing the Coronation of the Virgin. The chapel on the N side of the ambulatory contains an altarpiece painted with the Tree of Jesse (1554) and the Lady Chapel behind the choir 13C glass showing the legend of Mary Magdalen, restored by Viollet-le-Duc.

The site of the fortress on the headland beyond the four big drum towers is now a pleasant 18C quarter with a tree-lined walk following the old walls. Beyond the E end of Notre-Dame are the Place de l'Ancienne-Comédie and, on the neighbouring Rue J.-J.-Collenot, the local **Museum**. The most interesting items are on the second floor: ex-votos from the source of the Seine and Massingy-lès-Vitteaux; three paintings by Corot, including 'Young Boy wearing a Cap'; and, in the medieval room, two carved angels from an Entombment attributed to Antoine Le Moiturier, one of the sculptors who made Jean sans Peur's tomb at Dijon.

The Course de la Bague, run from Villenotte to Semur every 31 May, is the oldest horse-race in France, dating back to 1639.

From Semur D954 heads E and then N to the plain where the Auxois rivers flow together near (13km) **Venarey-les-Laumes** (3540 people; Tourist Information), a depressing place dominated by its railway junction but a useful jumping-off point for the rich group of places in the hills further E. **Alise-Ste-Reine** (670 people), 2km away, compresses the salient history of the region into its name. St Reine was martyred in 262. Legend identifies the spot where she died as the little spring, supposedly miraculous in origin and credited with healing powers, which rises in the village near the interesting 17C hospital. Alesia (Alésia in modern French) is the Roman name for *Mont Auxois (407m), above the village, where Caesar defeated Vercingetorix in 52 BC and so completed the conquest of Gaul he had begun some six years earlier. Vercingetorix, an Arvernian chieftain the rebellious Gauls had chosen as leader, hoped to score a surprise victory over Caesar's army as it made its way through Burgundy towards the Saône. Instead, he found himself trapped on Alesia, the capital of the Mandubii and a holy shrine of such antiquity that the Greek historian Diodorus Siculus traced its foundation to Hercules. Around the base of the hill Caesar established a double line whose outer ring successfully fought off attempts to raise the siege. Vercingetorix surrendered after six weeks and was eventually executed after being paraded through Rome in Caesar's triumph.

Most of the finds from the battlefield are in the museum at St-Germain-en-Laye, while the Archéodrome near Beaune (see Route 6) has a reconstruction of Caesar's formidable siege line. The *Musée Alésia in the village here has a fine collection from the Gallo-Roman oppidum that succeeded the Mandubian capital and flourished on the hill in the 1–4C: brooches and clasps, bronze figures (including the expressive Dying Gaul), a bas-relief of Jupiter with Juno and Minerva, and small statues of fertility goddesses and Epona, the Gallic horse goddess. The most prominent landmark on Mont Auxois itself is now the huge statue of Vercingetorix by Aimé Millet, erected in 1865 to commemorate the first organised excavations and bearing a noticeable resemblance to their patron, Napoléon III. It commands a superb view, though not the one surveyed by Vercingetorix, who was camped to the E. The excavated site of the Gallo-Roman town gives a vivid sense of its size and layout, with theatre, civic forum, streets and shops. Note particularly the headquarters and sanctuary of the metalworkers responsible for some of the finest work in the Musée Alésia and, still littered with stone coffins, the site of the basilica added in the 7C to house the relics of St Reine. They were later moved to Flavigny but are brought back to Alise-Ste-Reine each year for the pilgrimage and procession on the weekend nearest 7 September, when the 'Mystère de Ste Reine' is also performed in the imitation Roman theatre near Vercingetorix's statue. On the flank of the hill between the statue and the Gallo-Roman town is the heavily restored church of St-Léger, largely 9–10C but incorporating a fragment of the original building started soon after the saint's death in 678 and destroyed in Norman raids. The outside wall has a monument to the colourful 20C mayor of Dijon, Canon Kir, born and buried here.

The statue of Vercingetorix on Mont Auxois

The *château of **Bussy-Rabutin** (Caisse Nationale, open), off D954 about 4km NE of Alise-Ste-Reine, is everywhere stamped with the proud, caustic personality of its 17C owner. Roger de Rabutin, comte de Bussy, was a soldier and wit whose satirical 'Histoire amoureuse des Gaules' (1665) provoked Louis XIV to exile him from court. Bussy had already completed the alterations which swept away all but the corner towers of the medieval château: the handsome central block was finished in 1649. In exile he devoted himself to filling the interior with paintings and portraits. Few have any artistic value (and some have been rather clumsily restored) but collectively they express his preoccupation with sex, war, family history and the bitterness of exile. The panelled walls of the Salle des Devises bear cryptic emblems that comment obliquely on, for example, the infidelities of his mistress, Madame de Monglat. The bedroom is a gallery of royal mistresses from Diane de Poitiers onwards; note also the portrait of Bussy's cousin Madame de Sévigné, part of a triptych by Mignard. The lavish Tour Dorée is devoted to the king and his court, unflatteringly characterised in the captions.

Bussy-le-Grand, facing the château across the valley to the N, has a Romanesque church with a tall nave, a dome over the crossing and some interesting primitive capitals; two, on the E side of the crossing, show Daniel in the lions' den and the lions turning on their keepers. The wooden furnishings are 17–18C. Andoche Junot ('La Tempête'), who rose from the ranks to become one of Napoléon's generals and Duc d'Abrantès, was born in the village in 1771. The little village of **Frôlois** is perched on a rocky bluff overlooking a tributary of the Oze, 12km E of Bussy-Rabutin on the way to the Châtillon–Dijon road (Route 2). All that remains of its medieval fortress is a rectangular block rebuilt in the 17–18C (open). It contains painted ceilings and so-called Bergame tapestries, in fact painted cloth hangings.

***Flavigny-sur-Ozerain** (410 people), 5km SE of Alise-Ste-Reine, is one of the loveliest medieval hill towns in Burgundy, even if the view of it perched on its rocky summit does not live up to Lamartine's extravagant comparison with the view of Jerusalem. A fortified miniature city that declined until its picturesque charm began to attract visitors (Flavigny was a favourite haunt of Augustus John and William Rothenstein in the era of the New English Art Club), it is now often overrun by coach parties in the summer.

On the little esplanade at the S end of the town the old ramparts are broken by the 18C Porte Ste-Barbe and the 15C Porte du Bourg. The older gate belonged to the defences of the Benedictine abbey of St-Pierre, immediately beyond the Porte Ste-Barbe. The abbey now houses a factory making the aniseed sweets on sale in gift and souvenir shops throughout Burgundy. Its buildings are largely 17C but keep some fragments of the Romanesque abbey church, whose nave is marked by the lane running along the side of the factory. At the end are ruins of the Gothic choir added in 1250–1350. Nearby is the entrance to the Carolingian crypt begun in the 9C to shelter the relics of St Reine, built on a plan similar the crypt at St-Germain in Auxerre. The confessio has primitive capitals on re-used Roman columns. The hexagonal chapel adjoining it to the E, rediscovered during excavations in 1957–1960, is 11C work on the foundations of the original rotunda.

St Reine's relics were moved after the Revolution to the parish church of St-Genès, though before that date the number of pilgrims crowding into Flavigny had already given the church its most distinctive feature: the 13C tribunes running above the aisles of the nave and over the crossing like an elaborate rood loft. Note the charming Flamboyant pulpit. The side-chapels below were mainly added in the 16C; the third one on the S side of the nave contains a delicate 15C Angel of the Annunciation. The choir was expanded and refurbished in 1434–1438 when Quentin Menard (one of Philippe le Bon's ambassadors and, at the end of his life, archbishop of Besançon) founded a Société des Chapelains for priests born and baptised in Flavigny. The carvings on the *stalls, earlier than the Rigolley brothers' work at Montréal, show a highly developed taste for comic realism. On the S side of the choir is a striking 15C Vierge de Douleur, or hooded Virgin, in painted wood.

The medieval and Renaissance houses lining the street on the way up to St-Genès are typical of Flavigny's rich domestic architecture. From the E end of the church the road continues to the 15C postern. An interesting walk through the W side of the town follows the Rue Voltaire and Rue Lacordaire to the Porte du Val, really a 13C and a 15C gate joined together. Next to it is the building, once the bailiff's house, where Henri Lacordaire (born at Recey-sur-Ource) founded a religious community in 1848 as part of his campaign to revive the Dominican Order in France.

Beyond Venarey-les-Laumes D905 heads S, up the narrowing valley of the Brenne. D117b, a winding little road that branches right at 11km, is worth following for its views over the valley. It leads through (1km) Arnay-sous-Vitteaux to the neighbouring valley of the Lochère and (5km) **Marigny-le-Cahouet**, where the moated medieval château, restored in the 19C, has a half-timbered gallery (access to outside only). D905 continues S through (4km) **Posanges**, with its 15C château (not open), to (6km) **Vitteaux** (1060 people; Tourist Information), where the ruined fortress, medieval market hall and old houses make a pleasant, though still scruffy town centre. The furnishings in the church include a 15C organ loft and choir stalls.

The main route continues to St-Thibault, but it would be foolish to miss the chance of exploring the roads that head E and W from Vitteaux across the full width of the Auxois. The *D26 takes a breathtaking switchback course over the hills and valleys to (26km) St-Seine-l'Abbaye (see Route 2). **Verrey-sous-Salmaise**, in the valley where the Drenne and the Oze meet at 15km, has the sleepy pre-war atmosphere that lingers in many of the region's industrial or railway towns, but **Salmaise**, clinging to the steep hillside 3km to the N, is a picturesque place with a medieval market hall and a 13–15C château (not open). D90 follows a wide, straight course through the gently rolling countryside W of Vitteaux, joining N6 on the edge of the Morvan at 31km (see Route 12). The hill of **Thil** makes a prominent landmark, visible for miles. A side-road from (18km) **Précy-sous-Thil** (600 people) winds through Maison-Dieu up to the quiet, wooded summit with its ruined 12C castle and big 14C collegiate church.

The village of **St-Thibault**, off D70 7km SW of Vitteaux, stands on the broad Armançon plain through which the Canal de Bourgogne runs. The setting makes the *church look all the more dramatically disproportioned, its Gothic E end rearing high above the stubby 18C nave and overshadowing the 19C W tower. The bizarre effect vividly expresses the decline of the priory that originally built the church in about 1290–1320 to shelter the relics of St Theobald, but allowed it to sink from a great pilgrimage centre into partial ruin by the 18C. The N doorway has scenes from the life of the Virgin Mary on the tympanum above the central figure of the saint, whose life is depicted on the panels of the 16C doors. The figures on either side have been identified as either biblical or local: on the right, Aaron with

David or Robert II with his son Hugues V, the two Capetian dukes of Burgundy who endowed the church; on the left, Solomon with the Queen of Sheba or Hugues d'Arcy, bishop of Autun, with Agnès de France, Hugues' wife and the daughter of St Louis. Seen from the outside, the choir may now contribute to the oddity of the church, but inside it is still as powerful and pure as any Gothic work in Burgundy: a three-storey elevation which pulls the eye irresistibly up to the tall clerestory windows at the top. Its grandeur overwhelms details that would focus attention in a lesser building, like the 14C altarpiece in carved and painted wood showing scenes from St Theobald's life and the 14C tomb effigy thought to be the priory's founder, Guy de Thil. The elegant Chapelle St-Gilles on the N side of the church contains Theobald's relics.

From St-Thibault D970 follows the canal and runs close to A6, a setting that does little to help the château of **Éguilly** (open), to the right at 8km. It keeps its medieval plan with four corner towers but was otherwise rebuilt in the 17C. The canal runs through a 3.3km tunnel at (6km) **Pouilly-en-Auxois** (1370 Polliens; Tourist Information), a dull town that serves as a regional centre for much of the southern Auxois and the Montagne. The church of Notre-Dame-Trouvée on the hillside N of the town contains a 16C Entombment.

At **Chailly-sur-Armançon**, 6km W of Pouilly, the Renaissance château is now a hotel. At the quiet hill village of *Mont-St-Jean, 12km further, the western boundary of the Auxois is marked by the superbly placed 12–15C castle, which retains its keep (not open) and a lovely shaded walk beneath the ruined ramparts that rise from solid rock. The church within the enceinte has a Romanesque choir and crypt sheltering relics brought back from the Crusades, including (supposedly) those of St Pelagia. The neighbouring hill of **Croix St-Thomas** (578m), about 3km NE, makes another fine look-out point over the Auxois and the Morvan.

The tangle of roads and autoroutes S of Pouilly complicates the way towards the more rugged landscape of the Montagne. Follow, if you can find it, D18 through the village of (8km) Vandenesse-en-Auxois to the junction with the little D18a, 2km beyond. **Ste-Sabine**, 2km SW of the junction, has a tall 14C tower and porch awkwardly grafted on to its church. D18a heads N across A6, the canal and the river for the summit of the hill where (2km) *Châteauneuf-en-Auxois* stands. The castle (Caisse Nationale, open) that commands the valley so emphatically also dominates the huddle of pleasant old houses that make up this once important village, now shrunk to 63 inhabitants. The original fortress, with its square keep, round towers and curtain wall, dates from the late 12C to the 14C. After the châtelaine poisoned her husband in 1455 it was confiscated by Philippe le Bon and awarded to his seneschal, Philippe Pot, the owner of La Rochepot. His alterations and enlargements gave the castle its Flamboyant central block, the only part whose rooms are now open: note the Salle des Gardes and the chapel with frescoes of Christ and the Apostles in bands of colour recalling Pot's armorial bearings. From the car park at the other end of the village signposted walks lead to local viewpoints, including the nearby Croix de la Mission.

Châteauneuf appears in the novels of Henri Vincenot, a proud son of the Montagne who spent his childhood in the village and retired to **Commarin**, 6km N. The château (open) harmoniously combines the moat and round towers from the medieval castle with a central block built in the 17–18C. The interior is disappointing in its present state of decay, though the chapel has a small 17C Italian Entombment in terracotta and one room contains

15–16C heraldic tapestries. D977 bis continues N from Commarin to (6km) the high-lying **Sombernon** (770 people; Tourist Information), near A38 and a quick way into Dijon.

The present route follows a more devious course S on D18, still flanked by the canal and intermittently tangled up with A6, to the valley of the Ouche, where the Auxois confronts the N–S range of the Hautes-Côtes between Dijon and Beaune. The bridge that now dominates (6km) **Pont-d'Ouche** carries the autoroute on its way S to Beaune. **Bligny-sur-Ouche** (740 people; Tourist Information), picturesquely sited near the head of the valley 7.5km S, is descended from a Celtic settlement that grew up near the river's source. The church, once belonging to the castle destroyed on the orders of Louis XI after the death of Charles le Téméraire, has a Romanesque tower with Lombardic bands. The steam railway line running down the valley—one of the oldest in France, built in 1829–1835—has been reopened for tourists.

D33 and the canal follow the wooded valley N from Pont-d'Ouche towards Dijon. The Cistercian abbey at (6km) **La Bussière-sur-Ouche** was founded in 1130 and its buildings completed in 1172. Its history gave Henri Vincenot the idea for his novel 'Les Étoiles de Compostelle'. The domestic quarters (now a religious study centre) were largely rebuilt in the 19C but, with their woods, streams and little waterfalls, the grounds preserve the beauty of the site and, despite many alterations, the church still has some of its original Cistercian restraint. Note the echo of Fontenay in the square-ended choir and the simple pattern of windows lighting the N transept. 14km further, between Ste-Marie-sur-Ouche and Pont-de-Pany, D33 joins A38 for the last lap of the journey to Dijon. The little D35 twists its way up the steep cliffs SE of Pont-de-Pany to the 18C château (not open) at (4km) **Montculot**, where the young Lamartine stayed with his uncle. He inherited it in 1826, and a plaque outside records his regret at having to sell the scene of his childhood memories.

A38 runs a smoothly engineered course along the Ouche valley as it makes its way between the hills guarding the western approach to Dijon. At 4km D104 branches N through Fleurey-sur-Ouche to (4km) **Lantenay**, with the 17–18C château originally built by the Dijonnais *parlementaire* Jean Bouhier (open). On the hillside S of **Velars-sur-Ouche** (1420 people), another 5km beyond Fleurey, stand a statue of Notre-Dame d'Étang and its adjoining 19C chapel. The little D108 climbs S through Corcelles-les-Monts to (5km) the crater of **Mont Afrique** (600m), a vantage point over the Hautes-Côtes and Dijon. From this view Dijon's spreading suburban development seems almost to swamp the old centre. Steep roads drop down directly to the city and to Marsannay-la-Côte (see Route 6). In the valley below, A38 reaches the ugly tower blocks that announce the western suburbs of **Dijon** and N5 continues past Lac Kir to the centre, both described in the next route.

5 Dijon

Tourist Information. Place Darcy, phone 80 43 42 12, telex 350 912, fax 80 30 90 02. Cour d'Honneur, Hôtel de Ville, Place de la Libération, phone 80 67 12 12. 34, rue des Forges, phone 80 30 35 39, telex 351 444, fax 80 30 90 02. Aire de Dijon-Brognon on A31, phone 80 23 30 00.

Connections with other routes. Dijon is the goal of previous routes through the Vingeanne valley from Langres (Route 1), through the Châtillonnais from Châtillon (Route 2) and through the Auxois from Semur (Route 4). It is also the starting point for the Côte d'Or (Route 6) and the Bresse (Route 9).

˙˙Dijon comes as a welcome surprise in a country where the general rule is that provincial cities are more obviously provincial than they are cities. Though not very large (there are currently about 146,700 Dijonnais), it has a history that makes its present rôle as *préfecture* of the Côte d'Or and administrative centre of modern Burgundy more than a bureaucratic formality. Before such boundaries appeared on the map Dijon had established itself as the capital first of a medieval duchy that dreamt of being a kingdom and then of an independent-minded province that did not forget its past grandeur. Nor does Dijon today. Its history lies not just in archives—nor even the rich contents of its museums—but in architecture ranging from grand urban effects like the Place de la Libération and Palais des Ducs to the private houses that make walking its side-streets a continual delight.

Surprisingly, Dijon had no ancient importance. The trading routes that nourished prehistoric Burgundy did not exploit its strategic position where the river Ouche forces its way through the chain of limestone hills overlooking the Saône plain, a major crossroad in a region of crossroads. Nor was Divio (or Dibio), the *castrum* on the Roman road to Lyons, more than a small settlement. The city began its rise to power only when the bishops of Langres, while keeping their ecclesiastical control over Dijon, surrendered feudal control to the crown in 1016 and so paved the way for the first Capetian duke, Robert I, to declare it his capital in 1032. Even this dignity long remained nominal, the Capetians still preferring their castles at nearby Talant and Rouvres-en-Plaine, and the grandest monument in the early Middle Ages was Guillaume de Volpiano's church honouring the legendary local martyr Benignus. The accession of Philippe le Hardi, first of the Valois dynasty, in 1364 made Dijon capital of the duchy in a real sense: a centre of financial administration as well as of the feasts, tournaments and entertainments in which the court took delight. The ducal palace and particularly the ducal mausoleum at the Chartreuse de Champmol drew on the talents of artists, like Claus Sluter, attracted from the dukes' Flemish territories.

Dijon suffered with the death of Charles le Téméraire and the collapse of the Valois duchy in 1477. The continuing ambitions of Charles' granddaughter Marguerite d'Autriche could still bring an army of Swiss, German and Franc-Comtois to its gates in 1513, though the governor's adroit use of money and wine lifted the siege. Yet, after it fell under the control of the crown and a succession of royally appointed governors (notably the Condé family), Dijon never became a country backwater. Indeed, it gained new importance as the seat of the region's *parlement*, or High Court, and later of its *États*, or provincial assemblies. The *parlement* in particular bred its own powerful families, a *noblesse de robe* taking over from the *noblesse*

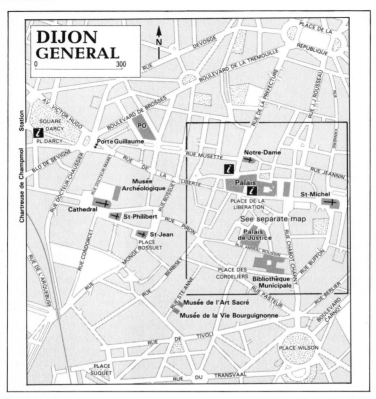

d'épée which had served the Valois dukes. Charles de Brosses (1709–1777), scholar, writer, womaniser and president of the *parlement* was typical of the men who set the tone of Dijon society and made it a centre of culture during the Enlightenment. The period saw the foundation of a learned academy which honoured Rousseau in 1750, a law school which grew into the university, a drawing school which nourished artists like François Rude and Pierre-Paul Prud'hon, and the Musée des Beaux-Arts.

Architecturally the *noblesse de robe* left monuments in the Renaissance Palace of Justice, the neo-classical Palais des États that replaced the ducal palace and, perhaps most important of all, the many *hôtels particuliers*, or town mansions, whose frontages, entrance porticos and wrought-iron grilles line the side-streets round the city centre. Making as rich an urban landscape as any you will find in France outside Paris, they reflect the successive architectural styles of the centuries when the *parlementaires* held sway: *échaugettes* and Flamboyant curls over doors and windows yielding to the exuberant decoration associated with the name of the local carver Hugues Sambin, and this in turn yielding to the Italian Renaissance and later neo-classical schools.

The tradition of urbane culture did not die with the Revolution or the 19C. The Musée Magnin, for example, is an art collection assembled by an official in the Audit Office during the opening decades of this century. But by then Dijon had greatly changed from the city which, for all its vitality, still numbered only 21,000 inhabitants in 1800. The 19C trebled that figure by making Dijon the chief railway junction on the Paris–Lyon line and indeed in eastern France. The railway remains a major employer and its yards still dominate the approach to the city centre from the W, yet there are signs that Dijon is losing its traditional rôle as a centre of communications: the Paris–Lyon TGV line runs via Mâcon and the Autoroute du Soleil via Beaune. The city has come to depend on service industries, among which tourism plays an increasingly important part. The visitors relish its traditional qualities and its traditional products: mustard, *pain d'épice* (gingerbread) and *cassis* or *crème de cassis*, the liqueur made from blackcurrants grown in the Hautes-Côtes. In *kir*, a mixture of *cassis* and dry white wine, Dijon has given the world an apéritif named after Félix Kir (1876–1968), the flamboyant post-war mayor who promoted its virtues.

The Rue de la Liberté, the main shopping street and axis of the city centre, runs between the Place de la Libération in the E and the Square Darcy in the W. These make convenient starting points for the five routes sketched below, all but the last emphatically walking routes.

The Place de la Libération, Palais des Ducs and Musée des Beaux-Arts

At the heart of the modern city, the ***Palais des Ducs et des États de Bourgogne** and the semicircular Place de la Libération it overlooks make a splendid neo-classical ensemble, still managing to keep its dignity despite the swarming traffic. The changes of name the Place de la Libération has undergone over the centuries ring the changes of French history: Place Royale, Place de la Révolution, Place Impériale, Place Royale again and then Place d'Armes until it got its present name in 1944.

The Palais has seen as many changes. It began life as the palace which the Capetian dukes and then, on a much more ambitious scale, the Valois dukes made the centre of their court. With the death of Charles le Téméraire and the absorption of Burgundy by Louis XI in 1477, it became the Logis du Roi. From the late 17C it served as the headquarters of the États de Bourgogne, the provincial assemblies of the three estates (nobility, clergy and commoners), and their bureaucracy, the Élus. Fragments of the Valois palace were incorporated in the grand new design by the king's architect Jules Hardouin-Mansart and his assistant Martin de Joinville, begun in 1681 and sporadically continued throughout the 18C. The main façade and the Place de la Libération recall Hardouin-Mansart's Place des Victoires in Paris, another urban scheme that had a statue of Louis XIV on horseback as its centrepiece. The Revolution swept both statues away and, while leaving the rest of the buildings at Dijon largely intact, demoted the Palais des États to the Hôtel de Ville. The E wing was added in the mid 19C to house the collections acquired by the Musée des Beaux-Arts since its foundation in 1787.

So, despite the impression of unity it gives on first view, the resulting group of buildings spans many centuries and several styles. Wrought-iron gates lead from the Place into the central Cour d'Honneur, with its 17C façades (and a Tourist Information Centre). The Cour de Flore, to the left, contains the most impressive relics of the 18C Palais des États. The

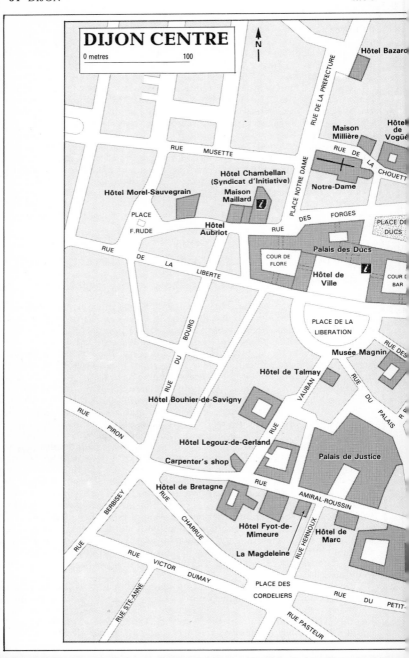

DIJON CENTRE

0 metres   100

N

Hôtel Bazard

RUE DE LA PREFECTURE

Maison Millière

Hôtel de Vogüé

RUE MUSETTE

RUE DE LA CHOUETTE

Hôtel Chambellan (Syndicat d'Initiative)

Hôtel Morel-Sauvegrain

Maison Maillard

PLACE NOTRE DAME

Notre-Dame

PLACE F.RUDE

Hôtel Aubriot

DES FORGES

PLACE DES DUCS

RUE

Palais des Ducs

COUR DE FLORE

RUE DE LA LIBERTE

Hôtel de Ville

COUR DE BAR

PLACE DE LA LIBERATION

RUE DU BOURG

RUE DES

Musée Magnin

Hôtel de Talmay

RUE VAUBAN

RUE DU PALAIS

Hôtel Bouhier-de-Savigny

RUE PIRON

Hôtel Legouz-de-Gerland

Carpenter's shop

Palais de Justice

RUE BERBISEY

Hôtel de Bretagne

RUE CHARRUE

RUE

AMIRAL-ROUSSIN

RUE STE-ANNE

RUE

Hôtel Fyot-de-Mimeure

RUE HERNIOUX

Hôtel de Marc

VICTOR DUMAY

La Magdeleine

PLACE DES CORDELIERS

RUE DU PETIT-

RUE PASTEUR

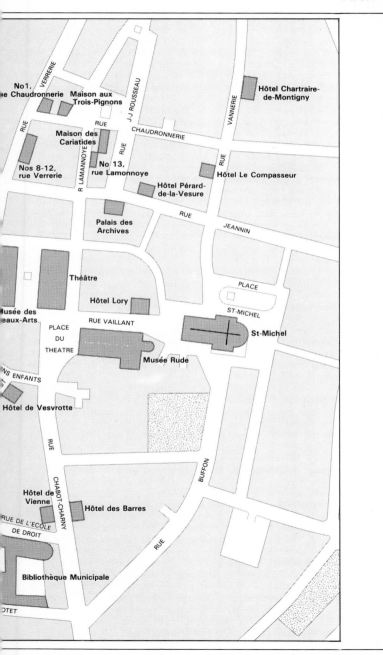

magnificent Escalier Gabriel leads up to the Salle des États, sumptuously decorated with false marble columns and *trompe l'oeil* paintings (open for temporary exhibitions). The staircase is named after Jacques Gabriel, who also designed the rococo Chapelle des Élus of 1733–1739 (open). The roofline of the Cour d'Honneur is broken by the Tour Philippe-le-Bon (open), built by the duke in 1440–1457 to serve as a look-out post and so commanding a wide view from the top. It also dominates the pleasant little Place des Ducs-de-Bourgogne behind the Cour d'Honneur, with the 15C façade of the Salle des Gardes. Earlier fragments of the palace, dating from Philippe le Hardi's building campaign in c 1365, survive in the Cour de Bar to the E. Its name recalls that the Duc de Bar (and titular King of Sicily), René d'Anjou, was held as Philippe le Bon's prisoner in the Tour de Bar, or Tour Neuve, in 1431–1437 after being captured in battle by the Burgundians. The 17C Escalier Bellegarde leads up to an enclosed gallery. At its foot stands a 19C statue of the sculptor Claus Sluter, and in the opposite corner is the well outside the ducal kitchens.

With the Salle des Gardes and other fragments of the medieval palace, the kitchens were incorporated in the 19C Musée des Beaux-Arts. Its main entrance lies beyond the end of the E wing in the Place de la Ste-Chapelle, named from the ducal chapel demolished at the beginning of the 19C.

The * *Musée des Beaux-Arts** has the best art collection in Burgundy and one of the best in any French province, rich enough to defeat casual prowling from room to room (which the building's complicated layout anyway discourages) and to prompt separate visits concentrating on its different aspects. These are: the rooms that survive from the medieval palace and now display the art of the Valois court, most famously the great tombs of the first two dukes in the Salle des Gardes; the paintings and sculptures from the 16C to 18C which, while emphasising the continued strength of Dijonnais and Burgundian art, are not just of local importance but cover several major European schools; and the recently installed Donation Granville with its generous holdings of Romantic, Impressionist and 20C work.

Even if you do not have the time or inclination to attempt a tour on the lines suggested in the detailed description below, you should still make sure to see at least the following highlights: the ducal tombs and other works from the Valois court in the Salle des Gardes, the 'Adoration of the Shepherds' by the Master of Flémalle next door, and the doors from the abbey at St-Omer among Flemish and Dutch works from the post-Valois era; the collection of work by German and Swiss Primitives; the carved doors of the Palais de Justice, the anonymous portrait from the Fontaine-bleau school, Nattier's portrait of Marie Leczinska, and the Salle des Statues, in the French galleries; and, in the Donation Granville, the paintings by Georges de la Tour, Géricault, Delacroix and the Impressionists.

The **Salle Pierre-Quarré**, next to the entrance foyer, explains the history of the building. Elsewhere on the ground floor, three rooms survive from the ducal palace. The **Salle du Chapitre**, the 14C chapter house of Ste-Chapelle, contains sculpture and some interesting smaller items: Philippe le Hardi's funeral crown, the filigree crosier of St Robert of Molesmes (founder of the Cistercians) and St Bernard's porringer. The vast **Kitchens** (c 1425) have six hearths and chimneys surrounding a dome with a central ventilating shaft. If they now seem rather bleak, Jan Huizinga's 'Waning of the Middle Ages' helps evoke the atmosphere when the head cook presided over the work from his central dais, observing the passion for ceremony and etiquette which governed all levels of the Valois court. The vaulted **Salle des Armes**, on the other side of the courtyard, has medieval arms and armour, including what is claimed to be Jeanne d'Arc's sword.

The **Salle des Gardes** on the first floor got its name when the Condés became governors of Burgundy in the 17C but, beneath the alterations of the centuries, is still essentially the great hall that Philippe le Bon added to the Valois palace. It makes an appropriate resting place for the tombs of the first two Valois dukes. Originally in the Chartreuse de Champmol (see Outskirts, below), they were moved to a place of honour in St-Bénigne during the early days of the Revolution, when the dukes could still be admired for their enmity to the French crown. As ideology changed, the tombs were banished and broken up before finally being restored and installed here in 1827. Meant as permanent witness to the dukes' power, they now speak more eloquently of the artists whom the dukes patronised: particularly Claus Sluter from Haarlem, who came to Dijon in about 1385 and succeeded Jean de Marville as court sculptor (*tailleur d'ymages* and *varlet de chambre*) in 1389, and his nephew and pupil Claus de Werve, who took over the post on Sluter's death in 1406.

Philippe le Hardi commissioned his tomb in the 1380s and Jean de Marville prepared the design before the duke's death in 1404. First Sluter and then de Werve carved the figures. De Werve's effigy of Philippe, now heavily restored, lies on a black marble slab watched over by two delicate angels. The sides of the plinth form miniature Gothic arcades filled with a procession of forty *pleurants*, or mourners, begun by Sluter and finished by de Werve. (Three of the original figures, and one from Jean sans Peur's tomb, have found their way to the Cleveland Museum of Art in the USA.) This procession is the great artistic achievement of the tomb and, indeed, one of the great achievements of Gothic sculpture. Like Sluter's Calvary (Puits de Moïse) and chapel doorway at the Chartreuse de Champmol, it turns a formal design into a dramatic tableau rich with human detail and expressive individual gesture. Note, for example, how the *pleurants* are not isolated within their separates niches and how the poses of even the conventional hooded mourners are skilfully varied.

The tomb of Jean sans Peur and his duchess, Marguerite de Bavière, was commissioned by Philippe le Bon in 1443. The Aragonese sculptor Juan de la Huerta began it and Antoine Le Moiturier of Avignon finished it in 1470. They copied the earlier tomb closely enough to suggest that court culture was hardening into archaism, marking the years that had passed only in details—the canopies of the miniature arcade have become Flamboyant, with angels holding musical instruments added as an extra flourish—and in a decline of workmanship that makes the carving of the *pleurants* look almost perfunctory by comparison to Sluter's work.

For all their magnificence, the tombs do not entirely overshadow the other contents of the Salle des Gardes, particularly the two Flemish altarpieces from the Chartreuse carved by Jacques de Baerze and gilded and painted by Melchior Broederlam of Ypres in the 1390s. The first has the Crucifixion as its central subject, with tempera paintings of the Annunciation, Visitation, Presentation in the Temple and Flight into Egypt. The Sienese influence on Broederlam's work is a reminder that Philippe le Hardi numbered a Simone Martini polyptych among his treasures. The second, now lacking its painted leaves, shows saints and martyrs. A third altarpiece, of the Passion, belongs to the late 15C Antwerp School. The portrait of Philippe le Bon from the studio of Roger van der Weyden (c 1445) presents an image of political power in sober, businesslike contrast to the chivalric bugles and trumpets of the ducal tombs. The tapestries above include one showing the unsuccessful siege of Dijon by Swiss, German and Franc-Comtois troops in 1513. At one end of the room is a Flamboyant chimney-piece, at the other a wooden gallery worth mounting for its view of the tombs.

The little room next to the Salle des Gardes has another treasure from the Chartreuse de Champmol, 'Adoration of the Shepherds' by the Master of Flémalle (usually identified as Robert Campin), in a lovely collection of 15–16C **Flemish and Burgundian** art that also includes: Aelbrecht Bouts ('Head of Christ'), two portraits by the Master of St-Jean-de-Luze and carved fragments of altarpieces.

The rest of the gallery's main collection of paintings, sculpture and furniture is loosely arranged by national schools and periods on the first floor (with, currently, a stray Flemish room on the second floor). **Flemish and Dutch** painting of the post-Valois era includes: the early 16C doors from the abbey at St-Omer, Jan 'Velvet' Bruegel, Franz Hals and Rubens (notably 'The Virgin presenting the Infant Christ to St Francis of Assisi'). An unusual and important group of **German and Swiss Primitives** includes Martin Schongauer, Konrad Witz and the Master of the Carnation of Baden. Italian painting, more strongly represented in the later schools, includes: Taddeo Gaddi, Pietro Lorenzetti, the 15C Sienese Master of the Osservanza, Domenico di Michelino, Titian ('Virgin and Child with St Agnes and John the Baptist'), Veronese ('The Infant Moses rescued from the Water' notable among several canvases), Lorenzo Lotto, Jacopo Bassano, Strozzi, Reni, Batoni and Guardi.

Inevitably, **French** art predominates. The collection from the 16C to the late 18C includes many artists to be expected in a museum of this size and importance: Charles Le Brun, Philippe de Champaigne, Eustache Le Sueur, Jean-Bapiste Corneille, François Boucher, Joseph Vernet and Oudry. An anonymous 16C work from the Fontainebleau school, 'Woman at her Toilet', comes as a pleasant surprise. It is particularly worth studying the Dijonnais and Burgundian artists who show that the city remained a centre of culture long after the end of the duchy. The carved Renaissance doors of the Palais de Justice are attributed to Hugues Sambin, whose name is also rather freely attached to the ornate façades of Dijon's *hôtels particuliers*, with their distinctive *chou bourguignon* (Burgundian cabbage). The doors stand at the top of the main staircase as prelude to a series of rooms largely devoted to Renaissance furniture and woodwork. The 17–18C rooms contain: bas-reliefs (notably of a *parlementaire* and his wife) by the Baroque sculptor Jean Dubois, whose surviving masterpiece is in the city's Musée de l'Art Sacré; portraits by Jean Tassel of Langres (of Catherine de Montholon) and Gabriel Revel (of Jean Dubois); and paintings by Philippe Quantin and Jean-François Gilles, known as Colson. Other artists from outside the region further strengthen a range of portraits and portrait busts which still retains some obvious local connections: Nicolas de Largillière (of Jean Bouhier, president of the Burgundian *parlement*), Pierre Mignard, Hyacinthe Rigaud (of Girardon), Greuze (of Abbé Gouguenot), Carle van Loo (of Louis XV), Jean-Marc Nattier (of Marie Leczinska, Louis XV's queen), Houdon (bust of Buffon), Caffieri (busts of Piron and Rameau) and Coysevox (bust of Louis XIV).

The **Salle des Statues** makes a particularly interesting period piece, preserving the decor created by the early pupils of the drawing school which François Devosges started in 1766. Its centrepiece, 'Hebe and the Eagle of Jupiter' is by Devosges' most famous pupil, the monumental sculptor François Rude (1784–1855); he also has a museum of his own around the corner from the Beaux-Arts. The ceiling by another student, Pierre-Paul Prud'hon (from Cluny, 1758–1823), is one of several examples of his work in the galleries.

The 19–20C rooms represent several local artists: the Romantic painter Félix Trutat; Alphonse Legros, better known for his career as an engraver in England; and the sculptor Jean Dampt. They set the tone for a rather undistinguished collection which does, however, include Géricault (copy of portrait by Rigaud) and Tissot.

The second and third floors, reached by a staircase from the 19C corner of the first floor, make up for the main collection's weakness in 19–20C art. On the second floor a room is devoted to François Pompon (1855–1933), the refreshingly unacademic animal sculptor from Saulieu to whom Dijon owes its polar bear in the Square Darcy; the museum at Saulieu also has a collection of his work. Near by is the entrance to the **Donation Granville**, installed in the two upper storeys since the 1960s and displayed in an informal, even intimate way that contrasts with the arrangement of the previous rooms. Its single most famous item is from the 17C: Georges de la Tour's serene candlelight painting 'Blowing out the Lamp'. Otherwise, it represents a wide range of French and French-dominated art movements of the 19–20C.

It begins with sculptures by Maillol and Rodin, and sketches, water-colours and oils by Guercino, Salvator Rosa, Prud'hon, Isabey, Corot and, particularly, Géricault ('Horses at Pasture'), Delacroix (study for 'The Sultan of Morocco receiving the French Ambassador') and Bonington, one of the few English painters to appear in French galleries. The Barbizon school (Rousseau, Millet, Daubigny) is strongly represented in a 19C collection that continues with Adolphe Hervier, Daumier, Auguste Boulard, Courbet, Gustave Moreau and oils, as well as sculptures, by Barye. Another unusual item is the group of watercolour sketches by Victor Hugo, in a display at the end of this floor which also includes work by Odilon Redon and Doré.

The next floor moves progressively into the 20C with good representative holdings of the Impressionists (Manet, Monet, Vuillard, Cézanne, Boudin, Sisley) and their Post-Impressionist and Cubist successors (Claude Domec, Adolphe Peterelle, Jan Meijer, and small specimens by Kandinsky, Picasso, Braque, Gris, Modigliani, Robert de la Fresnaye and Robert Delaunay). It ends with several large groups of contemporary or near contemporary work by: Étienne Hajdu, Charles Lapicque, Nicolas de Staël ('Footballers' series), Maria-Helena Vieira da Silva and Arpad Szenes.

East from the Palais des Ducs to St-Michel

This short walk heads E from the Palais along the Rue Vaillant, where the façade of St-Michel makes a handsome climax to a fine streetscape. Next to the Musée des Beaux-Arts stands the early 19C **Théâtre**, looking out across a square where several buildings have good wrought-iron balconies. On the left-hand side of the Rue Vaillant No 5 was the birthplace of the composer Jean-Philippe Rameau (1683–1764), while No 11 is the late 18C Hôtel Lory. On the opposite side stands the former church of **St-Étienne**, largely 15–17C but keeping a few Romanesque features, built by the abbey which once dominated this quarter of the city. Part of it has become the Chamber of Commerce, while the transept and choir shelter the **Musée Rude** with casts of monumental work by the Dijonnais sculptor, including his statue of Napoléon at Fixin (Route 6) and 'La Marseillaise' on the Arc de Triomphe.

St-Michel was begun in 1499, its Flamboyant Gothic modulating into the Renaissance style by the time the W façade was reached in the next century. The main doorway of the three in the richly decorated porch has a tympanum of the Last Judgement by Nicolas de la Cour, though his son-in-law Hugues Sambin used to be given the credit for it. The most striking features inside are the 18C pulpit and woodwork in the choir. The first chapel on the right as you enter the church contains figures from a 16C Entombment.

North of the Palais des Ducs: St-Michel to Notre-Dame

The streets N of the Palais des Ducs are especially rich in *hôtels particuliers* from the Middles Ages to the 18C, marked with very informative plaques. They can be explored on more or less any system, or no system at all, but a convenient route from St-Michel at the end of the previous walk begins by heading N on the Rue Vannerie. The stretch beyond the junction with the Rue Jeannin has several good buildings, notably No 66 on the left, the 16C **Hôtel Le Compasseur**, with an *échaugette*, satyr-mask and *chou bourguignon* in the style of Hugues Sambin. On the right-hand side further N are the striking gateway of No 41, the **Hôtel du Commandant-Militaire**, and its neighbour at No 39, the restrained **Hôtel Chartraire-de-Montigny** (1744–1750).

On its journey W toward Notre-Dame the Rue Jeannin passes the **Hôtel Pérard-de-la-Vesure** (1661) at No 19 on the right-hand side and the handsome doorway of the **Palais des Archives** (1708) opposite the end of the Rue Jean-Jacques Rousseau. This leads N to the Rue Chaudronnerie, where a left turn soon brings you to No 28, the superb ***Maison des Cariatides** (1603). Its façade, vigorously ornamented in the tradition of Hugues Sambin, amply justifies the name. No 13 around the corner in the Rue Lamonnoye has a half-timbered gallery. The Rue Chaudronnerie ends with a fine medley of houses on the right: note the 15C **Maison aux Trois-Pignons**, one of the oldest half-timbered houses in the city, and No 1, late 16C, with rusticated stonework in the Italian Renaissance manner.

The Rue Verrerie is lined with good houses on both sides. Note particularly the carvings on the half-timbered Nos 8–10, which include a vignette of a man shooting a rabbit, and the Greek inscription on the stone-built No 21 (1570). The little Rue de la Chouette leads right towards Notre-Dame. The ***Hôtel de Vogüé** at No 12, built for the *parlementaire* Étienne Bouhier in about 1610, is probably the finest house in Dijon. Decorated in the Renaissance manner, its entrance portico makes charming use of pink and white stone. The neighbouring **Maison Millière** at No 10 has restored half-timbering.

The opposite side of the Rue de la Chouette runs along the N wall of the church, passing the carved owl from which the street is named, a talisman worn smooth by the hands of passers-by. The early 13C Gothic ***Notre-Dame** has a W façade which would alone make it the best of the city's churches. Ingeniously suited to its crowded urban site, the design abandons the harmonic façade of the great northern French cathedrals and creates something as close to a flat wall as Gothic engineering would permit. The tall three-bayed porch stands below two storeys of blind arcades, separated by rows of gargoyles (some of them 19C replacements). The sculptured doorways were mutilated at the Revolution as efficiently as any in Burgundy. The W towers were never built, though a turret at the S corner supports the *jaquemart* clock that Philippe le Hardi plundered from Courtrai and presented to the city for its help in crushing the Flemish revolt in 1382. The crossing tower and spire were rebuilt in the 19C. The Burgundian Gothic nave is characterised by clusters of colonnettes and wall passages in both its upper storeys. Note the 13C glass in the N transept. The chapel to the right of the choir shelters an 11C or 12C Black Madonna credited by the pious with delivering the city from the siege by German, Swiss and Franc-Comtois troops in 1513. A modern Gobelins tapestry commemorates Liberation in 1944. A late 19C organ replaces the one Rameau played.

The courtyard of the Hôtel Chambellan (now the Syndicat d'Initiative) in the Rue des Forges

The Rue de la Préfecture, running N from the W end of the church, has several good 17–18C houses on its right-hand side: No 22, the **Hôtel Bazard** (1772); No 38, the **Hôtel Mochot-Coppin** (1681–1684); and No 40, the **Hôtel Esmonin-Dampierre** (by Jacques Cellerier, 1780). The large, dignified **Hôtel Bouhier-de-Lantenay** (1758–1759), further N on the left-hand side, has been the Préfecture since 1800.

The *Rue des Forges takes in a particularly fine group of houses on its way from the Place Notre-Dame, S of the church, to the Place François-Rude and the Rue de la Liberté. At No 34 the **Hôtel Chambellan**, built for the mayor of Dijon in about 1490, is now the **Syndicat d'Initiative**. Its unremarkable façade conceals a Flamboyant courtyard. The spiral staircase in the corner is well worth climbing to see the palm vaulting that springs from the gardener's basket, a conceit both witty and beautiful. No 38, the **Maison Maillard** (or Milsand), was built for another mayor of the city in 1560. Its façade with richly festooned windows has been attributed to Hugues Sambin; the courtyard contains an arcade with atlantes which is certainly his work. No 40, the **Hôtel Aubriot**, has a 13C façade altered and restored by successive owners, including the poet and civil servant Stéphen Liégeard (see also the Hôtel Legouz-de-Gerland on the next walk and Brochon in Route 6). Note the row of corbels below its string course. The Rue Stéphen-Liégeard opposite is a handsome little street. At Nos 52–56 on the Rue des Forges the 15C **Hôtel Morel-Sauvegrain** was built for Jean Morel, an intimate of Charles le Téméraire. Note its Flamboyant doors and windows.

The little Place François-Rude, on the edge of the Rue de la Liberté, was the birthplace of the sculptor. He was not responsible for the central fountain with its statue of Le Bareuzai, a naked vineyard worker treading grapes, which has become a much-loved local landmark in the way that really ugly monuments so often do. The Place hosts a market on Tuesday and Wednesday mornings and on Saturdays. On the opposite side of the Rue de la Liberté is the 18C frontage of No 68, the **Hôtel de Villemeureux**.

South from the Palais des Ducs to the Palais de Justice

Three streets—the Rue Vauban, the Rue du Palais and the little Rue des Bons-Enfants—lead S from the semicircular Place de la Libération towards the Palais de Justice. This walk starts on the Rue des Bons-Enfants and returns via the Rue Vauban.

The ***Musée Magnin**, on the right-hand side of the Rue des Bons-Enfants, houses the art collection which Maurice Magnin and his sister Jeanne presented to the State in 1937. It mixes paintings of varying quality in an indiscriminate way that invites neglect of its good but often small items, and it is strongest in schools unlikely to appeal to casual visitors. A well-calculated guide to a selected handful of the contents, available in the foyer, helps to overcome these problems. Besides, the museum holds all the charm of a collection born of private enthusiasm and still displayed in its original setting: the 17C Hôtel Lantin, with a handsome staircase and courtyard. A domestic atmosphere lingers upstairs, where the French works are displayed, and the quality of the furniture and smaller objects in the bedroom, boudoir and parlour overshadows the paintings.

The French paintings begin with the 17C–18C: Laurent de la Hyre (two musical putti from a series allegorising the liberal arts), Eustache Le Sueur, Sébastien Bourdon, Jean-Baptiste de Champaigne (nephew of the better-known Philippe represented in the Musée des Beaux-Arts), François-Michel Dandré-Bardon, and an evening landscape attributed to the elder Moreau. The drawings in the Oratory include a drapery study by David. The Galerie Perret, beyond the bedroom, boudoir and parlour, has work by two of David's pupils, François-Xavier Fabre and Anne-Louis Girodet, as well as François-Marius Granet and Géricault (oil study). David's influence continues in the Salon Doré with work by another pupil, Jean-Antoine Gros, and a portrait attributed to Pierre-Narcisse Guérin. Here and in the Salon Rouge the various tendencies of 19C art are well represented by Eugène Dévéira (powerful Orientalist portrait), Paul Delaroche (characteristic historical essay) and Isabey (seascape).

The downstairs rooms, generally less well furnished, begin with northern European schools: Jan van Biljert ('Feast of the Gods'), Bartholomeus van der Helst ('Woman holding a Book'), Rembrandt's master Pieter Lastman, and Mengs (striking self-portrait). Early Italian painting is represented by the Pisan Master of San Torpè but the strength of the Italian collection lies in the 16–18C: Cariani, Schiavone, Strozzi, Romanelli, Ricci and Tiepolo. A leering interpretation of Susannah and the Elders by Allessandro Allori prompts comparison with Pellegrini's handling of the subject near by.

Shortly beyond the museum the Rue Philippe-Pot branches right from the Rue des Bons-Enfants and leads down to the entrance of the Palais de Justice. Do not miss the rear courtyard of the **Hôtel de Vesvrotte** at No 3, where the early 19C owner studded the wall with fragments and copies of Gallo-Roman work.

The **Palais de Justice** was the seat of the *parlement* or High Court of the province installed by Louis XII after the fall of the Valois dukes in 1477. It keeps its gabled Renaissance façade amid the alterations and additions of later centuries; the carved wooden doors are 20C copies of the originals attributed to Hugues Sambin, now in the Musée des Beaux-Arts. The main hall, or Salle des Pas-Perdus, has a wooden barrel vault with tie-beams and there are magnificently decorated ceilings in two adjoining court rooms (open when not in session): a 16C one in the Chambre Dorée and a 17C one, moved from the old audit office, in the Cour d'Assises. The chapel has a wooden screen attributed to Hugues Sambin on which the *chou bourguignon* appears.

The Rue du Palais makes its way round the side of the courts to the junction of the Rue Amiral-Roussin and the Rue de l'École-de-Droit. The buildings of the **Bibliothèque Municipale** opposite incorporate the former chapel of the Collège des Godrans, a Jesuit school founded in 1587 and attended by Buffon, Bossuet and Rameau. Note also the Puits d'Amour, a 16C well re-erected in the courtyard entered from No 5. The library's collection is notable for manuscripts from Cîteaux and the 11C St-Bénigne Bible.

The Rue de l'École-de-Droit ends at the wide, rather bleak Rue Chabot-Charny. Just to the N stands No 32, the 15–17C **Hôtel de Vienne**, with a Gothic gallery in its courtyard. On the opposite side No 43, the 17C **Hôtel des Barres**, has an 18C porch.

The Rue Amiral-Roussin has several good buildings as it runs along the S side of the Palais de Justice. Note particularly the 17C **Hôtel de Marc**, the doorway (1514) of the church belonging to the Commanderie de la Magdeleine beyond the junction with the Rue Hernoux, and No 23, the **Hôtel Fyot-de-Mimeure**, with a façade and courtyard in the style of Hugues

Sambin. No 29, the **Hôtel de Bretagne**, faces the Rue Vauban. No 16, one of the half-timbered houses on the left-hand corner, has an inset panel above the ground-floor window which clearly identifies it as a carpenter's shop. The **Hôtel Legouz-de-Gerland** on the opposite corner is one of the city's grandest houses, spreading across to the Rue J.-B.-Liégeard, where its E façade was restored by Stéphen Liégeard in the 1890s (see the Hôtel Aubriot in the previous walk). An *échaugette* overlooks the Rue Amiral-Roussin, while the entrance from the Rue Vauban leads into the semi-circular late 17C courtyard with festooned windows.

The Rue Vauban leads back to the Place de la Libération, but before heading this way you may want to explore the area S of the Rue Amiral-Roussin. Follow the Rue Hernoux to the pleasant little Place des Cordeliers with, among other buildings, the 17C **Hôtel Rigoley-de-Chevigny**. The Rue Victor-Dumay leads to the Rue Ste-Anne, on the left, with two of the city's smaller museums as well as several good hôtels. The **Musée d'Art Sacré** in the late 17C chapel of the Bernardine convent provides a home for endangered works of art from churches in the Côte d'Or. Its collection of paintings, sculptures and liturgical objects includes a Baroque *altarpiece by the Dijonnais sculptor Jean Dubois, the most important of his works to have survived. The **Musée de la Vie Bourguignonne** in the 17C cloister brings the region's history to life with domestic objects and costumes spanning the cradle to the grave. The displays about food and cooking include a reconstructed Bresse kitchen.

On its way to the Place de la Libération the Rue Vauban passes the 17–18C **Hôtel Bouhier-de-Savigny** at No 12, facing the Place St-Fiacre. It was the birthplace of Jean Bouhier, the president of the *parlement* whose portrait by Largillière hangs in the Musée des Beaux-Arts. The **Hôtel de Talmay**, at No 3 on the right, has a mid 16C façade.

From the Square Darcy to the cathedral of St-Bénigne

The Square Darcy and Place Darcy form a busy road junction at the W end of the Rue de la Liberté. (Henri Darcy was the 19C municipal engineer who reformed the city's water supply and took a leading role in making Dijon a railway centre.) The pleasant gardens include a polar bear by François Pompon, the sculptor from Saulieu whose work can also be seen in the Musée des Beaux-Arts. A **Syndicat d'Initiative** stands on the S side. A plaque at No 9 bis on the nearby Rue Docteur-Chassier marks the Gestapo headquarters during the Occupation.

The **Porte Guillaume**, the 18C triumphal arch at the E end of the Square, stands on the site of the medieval city gate. Its name remembers Guillaume de Volpiano, the abbot who built the great Romanesque church of **St-Bénigne**, which lies at the end of the nearby Rue Docteur-Maret. It has been Dijon's cathedral since the city, for centuries part of the diocese of Langres, became the seat of an independent bishopric in 1731.

The Bishop of Langres built the first church in the 6C to honour what was piously supposed to be the tomb of St Benignus, a legendary figure credited with bringing Christianity to Dijon and suffering martyrdom in the 2C. It became a goal of pilgrimage and the centre of a religious community. In 1001 Guillaume de Volpiano, sent by Cluny to reform the monastery, began to build the grandest Romanesque church of its time in Burgundy, culminating at the E end in a three-storey rotunda derived from the example of the Holy Sepulchre in Jerusalem. The rotunda survived the rebuilding campaign begun in about 1280 but its two upper storeys were demolished at the Revolution. Its ground floor, or crypt, is the most interesting feature of a church which is now otherwise predominantly Gothic.

The heavily buttressed W façade has two octagonal towers with the multicoloured tile roofs characteristic of the region. The spire over the crossing was rebuilt in the 19C. Though the central Romanesque doorway survives beneath the elegant little balustrade of the porch, its sculpture was mutilated by Revolutionary mallets and the tympanum showing St Stephen's martyrdom is 19C work. But note the defaced tympana now set into the walls on either side: the background pattern of wavy lines which can just be made out also appears on the tympana from the side-doorways of St-Bénigne preserved in the neighbouring Musée Archéologique. The Burgundian Gothic interior is pure, severe and oddly lifeless in its effect. There is little to delay a visit to the *crypt, entered from the sacristy on the S side. Stairs lead down into the surviving fragment of the S transept and its two chapels. The capitals, apparently Carolingian, are striking in their primitive force: note particularly the man with extended arms emerging from a background of foliage. None of the capitals is in its original place, for the whole of the crypt was heavily restored and rebuilt when the remains of the upper storeys were cleared out in the mid 19C. A smaller portion of the N transept survives, separated from its fellow by an ambulatory built over the ditch containing St Benignus' tomb. The rotunda itself opens to the E, a wide circle divided into three ambulatories by concentric rings of columns. The central octagon was originally open to admit light from the top of the building. Note the motif on the capitals of a man praying with raised arms rather than clasped hands. E of the rotunda a passage leads to a little rectangular chapel of uncertain date, though perhaps 10C, which was originally above ground level. It stands on the site of the Gallo-Roman cemetery outside the walls of the *castrum*.

The **Musée Archéologique** occupies a former abbey building on the N side of St-Bénigne, its Gallo-Roman collection in the Romanesque cellar that contained Guillaume's chapter house and its medieval sculpture in the superbly appropriate setting of the 13C monks' dormitory.

It makes sense to start on the top floor, where a well-arranged display introduces the region's prehistory and early history. Palaeolithic finds include flint implements and a cast of a Neanderthal skull from Genay. The Bronze Age is represented by a gold bracelet from near La Rochepot and the *Blanot hoard of hammered bronze jewellery (necklace, belt, bracelets and anklets), uncovered when a storm blew an oak tree over in 1982; modern copies help one appreciate the originals. The wide range of Gallo-Roman artefacts embraces small bronze figure sets that pair Celtic with Roman deities and the huge, enigmatic stone heads from Chorey. Merovingian weapons, buckles and clasps complete the display.

The Gallo-Roman collection in the basement includes, among its architectural fragments, the Mavilly pillar carved with both Roman and Celtic gods and a reconstruction of the stone offering chest from Crain. Among the many funeral monuments, one from Til-Châtel shows a wine merchant with his pots arranged by size around his counter. The *finds from site of the Gallic and Gallo-Roman temples at the Source of the Seine make the largest and richest display. Its centrepiece is a bronze statue of the goddess Sequana in her boat, discovered together with a bronze faun. Numerous ex-votos representing limbs, eyes, genitals and internal organs testify to belief in Sequana's healing powers. The wooden carvings, particularly the *pèlerins* (pilgrims), have a starkly primitive look; those in stone are more realistically detailed.

The medieval sculpture in the vaulted dormitory has at least one masterpiece in the *bust of Christ from Claus Sluter's Calvary (the so-called Puits de Moïse) at the Chartreuse de Champmol. It invites comparison with the much sweeter Christ on the Cross from St-Bénigne attributed to Sluter's pupil Claus de Werve. This is displayed between two of St-Bénigne's Romanesque tympana, showing the Last Supper and Christ in Majesty; both use the same wavy lines to represent the sky just visible on the defaced tympana set into the walls on either side of the cathedral entrance. Other Romanesque fragments include capitals from Dijon's St-Philibert and the abbey at Moutiers-St-Jean. A 15C Holy Family in painted stone is striking for its realism.

The Rue Condorcet, running S from St-Bénigne, has some pleasantly shabby old buildings and the **Collège Marcel-Pardé**, built as an orphanage in 1682.

The church of **St-Philibert** (not open) near the E end of the cathedral has a handsome Flamboyant spire but otherwise keeps its Romanesque character. The Rue Danton continues to the mutilated Flamboyant church of **St-Jean**, now a theatre, facing the Place Bossuet. The bishop and preacher Jacques Bénigne Bossuet (1627–1704) was born at No 18, to the N, and baptised in St-Jean; he is remembered by a statue. The grandest house in the square is the **Hôtel Févret-de-Saint-Mesmin**, beyond Bossuet's birthplace, built to a design by Hardouin-Mansart in 1698–1700. The buildings opposite include No 17, the 18C **Hôtel Guyton-de-Morveau**; No 23, the 17–18C **Hôtel Perreney-de-Baleure**; and No 27, the 17–18C **Hôtel Brulard**.

The Rue Piron, where the comic poet Alexis Piron (1689–1773) was born, heads E towards the Place des Cordeliers, near the end of the previous walk. It is also worth walking S on the Rue Monge, which begins splendidly at No 1 with the **Hôtel Bouchu**—perhaps the work of Pierre Le Muet, the Dijonnais architect who completed the château at Tanlay (Route 3)—and descends into pleasant shabbiness by the time it reaches the birthplace at No 32 of the playwright Prosper Jolyot de Crébillon (1674–1762).

The Rue Bossuet leads N from the square and ends handsomely at the Rue de la Liberté with the half-timbered **Maison aux Trois-Visages** (1450–1470) and the late 16C **Hôtel Millière**, with an *échaugette*.

Outskirts

By far the most important sight on the outskirts of the city is the **Chartreuse de Champmol**, or rather the surviving fragments of it, which are now incorporated in the grounds and buildings of the psychiatric hospital about 1km W of the Square Darcy. Follow the Boulevard de Sévigné from the Square (or the Rue Mariotte from St-Bénigne) to join the Avenue Albert-1er on the other side of the railway line, and then turn left on the Boulevard Chanoine-Kir.

The charterhouse, or Carthusian monastery, lay outside the walls of the medieval city. Philippe le Hardi founded it in 1383 as the burial place for the Valois dukes (their Capetian predecessors had been buried in the abbey at Cîteaux) and his charter of 1385 made provision for a prior and 24 monks to pray for the souls of the family. Drouet de Dammartin, who had worked

*Claus Sluter's Puits de Moïse (Moses' Well) at the Chartreuse
de Champmol*

for Philippe's brother Charles V on the Louvre, was architect in charge. The
court sculptor Jean de Marville was succeeded by Claus Sluter in 1389 and
Sluter's work was completed after his death in 1406 by Claus de Werve, his
nephew and pupil. The Chartreuse was largely dismantled at the Revolution and all that survives on the site today is the W doorway of the chapel,
now an otherwise 19C building, and the so-called Puits de Moïse (Moses'
Well), protected from the weather by a glazed shelter. The tombs of Philippe
and his son Jean sans Peur are preserved in the Musée des Beaux-Arts
together with several works of art commissioned for the Chartreuse,
notably the two altarpieces by Jacques de Baerze and Melchior Broederlam

and the 'Adoration of the Shepherds' by the Master of Flémalle. Jan van Eyck's 'Annunciation', another treasure, hangs in the National Gallery of Art in Washington DC.

Claus Sluter's W doorway, added to the chapel shortly after the rest of the building was finished in 1388, is the earliest of his works to survive. It already proclaims his distinctive genius. Placing Philippe and his wife Marguerite de Flandre with their patron saints John the Baptist and St Catherine on either side of the doorway, praying to the figure of the Virgin Mary on the central pier, his composition transforms the traditional Gothic statue-columns into a dramatic group, further animated by the richly swirling drapery (particularly of the Virgin's robes).

The Puits de Moïse is really the base of the massive Calvary which Sluter carved at the end of his life, the crowning masterpiece of his career and hence of late Gothic sculpture. It stood over the well in the centre of the monastery's great cloister, transforming the literal source of water into a celebration of Christ's Passion as the fountain of life. The head of Christ is preserved in the Musée Archéologique but the rest of the figure and the figures of the Virgin Mary, St John and Mary Magdalen have disappeared. The pedestal itself is a hexagon topped by a corniche with mourning angels (carved by Claus de Werve). Around its sides stand statues of the six Old Testament prophets who foretold Christ's death: Moses, David, Jeremiah, Zachariah, Daniel and Isaiah. The scrolls they carry remind the spectator of the pertinent texts: 'And the whole assembly of the congregation of Israel shall kill it in the evening' (Exodus 12:6) for Moses, 'They pierced my hands and my feet. I may tell all my bones' (Psalms 22:16–17) for David, 'All ye that pass by, behold, and see if there be any sorrow like unto my sorrow' (Lamentations 1:12) for Jeremiah, and so forth. Yet characteristically Sluter went far beyond announcing the prophets' role in the theological scheme of the Calvary, using the variety of their poses and arrangement of their robes to create a series of individualised figures that ranges from the powerful, visionary Moses to the calmly regal David with his harp and the aged, enfeebled Jeremiah. The original decoration by Jean Malouel from Zutphen and Herman de Cologne heightened Sluter's realism, colouring the prophets' robes in red, azure and gold, and even giving Jeremiah a pair of spectacles. The pedestal itself was painted green and the cross above gilded and emblazoned with the coats of arms of Flanders and Burgundy. Such touches, suggests Jan Huizinga, link the composition with the *tableaux vivants* that were a favourite feature of the state occasions and public entertainments of the Valois court. Their loss emphasises the expressive dynamism of Sluter's sculpture, which (to quote Erwin Panofsky) 'contains potentially Michelangelo and Bernini'.

The route along the Avenue Albert-1er from the railway line to the Chartreuse begins at the **Jardin de l'Arquebuse**, with botanic gardens handsomely laid out on a site once used by the regiment of harquebusiers (the harquebus being an early type of musket). The **Musée d'Histoire Naturelle** in the 17C barracks contains displays of geology and fauna from the region and around the world, with a fine specimen of a glyptodon, ancestor of the armadillo. The Espace Grévin on the Avenue Albert-1er has a **Musée de Cire** (Wax Museum) with tableaux from Burgundian history and effigies of famous Burgundians. Beyond the Chartreuse the avenue continues as N5 past the artificial **Lac Kir**, a popular centre for outdoor activities and water sports. Completed in 1964, it is named after the mayor who had urged its creation. For Talant, see the end of Route 2.

The **Parc de la Colombière**, S of the Place Wilson by the Cours Général-de-Gaulle, was laid out for the Prince de Condé in the 17C. A fragment of Roman road survives.

6 The Côte d'Or: Dijon to Beaune and Chagny

Directions and distances. Total distance 42km (26 miles) to Beaune, 78km (49 miles) to Chagny. Route des Grands Crus from **Dijon** to (6km) Chenôve. D122 to (21km) Clos de Vougeot. N74 to (25km) **Nuits-St-Georges** and (42km) **Beaune**. N74, (44km) D973 to (45km) Pommard. D17, (54.5km) D17i, (59km) D111d to (60.5km) **La Rochepot**. D973, (61.5km) N6, (70.5km) D113a to (73.5km) Santenay. D974 to (78km) **Chagny**.

Connections with other routes. The previous route describes Dijon. Routes 14 and 15 reach Beaune and Chagny from Saulieu and Autun respectively. Santenay also lies near the end of Route 21, following the Canal du Centre from Paray-le-Monial via Le Creusot to Chalon. Chagny is described at the beginning of the next route, which heads through the Chalonnais.

The *Côte d'Or*, which gives its romantic name to the department for which Dijon serves as préfecture, is the great wine-producing region of Burgundy: a golden hillside indeed, when the vine leaves have turned at harvest time (*vendange*) in late September or early October. It stretches SW of Dijon through Nuits-St-Georges and Beaune to Santenay, a narrow strip hardly a mile wide and only about 35 miles or 56km long, on the slopes between the rugged, upper reaches of the Montagne and the flat plain of the Saône. The terrain is ideal for vines: enriched by mineral deposits washed down in the *combes* and watercourses that break up the hills, drained by the steep slope and the stony soil, protected by the heights above from cold wind and frost, yet exposed to the morning sun.

Nobody knows when the Côte first began to produce wine. The Vix treasure in the museum at Châtillon is proof that wine was known in Burgundy by about 500 BC, if only through importation, and the Romans certainly found vines growing in the region. But the earliest identifiable pioneers of today's vineyards were the monasteries. At Gevrey-Chambertin the Clos de Bèze was first cultivated by the abbey of Bèze in the 7C, while Cîteaux, on the nearby plain, cultivated Clos de Vougeot from the early 12C. From such work the industry has developed, surviving the ravages of phylloxera (a root-eating parasite) in the late 19C and the depression following World War I to achieve the present worldwide reputation that makes the list of its villages and vineyards a connoisseurs' index.

These places, so large in reputation, are small and modest. Land is at too much of a premium to permit the villages to sprawl and the strong local economy has largely preserved a sturdy, working look that not even fame and the tourists can destroy. There are churches with multicoloured tiles on their spires, the occasional big château, and narrow streets of houses ranged round the traditional courtyard with buildings for *cuveries* (vat-houses) and *caves* (cellars). A distinctive sight in the courtyards and on the roads are the *enjambeurs*, tractors specially designed to straddle the rows of vines. Nor are the vineyards themselves large. Chambertin Clos de Bèze and Chambertin cover only about 70 acres between them (yielding about 9000 dozen bottles of wine a year) while Clos de Vougeot, the largest *Grand*

Cru vineyard on the Côte, covers about 124 acres (about 16,500 dozen bottles). The fact that it is divided into more than 100 separate plots and shared between about 80 different owners makes Clos de Vougeot an extreme case, but great labels are now rarely if ever singly owned.

These labels belong to the complex *appellation d'origine contrôlée* (AOC) system which identifies and ranks wine from the precisely pinpointed *Grands Crus* in the highest category to the broad regional designations of the simpler products. These regional designations reflect the several divisions of the Côte. The Côte de Nuits stretches from Fixin through Nuits-St-Georges itself to Premeaux-Prissey. Red wine made from the Pinot Noir grape predominates and its most general *appellation* is Côte de Nuits-Villages. The Côte de Beaune stretches from near Aloxe-Corton through Beaune to Santenay. Less unified in character than the Côte de Nuits, it produces both famous reds and whites, the white coming from the Chardonnay and Pinot Blanc grapes. Its regional *appellation* is Côte de Beaune-Villages (Côte de Beaune being the regional label for Beaune itself). The rougher and more exposed reaches higher up the Montagne are known as the Hautes-Côtes, subdivided into the Hautes-Côtes de Nuits and the Hautes-Côtes de Beaune. They produce wine which in general lacks the prestige, though not always the quality, of its better-known neighbours, and the grapes used also include the Aligoté for whites and the Gamay, which produces only inferior red wine in Burgundy (sometimes combined with the Pinot Noir to make blends like the Passe-Tout-Grains) but comes into its own in the slaty Beaujolais hills. In the less favourable terrain of the Hautes-Côtes wine production is joined by soft-fruit growing (particularly of blackcurrants for *cassis* liqueur) and general farming.

Many *caves* are open to visitors, as their *dégustation* and *vente* signs announce. A full list is available from the Maison de Tourisme in Beaune.

From the centre of **Dijon** follow the signs for Beaune and then branch right on the Route des Grands Crus for (6km) **Chenôve**. Modern development makes Chenôve look like part of Dijon's suburban sprawl though it is in fact a separate town (19,530 people). The Rue Roger-Salengro in the old town keeps two early 15C winepresses (open) made for the Valois dukes' *clos* on the Côte de Dijon. The only vineyards of any size to have survived the spread of the city are further along D122 at (2km) **Marsannay-la-Côte** (5220 people) and its southern neighbour (2km) **Couchey**, known particularly for a rosé made from the Pinot Noir. At 'Le Pas de l'Arbre de Charlemagne', a passage of arms held at Marsannay in 1443, Pierre de Bauffremont and his companions from the court of Philippe le Bon challenged all comers to a jousting tournament. The steep D108 leads up via Corcelles-les-Monts to (6.5km) the viewpoint on Mont Afrique, described in Route 4. D122 continues to (2km) **Fixey**, with a simple early Romanesque church looking over the vineyards.

The **Côte de Nuits** formally begins at (1km) neighbouring **Fixin** (880 people; Tourist Information). The Parc Noisot is a lovely stretch of woodland laid out by Claude Noisot, a former captain of Napoléon's Imperial Guard, in honour of his Emperor: it includes a little museum of Napoleonic souvenirs, a flight of a hundred steps recalling the Hundred Days and 'Le Réveil de Napoléon', a statue by François Rude showing the defeated Emperor waking to take his place among the Immortals. Noisot's tomb and a bust of Rude stand at a respectful distance near by. The road leading to the park continues to a good viewpoint over the Côte. On its way out of the village the Route des Grands Crus passes an elegant *lavoir*. **Brochon** (590

Detail of François Rude's 'Le Réveil de Napoléon' in the Parc Noisot at Fixin

people), 1km beyond, has a château (not open) built by the poet and public servant Stéphen Liégeard (1830–1925), said to have provided Alphonse Daudet with the model for his *sous-préfet*. (Liégeard also coined the term 'Côte d'Azur' by analogy with 'Côte d'Or'.)

Gevrey-Chambertin (2830 people; Tourist Information), 2km further, is a handsome little place grouped around its 15–16C château, on the site of the castle built by the abbots of Cluny in the 13C (open). Originally just Gevrey, it was the first village on the Côte to double-barrel its name with that of its *Grands Crus*, of which it boasts more than any other commune. The two most famous lie to its S. Clos de Bèze (or Chambertin Clos de Bèze) was originally owned by the monks of Bèze, granted the land in about 630, before it passed into Cluniac hands. Neighbouring Chambertin is said to derive its name from the 'Champ de Bertin' or field of Bertin, a landowner who set out to emulate the monks' achievement.

You can explore the **Hautes-Côtes de Nuits** from Gevrey-Chambertin by following the steep, winding D31 up the **Combe de Lavaux**, with its limestone crags. Beyond (6.5km) **Chamboeuf** it joins D35 for (6km) **Ternant**, E of a wooded stretch of country with dolmens and caves. It is also worth branching left on the little D116, just before Chamboeuf, for (6.5km) **Reulle-Vergy** and the hill of Vergy, with a partly Romanesque church on its N flank and the largely 18C ruins of the Cluniac abbey of St-Vivant on its S flank. On the wooded hilltop stand a few ruined vestiges of the castle belonging to the powerful family which challenged the Capetian dukes until Eudes III solved the problem by marrying Alix de Vergy. The family is also remembered for the tragic love story first told in the late 13C 'La Chastellaine de Vergi'. Reulle-Vergy itself has an interesting local museum. The church at **L'Étang-Vergy**, 2km SW, contains a fragment of the 15C Tournai marble tomb of Pierre de Bauffremont. D25 and D35 make their way down to (8.5km) Nuits-St-Georges through a landscape mixing quarries and vineyards.

The Route des Grands Crus from Gevrey-Chambertin passes the *Grands Crus* of (4km) **Morey-St-Denis** (640 people) and (1km) **Chambolle-Musigny**: Clos de la Roche, Clos St-Denis, Clos de Tart, Les Bonnes Mares (straddling the two communes) and Les Musigny. The roster of famous names continues at (1km) **Vougeot**, where the Clos de Vougeot vineyards are flanked, higher up the hillside, by those of Les Grands-Échézeaux and Les Échézeaux.

Clos de Vougeot was acquired by the monks of Cîteaux soon after they had established their abbey in 1098 and cultivated by their *vignerons* and *maîtres de cellier* until the Revolution. The great wall that enclosed the vineyard from the 15C is still maintained. The *château (open) in its centre is deservedly one of the famous sights of the Côte. Its irregular courtyard combines a Renaissance block with earlier Cistercian buildings, notably the 13C *cuverie*, a cloister with massive oak winepresses standing at each of its angles. In 1944 the château was bought by the Confrérie des Chevaliers du Tastevin, founded in Nuits-St-Georges during the depression a decade earlier. Its convivial banquets and pseudo-medieval rituals make a highly successful exercise in public relations. There is an audio-visual display about the brotherhood and a display of the little winetasting cups from which it takes its name; the rooms shown include the much restored Romanesque *cellier* used for chapter meetings and the gathering that begins the Trois Glorieuses festival each November. Cîteaux itself, on the plain 13km SE, is described in Route 9.

Beyond the château N74 leads S via (2km) **Vosne-Romanée** (530 people) with its five *Grands Crus*: La Romanée-Conti, La Tâche, Le Richebourg, La Romanée, La Romanée-St-Vivant. **Nuits-St-Georges** (5570 Nuitons; Tourist Information), 2km beyond, is a centre of both vineyards and the wine trade. The original headquarters of the Confrérie des Chevaliers du Tastevin, it holds a Hospices wine auction like the one at Beaune on the Sunday before Palm Sunday and an unfermented wine festival, La Fête du Vin Bourru, near the beginning of November. Its cheeses should not be forgotten. Visually, it has little to offer and the polychrome tiles on the spire are the most cheerful thing about St-Symphorien, a church whose architectural interest as a late 13C mixture of Romanesque and Gothic does not relieve its grimness. The local museum has an interesting archaeological collection and souvenirs of the Battle of Nuits, an indecisive rearguard action against the invading armies in the Franco-Prussian War.

From Nuits D25 climbs up the Hautes-Côtes, passing the turning for D35 and the route via Vergy to Gevrey-Chambertin already described. D25 continues to (9km) **Arcenant** with its Resistance monument, the **Combe Perthuis** and a rugged country of caves, water sources and views from which perilous little roads lead over to the Ouche valley (Route 4) or back to Savigny-lès-Beaune (see below).

S of Nuits N74 runs through the fringes of the Côte de Nuits on the way to (3.5km) **Comblanchien** (570 people), with a memorial to the prisoners massacred by the Nazis in August 1944. The 'marble' from the local quarries is really a polished limestone, either the Rosé de Premeaux or the so-called Comblanchien marble, a beige stone used for the Paris Opéra and Orly Airport. The road enters the **Côte de Beaune** on the way to **Aloxe-Corton**, on the right 8km beyond, whose beautifully sited vineyards are unique on the Côte in producing both a great red (Corton) and a great white (Corton-Charlemagne). It shares the latter label with **Pernand-Vergelesses**, a village 2km N with a partly Romanesque church. **Savigny-lès-Beaune** (1390 people; Tourist Information), 4km SW, is known less for its wine than its château (open), really two 17C buildings, now displaying a collection of motorbikes, cars and aircraft. N74 continues from Aloxe-Corton to (5.5km) Beaune.

*BEAUNE (21,290 Beaunois; Tourist Information), for long a centre of the wine trade on the Côte, is nowadays also a centre of the tourist trade. The pervading atmosphere of wine, the narrow streets with their tall, sleepy houses, the church of Notre-Dame and, above all, the Hôtel-Dieu—most famous of Beaune's old buildings and one of Burgundy's great landmarks— ensure a steady flow of visitors breaking their journey down the autoroute or the Route des Grands Crus. Originally a Celtic settlement at the source of the Aigue (where the river god Belenos was worshipped) and then a Roman town, Beaune became one of the first strongholds of the duchy and the original seat of its *parlement*. The rise of Dijon as capital did not end the traditional rivalry between the two towns and, if Dijon has vastly outgrown Beaune in size since the coming of industry in the 19C, the autoroute system now puts Beaune at the crossroads of the region.

An obvious way to begin or end a tour is to make the circuit of the old walls (about 2.7km or 1.7 miles), starting in the N at the **Porte St-Nicolas** and walking clockwise. Though large fragments survive, their setting has little of the picturesque charm found at Avallon or even Autun: Beaune is not a hill town, and the rectangular *enceinte* now looks out on suburbs and the howling traffic of the boulevards. The walls and towers are largely 12–14C, while the five bastions were added in the 16C and 17C. Note the characteristic *échaugette* on the **Bastion Notre-Dame**, the first encountered on the walk E from the Porte St-Nicolas. The late 15C castle by the next bastion, the **Bastion St-Jean**, was dismantled by Henri IV at the demand of the Beaunois themselves after the town had been made a reluctant strong-hold of the Ligue during the Wars of Religion.

At several points the line of the old walls is broken by streets leading into the old centre. The ****Hôtel-Dieu** (open) is a precious survival, a medieval hospital founded by Philippe le Bon's chancellor Nicolas Rolin and his third wife Guigonne de Salins in 1443, after an outbreak of the plague in Beaune.

BEAUNE
0 metres   200

St-Nicolas & DIJON
BD MARECHAL FOCH
Bastion des Filles
Porte St-Nicolas
English Garden
R. DU COLLEGE
RUE DE LORRAINE
Hôtel de Ville
Bastion Notre-Dame
Musées
SQUARE DES LIONS
RUE MAREY
Tour Blondeau
CLEMENCEAU
Remparts
BOULEVARD
Collégiale Notre-Dame
DE LA REPUBLIQUE
PL. MONGE
Hospice de la Charité
R. DES TONNELIERS
Bastion St-Jean
SAULIEU
Bastion des Dames
Musée du Vin
THIERS
Station
PL. FLEURY
R. MALROUX
Hôtel Dieu
PLACE CARNOT
Bastion Ste-Anne
AUTUN
BD BRETONNIERE
Bastion de l'Hôtel Dieu
Remparts
RUE DU FAUBOURG MADELEINE
PLACE MADELEINE
Grosse Tour
CHALON-S-SAONE

Taking the St-Jacques hospital in Valenciennes as his model, their architect
(perhaps Jacques Wiscrère) married local Burgundian with Flemish traditions to create Flamboyant Gothic buildings that wonderfully evoke the
spirit of Valois culture. To the street they present a deliberately plain
appearance, and only the canopy over the main gate prepares the visitor
for the rich spectacle of the half-timbered buildings on the courtyard inside:
a Flemish cloth hall ripened by the southern sun into witty, genial fantasy.
Slender columns support the gallery below the steep-pitched expanse of
polychrome tiles, studded with dormer windows that sprout a small forest
of pinnacles. The Grande Salle des Pôvres (Paupers' Ward), with its carved
and painted roof, preserves the original arrangements for the sick. The
theatrical way they are now presented is the first of several jarring touches
that seek to make a stage-set of the hospital. Fourteen four-poster beds
flank each side of the room (the original beds were wider and often held
more than one patient), allowing the sick to see services in the chapel
beyond the screen at the E end. The room has lost many of its richer
furnishings, but note the 17C pewter in the display cases by each bed and
the fine 15C Flemish Ecce Homo in painted wood. The window and screen
at the E end are modern reproductions and the chapel itself was restored
in the 19C. A plaque marks the burial place of Guigonne de Salins, who
retired to Beaune after Rolin's death and died at the hospital in 1470.
Adjoining rooms include the Salle St-Hugues, a private ward for privileged
patients; the Salle St-Nicolas, with an exhibition about the history of the

hospital; the kitchen, with its array of copper pots; and the charming 18C pharmacy.

The Salle St-Louis, added to the courtyard in the 18C, now houses the choicest works of art with which the hospital was endowed. Irritatingly, it can be visited only as part of the guided tour. The main room contains 16C and 17C tapestries from Tournai (the Prodigal Son) and Brussels (the story of Jacob). In a darkened annexe specially constructed for the purpose hangs Roger van der Weyden's ****polyptych of the Last Judgement, commissioned by Rolin in 1443 as the altarpiece for the chapel and presumably complete by the time the chapel was dedicated in 1451. One of the greatest Flemish works produced by the Valois era in Burgundy, it takes a subject that in previous centuries had been a staple of Burgundian Romanesque sculptors and treats it afresh, with vivid realism and bright colour. The large magnifying lens permanently installed in front of it helps reveal the finer detail. On the upper register of the central panel—there are nine in all—Christ sits in Judgement on a rainbow, his feet resting on a globe. He is flanked by a lily and a fiery sword (power and justice) with Latin inscriptions from Matthew 25:34 and 41: 'Come, ye blessed of my Father, inherit the kingdom prepared for you from the foundation of the world'; and 'Depart from me, ye cursed, into everlasting fire, prepared for the devil and his angels'. The marvellously serene angels on the small adjoining leaves hold the instruments of the Passion. But St Michael, not Christ, is the focal point of the composition. He stands weighing souls in the lower register of the central panel, a graceful, white-robed figure whose every feature and gesture express calm and poise: judgement embodied as balance, in all the meanings of the word. The nude souls in his scales are labelled respectively 'virtutes' (virtues) and 'peccata' (sins). From the earth at his feet arise the naked figures of the dead, making their way gratefully towards Heaven on the left or, in larger numbers, fleeing in terror towards Hell on the right. Above them sit two groups, headed by the Virgin Mary and John the Baptist; among saints, apostles and several unidentified people a king, a cardinal and the pope appear, closest to Heaven, at the extreme left.

All the nudes were given clothing in the early 19C. These additions were removed, though not without some permanent damage to the painting, when it was restored at Paris in the 1870s. At the same time the polyptych was cut in half so that the backs of the panels, normally visible only when the wings were closed, could be hung separately. These bear grisaille paintings, simulating statues, of the Annunciation and the two patrons saints of the Hôtel-Dieu, St Sebastian and St Anthony. To the left and right appear the kneeling figures of Guigonne de Salins and Rolin, Rolin with the same severe features painted by van Eyck in his 'Madonna with Chancellor Rolin', which now hangs in the Louvre. His son, the cardinal, appears in the Nativity by the Master of Moulins in the Musée Rolin at Autun.

The endowment of the Hospices de Beaune (joint name for the Hôtel-Dieu and the Hospice de la Charité) includes some of the region's most valuable vineyards, between Aloxe-Corton and Meursault, among other landholdings. The auction of the Hospices de Beaune wines, billed as the largest charity auction in the world, is a central event in the Trois Glorieuses festival each November.

On the square adjoining the Hôtel-Dieu the old covered market has been restored to house, among other things, the **Maison de Tourisme**. The Place Carnot, further E, has a pleasant array of old buildings.

North of the Hôtel and the Place de la Halle is the former **Hôtel des Ducs**

de Bourgogne, later the Logis du Roi and now the wine museum. The Flamboyant façade of the main building and the half-timbered outhouses themselves are more impressive than the museum collection, though it does include winepresses in the *cuverie* and a tapestry celebrating wine by Jean Lurçat in the Ambassade des Vins de France.

A little further N stands the collegiate church of ***Notre-Dame**, begun in about 1119. Its debt to Cluniac Romanesque and affinity with its larger and greater contemporary, St-Lazare at Autun, have been partly submerged under the many later additions, like the 14C W porch with its carved 15C door panels. The E end presents an interesting medley. Romanesque elements inside include the fine elevation of the nave and a handful of carved capitals: note (all on the S wall or S arcade) the animal musicians, the Tree of Jesse, Noah's Ark, the stoning of St Stephen and the grape-pickers. On the N side of the nave the Rolin chapel (second from W) contains a late 15C fresco by Pierre Spicre showing Lazarus' resurrection and the neighbouring St-Martin chapel a carved 16C altarpiece. But by far the most striking furnishings are the five tapestries in the choir showing the life of the Virgin Mary: nineteen richly coloured tableaux in which the spirit of the Italian Renaissance begins to make itself felt. Based on drawings by Pierre Spicre, they were commissioned in 1474 by Cardinal Rolin of Autun and presented to the church by Hugues le Coq, who appears kneeling in front of Hugues, abbot of Cluny, in the last scene on the S side. The S transept door leads to the handsome 13C cloisters and chapter house.

Near the E end of the church stands a 14C belfry in the Flemish style. The neighbouring Place Monge is named after Gaspard Monge (1746–1818), the mathematician, physicist and Revolutionary politician from Beaune who is remembered by the names of streets and squares in several Burgundian towns. His statue is by François Rude. The **Hôtel de la Rochepot** (now No 9) has an early 16C Gothic façade.

The Rue de la Lorraine, leading N, is the best street of old buildings in Beaune. Note, at the corner of the Rue Rousseau-Deslandes on the right, the 15C house and the **Hospice de la Charité**, a hospital for orphans established in 1645. Further up the Rue de la Lorraine, on the right, the **Hôtel de Ville** occupies the 17C cloisters of a former Ursuline convent. One wing houses two museums: the **Musée des Beaux-Arts**, with works by the painter Félix Ziem (1821–1911), a native of Beaune; and the **Musée Étienne-Jules Marey**, dedicated to another Beaunois, the 19C physiologist who pioneered chronophotography, a technique for recording movement which played its part in the history of the cinema.

The Rue de la Lorraine ends in the N at the Porte St-Nicolas, where the walk around the walls conveniently begins. The church of **St-Nicolas**, further N, has a Romanesque tower and doorway. Its primitive tympanum shows the saint with the three children whom the popular legend claimed he rescued or resuscitated.

The **Montagne de Beaune**, about 4km W on D970, makes a good look-out point (359m) over the vineyards and the town. The road continues over the Hautes-Côtes, with another good viewpoint at the crest near Bessey-en-Chaume and junction with D23, to Bligny-sur-Ouche (Route 4), 19km from Beaune.

The ***Archéodrome** is by the side of the A6 6km S of Beaune, though determined mapreaders can also reach it by minor roads from Beaune or Chagny. It seeks to bring the archaeology of Burgundy to life through open-air reconstructions, audio-visual displays, models and casts, rather than original objects. The result is entertaining for children and at least interesting to adults. The indoor area introduces major sites and eras: La Solutré (Palaeolithic), Vix (Iron Age) and Alesia (Gallo-Roman). There is a room devoted to the use of aerial photography and, an imaginative touch, a Gallo-Roman garden planted in the centre of the exhibition hall. A section of Caesar's siege line at Alesia is the most striking of the open-air reconstructions, which range from Neolithic huts to a Gallo-Roman cemetery. Friends of the M6 might wish to note that the Archéodrome was financed by the Société des Autoroutes Paris–Rhin–Rhône as part of its policy to humanise and enliven French motorways.

Though its hotels and restaurants make Beaune an obvious stopping point, the town does not mark the end of the Côte and its vineyards, which continue S to the region of Santenay and Chagny. There are many possible ways of making the tour. The best start is to follow N74 SW from Beaune, branching right on D970 to (3km) **Pommard** (550 people), a great though once much-abused name among red wines. On a straight line between here and Santenay (16km SW) lie vineyards which mark the change from red to white. **Volnay**, at 2km, is a pleasant village. **Meursault** (1540 people; Tourist Information), 3km beyond, is the largest producer of white wines on the Côte. It has a striking church spire and, near the N74, the Romanesque doorway of a 12C leper hospital. **Puligny-Montrachet**, 4km further, and **Chassagne-Montrachet**, another 2km, share the Montrachet whites.

A more interesting route from Pommard goes via the **Hautes-Côtes de Beaune**, taking D17 W past (8km) **St-Romain**, among vineyards that produce both red and white wines. The ruins of the old castle in the upper village, on the crest of the ridge, make a good viewpoint. The town hall in the lower village has a local history display. D17i snakes along the ridge past limestone crags at (4km) **Orches** and joins D111d beyond Baubigny on the way into (3.5km) **La Rochepot**.

The distant view of the castle at La Rochepot (open), with its multi-coloured roofs and its cluster of towers, spires and pinnacles, is one of the most satisfyingly romantic sights of the Côte. It should come as no surprise to discover on closer view that the building is largely a modern reconstruction. Dating originally from the 12C, the castle was first rebuilt by Régnier Pot and Philippe Pot, powerful courtiers of the Valois dukes. Philippe Pot (1428–1494), the Burgundian ambassador to England, survived his master's fall to be appointed Grand Seneschal of Burgundy by Louis XI; his tomb is in the Louvre. The Revolution reduced La Rochepot to ruin, from which it was rescued and rebuilt in 1893–1926 by the son of Sadi Carnot, President of the Third Republic (see Nolay below). Very little of its former character survives in the buildings that surround the irregular courtyard, though there is a dramatic view from the terrace. Perhaps the best interior is the dining room, with a carved and painted wooden ceiling, Renaissance chimneypieces, 17C Aubusson tapestries and a painting attributed to Primaticcio. Also displayed here is a copy of the Bronze Age bracelet discovered in the neighbourhood; the original can be seen in the Musée Archéologique at Dijon. The Romanesque parish church is more authentic, despite mutilations and the loss of the vaulting over the nave. It belonged to a Benedictine priory and declares its affinity with the Cluniac style in the fluted pilasters and carved capitals: note particularly the Annunciation (first pillar from the W in the S arcade) and Balaam and his ass (second pillar from the W in the N arcade). The altarpiece, originally in the castle, is a 17C triptych of the Deposition and Entombment attributed to the Dijonnais painter Philippe Quantin.

Nolay (1550 people; Tourist Information), 4km SW of La Rochepot on D973, is a pleasant town with some old streets and a strikingly picturesque group of buildings by the 17–19C church. The 14C market hall has a framework of chestnut timbers supporting a roof made of the heavy limestone tiles locally called *laves*. A statue stands outside the birthplace of Lazare Carnot (1753–1823), military engineer, member of the Convention in the 1790s and uncle of Sadi Carnot, President of the Third Republic in the 19C. The little Flamboyant chapel of St-Pierre (1517) survives N of the town. It lies on the route following D111 up the narrow, winding *Vallon de la Tournée, past the little wine-producing villages of Cormot-le-Grand and Vauchignon to (4km) the remote and fittingly named **Cirque du Bout du Monde**, a natural rock amphitheatre with a waterfall. D33 and D1 run S from Nolay through vineyards to the handsome little town of (13km) **Couches** (1460 people), on the northern edge of the coalfields in the Blanzy basin. The castle (open) on a rocky spur 1km W by the Chalon road preserves its fortifications, 12C keep, 12C 'prison' tower and Flamboyant chapel built by Claude de Montaigu, chamberlain to Philippe le Bon and chevalier of the Toison d'Or. The chapel contains a good little collection of 15–16C Burgundian religious sculpture and a painting of Christ by Rouault. The buildings are sometimes called the castle of Marguerite de Bourgogne, from the belief that the repudiated wife of Louis X did not die before the king's remarriage in 1315, as the official histories have it, but spent the rest of her life here as the secret prisoner of her cousin's family.

The main route from La Rochepot to Chagny joins N6 S of the village. The road passes near **St-Aubin**, with a Romanesque church. St-Aubin produces red and white wine, while its sister village of **Gamay** gave its name to the grape. At 10km from La Rochepot D113a leads S to (3km) **Santenay** (1010 people; Tourist Information). The name embraces two distinct communities. Santenay-le-Bas, a spa since Roman times, has a casino and thermal baths. Santenay-le-Haut marks the southern tip of the Côte de Beaune. The vineyards rising up the flanks of the *Mont de Sène (or Montagne des Trois Croix; 521m) make one of the most charming landscapes on the Côte. The church of St-Jean-de-Narosse, near the foot, has a 15C choir with complex lierne vaulting. For the Canal du Centre S of Santenay, see Route 21. The present journey finishes by taking D974 3.5km E to **Chagny**, described at the beginning of the next route.

7   The Chalonnais: Chagny to Chalon-sur-Saône and Tournus

Directions and distances. Total distance 68km (42 miles). **Chagny**. D981 to (15km) Givry and (25km) Buxy. D977 to (41km) **Chalon-sur-Saône**. N6 to (68km) **Tournus**.

Connections with other routes. Chagny is reached at the end of the previous route, down the Côte d'Or; in Routes 14 and 15 from Saulieu and Autun respectively; and in Route 21, which follows the Canal du Centre from Paray-le-Monial via Le Creusot. Route 8 describes Tournus and continues through the Mâconnais.

The **Chalonnais**, or Côte Chalonnaise, is a little pocket of hilly country between Chagny and Buxy (only about 40 miles or 25km as the crow flies), bounded in the W by the Dheune valley and in the E by the Saône where

Chalon itself stands. Sandwiched between the Côte d'Or and the Mâconnais, and sharing with them the same favourable *climat*, it produces light red wines from the Pinot Noir and whites from the Chardonnay, as well as sparkling wines like Crémant de Bourgogne. The main vineyards are at Rully, Mercurey (the best known and arguably the centre of the region), Givry and Montagny. Though profiting from the post-war boom in all Burgundy wines, they have never been as well regarded as their powerful rivals; recovery from phylloxera, which attacked the Chalonnais more savagely than anywhere else in Burgundy, was harder and less complete. Nor is the landscape as completely given over to vineyards as the smooth, almost continuous slope of the Côte d'Or. In the broken-up hills vineyards alternate with pasture land for beef cattle and goats (look out for goat cheese). The towns and villages are like their wines, pleasant but less memorable than those of the Côte or the Mâconnais.

The journey down the Côte d'Or in the previous route ends at **Chagny** (5350 Chagnotins; Tourist Information), a commercial and industrial town known for making tiles, and the scene of a lively Sunday morning market. Chagny usually attracts travellers by its restaurants and its proximity to the N6, but also keeps a few old buildings. The church has a Romanesque tower and the hearts of Pierre Jeannin and his wife buried beneath the chancel; the rest of them is in St-Lazare at Autun.

This route ignores N6, which runs directly to Chalon, and instead follows the straight, tree-lined D981 S to the vineyards. The first wine-producing village is **Rully** (1640 people), to the right at 4km, with a big partly medieval château (access to outside only) on the spur of the hill to its S. **Fontaines** (1840 people), a spreading village to the left of D981 3.5km further on, has a good Gothic church.

Another 3.5km beyond is the junction with D978, the Autun road, leading in 4km to **Mercurey** (1280 people), whose red wines are the best known of the Côte Chalonnaise. The little village of **Touches**, about 1km to its S, is a picturesque place with a good 13C church. Side-roads lead 2km further S to **Mellecey**, where the church has Lombardic bands.

The quiet **Vallée des Vaux** runs SW from the junction of D981 and D978 through Mellecey. **Barizey**, on the left at 7km, has a neo-classical church (1778–1786) by Emiland Gauthey, simpler than the one at Givry and now in very poor condition. **Châtel-Moron**, marking the head of the valley 3km beyond, makes a good viewpoint.

Beyond the junction with D978, the main route and D981 continue S to (1km) **Germolles**, which keeps fragments of the medieval castle converted by Philippe le Hardi into a ducal lodge for his wife Marguerite de Flandre, notably chapels of the 13C and late 14C (open). **Givry** (3340 people), 3km beyond, produces wines once favoured by Henri IV, though they have lost in reputation to those of Mercurey. Several buildings give the town a neo-classical look. The most striking is Emiland Gauthey's *church (1770–1791), a dramatic design of three linked rotundas said to be the test model for the Panthéon in Paris, a project on which Gauthey advised Soufflot. His clock tower containing the Hôtel de Ville (1770) spans the street near the round market hall (1830). **Jambles**, 3km W on an alternative way of approaching the Vallée des Vaux, is a little village with *vignerons'* houses.

Buxy (2000 people; Tourist Information), 10km further S on D981, has a nice ensemble of old buildings round its church, though the hideously restored interior is best avoided. With neighbouring **Montagny**, it marks the end of the Chalonnais vineyards. **Bissy-sur-Fley**, 10km SW on D983, has a Romanesque church and the small early 16C château where the Renaissance poet Pontus de Tyard, a member of Ronsard's Pléiade, was born.

The main route from Buxy simply follows D977 NE to (16km) Chalon, described below. An alternative way avoids Chalon and continues S on D981 to (21km) Cormatin, where its joins the journey through the Mâconnais in Route 8. **St-Gengoux-le-National** (1010 people; Tourist Information), to the right at 11km, once flourished because of its wines and its connection with Cluny and the French crown. There are heartening signs of revival in the old *centre on the hill, where the streets often have names (Rue des Vertus, de l'Espérance, de l'Abondance) as pleasant as the buildings, which display the typical features of Burgundian vernacular: the encorbelled staircase turret rising above the front door, the *échaugette*, the Flamboyant curl over doorways and windows, and the occasional neo-classical doorcase added to an older house. The church is an unsatisfactory mixture of Romanesque, Flamboyant and 19C imitation Flamboyant.

CHALON-SUR-SAÔNE (54,580 Chalonnais; Tourist Information) stands where the river, after gathering tributaries on the way across the plain E of the Côte d'Or, swings S on its broad, straight course through Tournus and Mâcon to join the Rhône at Lyon. The Saône has determined the city's history since Celts and then Romans made it a trading port and crossroads on the route from Britain to the Mediterranean (see Châtillon, Route 2). It later became the market centre for the hunters of the Alps, the Jura and the Massif Central. The building of Emiland Gauthey's Canal du Centre (1783–1791), linking Chalon with the Loire at Digoin, confirmed its destiny as an industrial town. Le Petit Creusot, a subsidiary of the Schneider ironworks installed in 1839, was the first of the factories which now crowd its outskirts (Kodak, Philips, Framatome), making it the second largest but not the second most attractive city in Burgundy.

The calm waters of the Saône create the best scenery in a town centre that otherwise has only occasional pockets of interest. The **Pont St-Laurent**, blown up (like many Saône bridges) by the retreating German armies in 1944, has been rebuilt to Gauthey's original design of 1780. It leads across to the little suburban island where Jacques de Lalaing, the most extravagantly anachronistic knight errant who flourished at the court of Philippe le Bon, held his passage of arms, the 'Fontaine aux pleurs' (Fountain of Tears), in 1449–1450. Several buildings make a handsome view. The 16C **Hôpital** was built after Chalon had cold-shouldered Nicolas Rolin's offer of an Hôtel-Dieu and thus helped Beaune acquire its greatest building. (Still part of a working hospital, it is open about one day a month.) The charming brick 15C **Tour du Doyenné** (Deanery Tower) on the tip of the island used to stand near St-Vincent but was demolished and rebuilt here in the 1920s.

The ***Museum of Photography**, installed in an 18C building on the Quai des Messageries opposite the tower, is named after the early pioneer Joseph Nicéphore Niepce (1765–1833), born in Chalon. A fascinating collection, it has specimens of Niepce's own apparatus as well as that of successors like Daguerre and Fox Talbot.

From the nearby square the town's main commercial street—the Rue du Port-Villiers continued by the Rue du Général-Leclerc—leads up to the obelisk commemorating the opening of the Canal du Centre. Not far from the quay it passes the Place de l'Hôtel-de-Ville, where the late 17C church of **St-Pierre** (with good choir stalls) faces the **Musée Denon**. Géricault's 'Portrait of a Negro' is outstanding in a *collection that embraces several European schools: French (Nicolas de Largillière, Philippe de Champaigne,

Carle van Loo and the local Étienne Raffort); Italian (Bernardo Strozzi, Guercino, Salvator Rosa, Luca Giordano); and Dutch (fine landscape by Jacobus Koninck). The ground floor also displays Burgundian furniture. The archaeological collection in the basement includes the *'laurel-leaf' flint tools from Volgu (compare Solutré, Route 8) and, among local Gallo-Roman items, a fine statue of a gladiator and a lion. Among the medieval sculptures are the tomb effigy of Alexandre de Montaigu, 13C bishop of Chalon, and a capital from Cluny.

The pedestrianised Rue au Change leads from the Place de l'Hôtel-de-Ville and the main thoroughfare towards the little Place du Châtelet and the old quarter of Chalon. A market is held here on Fridays and Sundays. Note the 17C **Maison des Quatre Saisons** (No 37) on the right-hand side of the Rue du Châtelet; there are more old buildings on the Grande Rue, leading N. Further E, **St-Vincent**, which served as Chalon's cathedral until the 18C, stands in a square of old houses. Its W façade is 19C Gothic and the rest of the building a patchwork of different periods. The nave is 12C Romanesque below and early 14C Gothic above, with fluted pilasters being continued by clustered colonnettes. The Romanesque choir and apse were rebuilt in the 1230s. Note, among the few capitals in the nave to have escaped the hand of the restorer, Cain and Abel (on the fifth pillar from the W in the N arcade) and the disciples on the road to Emmaus and Christ appearing to Mary Magdalen (on the N side of the choir). The chapel off the S transept has a late 15C Pietà and a 16C tapestry of the Eucharist, and the Flamboyant chapel off the S side of the choir grisaille glass showing the Virgin of the Apocalypse. The altarpiece is a 17C triptych by Richard Tassel of Langres. A door in the S transept leads to the elegant Gothic cloister, where some heads, animals and foliage survive mutilation of the capitals.

St-Marcel (4120 people), 3km SE, has the Gothic church of the Cluniac priory where, thanks to the kindness of Pierre le Vénérable of Cluny, Abélard spent the last years of his life after his condemnation at Sens in 1140.

N6 heads S from Chalon, passing (9km) the junction with D6. At **La Ferté**, on the edge of the forest 6km SW, Stephen Harding founded the first daughter of Cîteaux in 1113. It was sacked by Protestant armies during the Wars of Religion, rebuilt but again dismantled after the Revolution. After N6 crosses the Grosne a distinctive ridge of hills announcing the northern fringe of the Mâconnais breaks the flat landscape of the Saône valley. At (8km) **Sennecey-le-Grand** (2570 people; Tourist Information) the neo-classical church, the Mairie and the Office de Tourisme stand inside the moated *enceinte* of its old castle. Two Romanesque churches with good towers survive nearby: St-Julien, in a little rural backwater overshadowed by the A6, and St-Martin-Laives, 3km W on the hill overlooking the autoroute. **Tournus**, 10km further, is described at the beginning of the next route.

8 The Mâconnais: Tournus to Mâcon via Cluny

Directions and distances. Total distance 110km (68 miles). D14 from **Tournus** to (24km) Cormatin. D187 to (30km) Chissey-lès-Mâcon and (30km) Prayes. D146 to (38km) Blanot. D446, (42km) D487, (44km) D187 via Col de la Pistole, (48km) D161 to (49km) Bissy-la-Mâconnaise. D82 to (55km) **Azé**. D15 to (67km) **Cluny**. D980, (71.5km) D22 to (83.5km) Tramayes. D45, (90.5km) D31, (94.5km) D185, (95.5km) D31/D23, (100km) D54 to (102km) **Solutré**. D54 to (110km) **Mâcon**.

Connections with other routes. Tournus lies at the end of the journey through the Chalonnais described in the previous route. Cormatin connects with the detour from Buxy in the previous route. Mâcon is also reached in Route 9, across the Saône plain and the Bresse from Dijon via Louhans and Bourg-en-Bresse (Brou), and in Route 22, through the Charolais from Paray-le-Monial.

If Burgundy is the country of transition between north and south, then the ****Mâconnais**—probably the most beautiful of all its *pays*—is where the south begins. Even drivers hurrying down the Autoroute du Soleil or the N6 from Chalon past Tournus and Mâcon cannot miss the change in, for example, the shallow roofs with warm, red pantiles that replace the steep, polychrome tile roofs of the Côte d'Or. Imperceptibly, the countryside leaves Dijon and its memories of Flanders behind and, like the river Saône, looks toward the Rhône and the Mediterranean.

The Mâconnais lies between the Saône and its western tributary the Grosne. The flat countryside by the Saône is cattle pasture. Around the Grosne, where Cluny stands at the centre of a little adjunct or neighbouring *pays*, the Clunisois, are thickly wooded hills merging with the Charolais further west. But the characteristic landscape of the Mâconnais is the range of hills that divides the two rivers, the last link in the loose chain connecting the Côte d'Or and the Chalonnais with the Beaujolais.

The names of Tournus and Cluny, sites of two great but very different abbeys, prepare the traveller for the Romanesque churches in the little villages that make up the heartland of the Mâconnais: at, for example, Brancion, Chapaize, Lancharre, Malay, Ougy, Taizé, Chissey-lès-Mâcon and, above all, Berzé-la-Ville. And as so often in Burgundy, Romanesque architecture goes hand in hand with vineyards. The Mâconnais produces both red and white wines, though the whites (from the Chardonnay grape) are the best regarded. Those from the vineyards of Lugny, Viré, Clessé and Azé in the northern Mâconnais are usually sold under regional *appellations*: Pinot-Chardonnay-Mâcon, Mâcon Blanc, Mâcon Supérieur, Mâcon-Villages. The southern vineyards in the shadow of the Solutré rock are known for more prestigious labels: Pouilly-Fuissé, Pouilly-Loché and Pouilly-Vinzelles. St-Véran is a modern *appellation*, officially acknowledged in 1971, bred from a Beaujolais white in a region where the Mâconnais vineyards begin to overlap with the Beaujolais.

Though easiest to list, wine and Romanesque architecture are not necessarily the region's greatest attributes. Mâconnais wines do not challenge those of the Côte d'Or in reputation, nor even benefit greatly from the current popularity of Beaujolais reds. Mâconnais churches form a less distinctive group than those of the Brionnais, and do not often rival Brionnais architecture in sculptural detail. Both vineyards and churches take their place in a landscape whose keynote is its variety. If you look down from the hill at Brancion, or pause on the way over the Col de la Pistole or Col de Grand-Vent, you will see slopes and valleys divided by hedges into a patchwork of fields for maize, sunflowers and potatoes, pasture land for the brown goats and even sheep as well as the ever-present staple of Burgundian agriculture, the Charolais, and orchards of walnuts and cherry trees. But it is the hills themselves to which your eyes will continually return. No longer a continuous ridge like the Côte d'Or but not yet the contorted mass of the Beaujolais mountains, they make a humanised, friendly landscape that can still spring surprises like the limestone crests of Vergisson and Solutré in the south. Usually wooded on top, stretching in rounded shapes to the blue horizon, the hills possess a shifting, elusive beauty that tested even the eloquence of Lamartine, loyal and impassioned native of the Mâconnais though he was.

Such country requires patient exploration with an eye on the passing scenery and not the mileometer. Both the main roads from Tournus to Mâcon, the Autoroute du Soleil (A6) and the N6, miss most of the region's character, and even the obvious ways of adding Cluny to the journey still leave many rewarding corners unvisited. After describing Tournus, the route suggested below follows a winding course on country roads which, even without its various detours and alternatives, more than triples the distance by the A6 or N6.

TOURNUS (6570 Tournusiens; Tourist Information) stands on a shelf of land overlooking the Saône. Its position makes it a centre for the flat country of the Bresse beyond the river as well as the hilly Mâconnais, and has guaranteed it a long history. Tournus began as a settlement of the Aedui, developing into the Roman supply post of Castrum Trenorchium on the Via Agrippa, and acquiring its first Christian martyr with the death of Valerian (Valérien) in 179.

The abbey church of ****St-Philibert**—one of the earliest, as well as greatest, Romanesque buildings of Burgundy—originated in the monastery established by the 6C to preserve Valerian's relics on the hill where he died. In 875 the community was joined by the monks from Noirmoutier at the end of their long odyssey after Norman raids had driven them from their island near Nantes some forty years earlier. Their arrival with the body of their founder St Philibert more than doubled the size of the monastery and gave it new importance, without bringing calm. The Magyars devastated Tournus in 937, and a schism in 945 caused the Philibertines to retreat to the Auvergne for several years. Work on the present church began soon after the quarrel was patched up in 949 and continued until the late 12C. Most scholars agree that St-Philibert belongs to at least three separate periods during this long and largely undocumented span, each of them critical to the development of Romanesque in Burgundy. The crypt for Valerian's tomb was dedicated in 979. The earliest part of the church above ground is clearly the narthex, with the Lombardic elements that characterise the first phase of Burgundian Romanesque; it may be the work of the masons who built the rotunda for Dijon's St-Bénigne. The nave, rebuilt after a ravaging fire in 1006, has curious vaulting apparently added in the mid 11C, while the choir was renovated for the final rededication in 1120. The two towers added later in the 12C belong to the last stage of Romanesque, the statue-columns on the narthex tower pointing the way forward to Gothic.

Two towers beyond the W end of St-Philibert form the entrance to the abbey. The irregular circle of streets round its buildings reflects the shape of the narrow fortified *enceinte* that the monks prudently adopted after the Magyar attack, and two more towers, the Tour du Portier and the Tour de Quincampoix, survive to the S. The W end of the church itself has a fortified look too, the surfaces of its walls relieved only by the pattern of Lombardic arcatures and strips. Though containing a narthex, it is clearly as much a defensive fortress as a ceremonial church entrance. The St-Michel chapel on its second storey, big enough for a church in its own right, shows the same massive simplicity as the exterior. The thick, unadorned columns and round arches of its three-bayed arcade exude such weight and power that they would be merely oppressive without the great height of the nave above, tall enough to admit a clerestory. From its E end a series of arched openings looks over the upper level of the nave. The central arch, its view now blocked by the back of the organ, is known as Gerlannus' Arch from the Latin inscription which appears halfway up the archivolt to the right. The foliage capitals and carved blocks above them, showing a shallowly incised face and human figure, represent the very first stage of Romanesque sculpture in Burgundy. The ground floor of the narthex shares the same plan, though the combination of groin vaulting in its central nave with transverse barrel vaulting in the aisles anticipates the experiments in the main church beyond. Note the fragments of wall painting: a 12C Christ in Majesty at the E end of its nave and a 14C Crucifixion in the N aisle.

Whether glimpsed first from the St-Michel chapel or from the low, rather gloomy confines of the ground-floor narthex, the nave of St-Philibert is one of the great dramas of Burgundian Romanesque. The unbroken height of its arcade establishes a powerful vertical accent, uninterrupted by decorative detail. The simple masonry emphasises the beauty of the warm, pink stone from Préty (on the Saône just S of Tournus), hewn into small blocks and laid in regular courses so that it looks almost like brick. The pink and white banding of the transverse arches, the only flourish, lends a Moorish touch that looks forward to the nave at Vézelay. The aisles are groin vaulted but the nave itself has barrel vaults running transversely across each of its five bays, a highly unusual arrangement that appears again only at Mont St-Vincent. Note how it helps to diffuse light throughout the building.

The drama and beauty of St-Philibert end at the crossing dome. In La Madeleine at Vézelay the disparity between nave and choir—the shift from Romanesque to Gothic and from warm, coloured stone to white stone—is miraculously successful. A similar change here, to a white stone from Tournus itself and to a later phase in Romanesque, is not. The bad modern glass and the 18–19C restoration are part of the problem but some of it is original: the choir is too small in comparison to the bold, generous proportions of the nave. Adding the finishing touch to the interior of the Romanesque church, the 12C builder was forced to follow the ground-plan of its earliest part, the crypt beneath. This has heavily restored foliage capitals, Roman in inspiration if not in origin, and a 12C fresco of Christ in Majesty in the chapel on the S side of its ambulatory. The relics of St Valerian lie in the apsidal chapel, below those of St Philibert in the choir—the arrangement finally adopted to settle the dispute between the two monastic factions over the status of their different founders.

What was once the monks' warming room, by the entrance to the narthex, now contains sculptures from the cloisters and from the narthex tower; though badly worn, the gaunt, elongated statue-columns of St Valerian and St Philibert are outstanding. Nearby is the N walk of the 11C cloisters. The rib-vaulted Gothic chapter house (1239), to its E, is used for temporary art exhibitions. The superb 11C store room and monks' refectory, marking the other sides of the cloisters, lie S of the abbey; now part of a centre of Romanesque studies, they shelter changing exhibitions and a good bookstall.

The buildings on the circle of streets round the abbey church include, on the E side, the 15C Abbot's Lodging and, on the N, the **Musée Bourguignon Perrin-de-Puycousin**, which displays everyday objects and traditional costumes in a series of reconstructed interiors and waxwork figures. The house itself was built for the treasurer of the college of canons which succeeded the monastery in the 17C and later belonged to the literary critic Albert Thibaudet (1874–1936). Though Tournus has nothing else to compare with St-Philibert, the rest of the town is interesting enough to justify a longish walk S from the abbey. The local museum, the **Musée Greuze** in the 17C buildings of a former Benedictine convent on the Rue du Collège, takes its name from Jean-Baptiste Greuze, born at Tournus in 1725. The two rooms devoted to his work contain a fine self-portrait and a large series of drawings. The **Office de Tourisme** on the corner of the Place Carnot occupies a half-timbered building which begins an interesting medley of 16–18C houses lining the Rue de la République. Note particularly the Hôtel de l'Escargot, with its *échaugette*, on the corner of the Place de l'Hôtel-de-Ville. The spruce **Hôtel de Ville** itself (1774–1777) is by Emiland Gauthey. The 17C Hôtel-Dieu behind it keeps its old pharmacy. The Rue Désiré-Mathivet continues S to **La Madeleine**, with a W doorway flanked by *roman fleuri* columns and capitals. There is a good view of the Romanesque tower and E end from the nearby Saône quay. Marking the site of the original Roman castrum, the church now stands in a pleasantly shabby old neighbourhood. Note the group of buildings to its S and the row of 16–18C chaplains' houses in the Rue du Quatre-Septembre to its W.

Route 9 describes Cuisery, Romenay and St-Trivier-de-Courtes in the Bresse E of Tournus.

N6, following the Saône directly to Mâcon, avoids Cluny and the best parts of the Mâconnais, though three places just to the W of its course have interesting Romanesque churches: (6km) **Farges-lès-Mâcon**, (2km) **Uchizy** (620 people) and (10km) **Clessé**.

The more devious route proposed here begins by taking the winding D14 into the wooded hills W of Tournus. **Ozenay**, in the valley of the Natouze at 6.5km, has a simple Romanesque church opposite its 15–17C château (not open). *Brancion, another 6.5km, commands the ridge between the valleys of the Saône and the Grosne. As the tourists have discovered, it is one of the most charming hill villages in Burgundy, a lovely southern cousin of Flavigny and Châteauneuf, with a castle, Romanesque church and old market hall. The castle (open), built in the 10C and refurbished by Philippe le Hardi in the 14C, has a restored keep with a splendid view over the village and surrounding countryside. The beautifully sited church, a masterpiece of Romanesque at its simplest and most quietly harmonious, contains 13C wall paintings and the effigy of the last Seigneur, Jocerand de Brancion, a cousin of Louis IX (St Louis) who died on the Sixth Crusade in 1250. The view from the W end of the church, as good as the one from the castle keep, looks down on the Romanesque church of La Chapelle-sous-Brancion, best admired from a distance.

The D14 runs through woods on the way to (6km) **Chapaize**, by the Bisançon. The tower of its early Romanesque *church, once part of a Benedictine priory, makes a prominent landmark. Note the Lombardic work outside and the massive pillars of the nave, without capitals. At **Lancharre**, a quiet rural enclave 3km NE, the church is the surviving E end and tower of the Romanesque building that belonged to the convent or, strictly, college of female canons founded by the Seigneurs de Brancion in the 11C or 12C. D14 meets the valley of the Grosne at (5km) **Cormatin**, where the *château (open) consists of two wings surviving from the Renaissance building of 1605–1608. The well-restored interior has a series of rooms superbly decorated in the Louis XIII style, with carved and painted woodwork and ceilings and a good collection of paintings (Nattier, Rigaud, Mignard).

Cormatin lies on the D981 which links Buxy, 25km N in the Chalonnais (Route 7), directly with Cluny, 13km S. There are Romanesque churches on or near its course N of Cormatin at (3km) **Malay** and (3.5km) **Ougy**, and S of Cormatin at (3km) **Ameugny**. **Taizé**, 1km S of Ameugny, has been made famous by the ecumenical religious community which the Swiss pastor Roger Schutz founded in the 1940s. It has restored the little Romanesque parish church and added its own modern Church of Reconciliation.

The longer but more interesting way from Cormatin to Cluny begins by heading SE on D187 through the village of (4km) **Lys**, with a Romanesque church. There is a better one at **Chissey-lès-Mâcon**, 1km beyond, with a tall tower and spire, and several good carved capitals on the N wall of its nave, including the Nativity, David fighting Goliath and a devil's head. At Prayes, 1km further E, D146 follows the valley of the Grison S as it skirts the granitic **Mont St-Romain** (579m). **Blanot**, at 8km, is a picturesque little place among vineyards that produce red and white wine. The rustic Romanesque church, almost overwhelmed by the height of its tower, stands on the site of a Merovingian cemetery; a few tombs survive near the buildings of the old Cluniac priory opposite. On its way out of the village in the direction of Fougnières D446 passes caves (open) with stalactites and stalagmites. The road then joins D487 on its way round the flank of Mont St-Romain. A little road on the left leads up to the top of the hill, with an orientation table explaining the wide view. D187 branches right, crossing the ridge by the *Col de la Pistole, a winding, perilous journey alternately closed in by forest and opening to wide views. There are vineyards on the last stage, as D187 joins D161 on the way into (11km) **Bissy-la-Mâconnaise**, where the late Romanesque church contains 15C and 16C statues. The vineyards of **Lugny** (730 people) lie to the E.

D82 heads S to (6km) **Azé** (650 people). The *cave system (open) created by the underground course of the river Verzé, rising on Mont St-Romain, is the largest in southern Burgundy and also, as modern excavations are still showing, one of its most significant archaeological sites. The river now flows through the larger of the two caves accessible to the public, where the romantic scenery includes a waterfall, fragile stalactites and stalagmites, grottoes with walls stained black by manganese or red by iron, and pools harbouring rare fauna. The smaller cave is a narrow cleft from which the sediment has been cleared since the 1960s, to a distance of about 200m, uncovering the bones of bears, lions, etc. from the Acheulean era (c 300,000 BC) onwards and traces of human habitation stretching from the Upper Palaeolithic period through the Bronze and Iron Ages and the Gallo-Roman era to the Middle Ages. The finds are now displayed in the cave itself and the small museum near the entrance.

D15 winds through the hills and woods via (5km) **Donzy-le-Pertuis**, beneath the **Montagne de Joux** (572m), before dropping down into the valley of the Grosne at (7km) Cluny.

CLUNY (4430 Clunisois; Tourist Information) is a little town dominated by its great *abbey, once the most magnificent in Europe and even now, two centuries after its destruction, a powerful magnet for visitors. The octagonal Romanesque tower rising over the town is virtually the only relic of the church left standing after the Revolution, though some important fragments of its sculpture have also miraculously survived. These are highlights on the guided tour provided by the Caisse Nationale, which now administers the core of a widely dispersed site, by turns fascinating and disappointing.

Cluniacum, a Frankish villa built on the site of a Roman station, belonged to Charlemagne's family and then became a favourite hunting lodge of Guillaume, duc d'Aquitaine. In 910 the duke gave the land to Bernon (St Berno), abbot of Baume-les-Messieurs, for a monastery observing the original purity of the Benedictine rule. The community grew from the 12 monks Bernon directed to about 70 by 1042, 200 by 1085, and 300 in 1109. Such numbers hardly convey the power that Cluny came to wield. Its foundation charter granted the Order (technically the Convocation and Order of Cluny) freedom from outside interference except by the pope himself should the house became gravely disordered. The Cluniacs used their independence to build a centralised organisation in which all daughter houses were directly ruled from Cluny itself, its abbot being technically abbot of all Cluniac foundations. In this fashion he came to control an empire of well over 1000 houses, most strongly concentrated in France but including almost 100 in Germany, almost 50 in England (where Lewes Priory was the chief house) and about 30 in Spain. At Cluny itself, where all the monks received their training, the abbot was a feudal baron who entertained cardinals and popes, kings and emperors as his guests, or gave them shelter when the turbulence of medieval politics made it necessary. The unhappy Pope Gelasius II, driven from Rome by the Holy Roman Emperor, died at Cluny and his successor Calixtus II was elected here in 1119. Such power, remote from Bernon's original purpose, brought its problems. Ponce de Melgeuil, one of the abbots responsible for building the great church, died in a papal prison on charges of corruption in 1126. St Bernard's attack on the lax standards of Cluny showed that the purifying energy of monasticism had already passed to the Cistercians, who themselves went on to follow the same career of spiritual decline through material success. The Hundred Years War and the Wars of Religion took their toll on Cluny, until the zealots of Mâcon—a town conspicuous for Revolutionary fervour—arrived to dismantle it.

The buildings of Cluny had always reflected its importance. Bernon's church, dedicated in 927, was soon replaced by a grander building, begun in 955, dedicated in 981 and extended in about 1010. In its final form Cluny II had a W narthex with belfry towers, a third tower over the crossing and a stepped apse enclosing a square sanctuary flanked by processional corridors. Its scale was about that of St-Philibert at Tournus, big by the standards of the time but modest in comparison to its great successor. Hugues de Semur (abbot in 1049–1109, later St Hugh of Cluny) began Cluny III in about 1085; Ponce de Melgueil and Pierre le Vénérable brought it to completion in about 1130. Pierre le Vénérable also added the monastic buildings. Cluny III was the largest church in Christendom until the building of the present St Peter's in Rome: 187m (just over 200 yards) long from narthex to E end, with its nave and aisles together about 41m (45 yards) wide. The W narthex had two towers as before, but on a larger scale. The lengthened nave was flanked by double aisles and roofed with the tunnel-

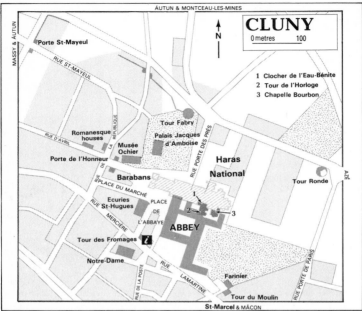

vaulting which the music-loving Cluniacs seem to have favoured for its acoustics. The towers over the crossing and transepts had grown from one to three, and the main transepts were supplemented by lesser transepts further E. The E end adopted what would become the familiar arrangement of a rounded apse with ambulatory and radiating chapels. Its proportions and sculptural detail made Cluny III the parent of the mature Romanesque style that flourished so widely in Burgundy. Essential elements of its design were echoed by La Charité-sur-Loire, Paray-le-Monial, Semur-en-Brionnais and Autun, while the carvings of Autun, Vézelay and the Brionnais churches frequently betray the hand of the Cluny workshop.

Cluny demands more imagination than any of these places, and a longish walk combining some private exploration with the Caisse Nationale guided tour. The obvious place to park is on the Rue Porte-de-Paris, which even today can still clearly be seen to mark the N edge of the abbey *enceinte*. The 12C **Tour Ronde** survives at its E end. Further W are the **Haras National** (open), a stud farm with stables built of stone pillaged from the abbey ruins. From the 14C **Tour Fabry** near by a signposted walk leads through pleasant gardens which contain two palaces named after the abbots who built them, the early 16C **Palais Jacques d'Amboise**, with a fine Flamboyant façade, and the 15C **Palais Jean de Bourbon**. They stand near the **Porte d'Honneur**, the double-arched Romanesque entrance gate of the abbey, at the junction of the Rue d'Avril and the Rue de la République. Both streets have Romanesque houses: note No 25, Rue de la République and No 6, Rue d'Avril, the Hôtel des Monnaies.

Jacques d'Amboise also built the abbots' town house in Paris, preserved as the Musée de Cluny, with a collection of medieval art that includes the tapestry series known as 'La Dame à la Licorne'. His palace at Cluny has become the Hôtel de Ville and Jean de Bourbon's palace the ***Musée**

Ochier. The splendid collection of sculptural fragments from the abbey housed in its basement includes the capitals, keystone and remains of the great W doorway unearthed after World War II by Kenneth J. Conant (the Harvard scholar whose lifetime investigation of Cluny shed light on virtually all aspects of its development), as well as finds from the re-excavation of the narthex completed in 1991. The first floor has sculptures and architectural fragments from local houses, and a library with many volumes from the abbey's collection. The ground floor displays a scale model of the town and the abbey, paving tiles, and paintings which include work by Pierre-Paul Prud'hon, born at Cluny in 1758 and sent to the drawing school in Dijon (see the Musée des Beaux-Arts).

The Musée Ochier is also the starting point for the guided tour of the abbey. Its first highlight is the site of the narthex immediately beyond the Porte d'Honneur, which recent excavation has greatly helped make intelligible to the visitor. The foundations of Les Barabans, the great W towers blown up with gunpowder at the Revolution, have been incorporated into two nearby houses. The bases of the pillars forming the central arcade are now marked in the pavement. The N aisle has disappeared beneath the Hôtel de Bourgogne but some fragments of the S wall survive.

The beginning of the Place de l'Abbaye corresponds roughly to the W door of the church, whose E end lay a good 155 metres (about 170 yards) beyond. The 12C **Écuries de St-Hugues** on the W side of the square contained the abbey guest house as well as the stables. The 11C **Tour des Fromages** (Cheese Tower), off the S side of the square, marks the boundary of the abbey *enceinte.* Now housing the **Syndicat d'Initiative**, it gives a good view of the town from the top. This is not part of the guided tour, which heads for the abbey buildings incorporated in the École Nationale des Arts et Métiers on the E side of the square. The rather ugly façade, originally 14C but heavily restored in the 19C, gives access to the 18C cloisters and then the few precious remains of Cluny III itself. The first is the S arm of the great transept, marked by the lovely octagonal **Clocher de l'Eau Bénite** (Holy Water Tower) rising above the cupola. Of the two transeptal chapels, St-Martial is Romanesque and St-Étienne is 14C Gothic. The bay near by shows the characteristic three-storey Cluniac elevation with its use of fluted pilasters and Corinthian capitals. The surviving E or lesser transept preserves a fragment of Romanesque work and the 15C Bourbon chapel, with some striking Flamboyant carving.

The tour continues through the decaying formal gardens of the abbey grounds to the 13C **Farinier** and 12C **Tour du Moulin**, the flour storeroom and mill, at the S corner. The ground floor of the Farinier contains sculptural fragments from several periods of the abbey's history but the room above is much more interesting, both for its architecture (note the fine timber roof) and its contents. Here the ****capitals** from the choir of Cluny III, found among the rubble after the Revolution, are displayed in a semicircle that reproduces their original position on the columns dividing the sanctuary from the ambulatory. If the S transept conveys the size of Cluny III more vividly than any mere recital of its dimensions, these capitals show the Cluniac style of carving which would enrich Autun, Vézelay, Saulieu and the Brionnais churches evolving from the formal shape of the Corinthian capital used in Roman art. The two capitals from the entrance to the sanctuary show the Fall and Abraham's sacrifice. Particularly interesting among the others are the two which together illustrate the eight tones of music, a reminder of the importance of plainsong in Cluniac worship. Near by stand Conant's models reconstructing the choir and W doorway.

The guided tour ends at the bookstall in the Tour du Moulin. To the SE stands the church of **St-Marcel**, with a handsome Romanesque tower and E end, marking the artisans' quarter outside the abbey walls. NW of the Tour du Moulin on the way back to the central square is another town church, the Gothic **Notre-Dame**, with a lofty nave and rose windows at the crossing. It stands near the Tour des Fromages, noted above.

Massy, off D980 (the Montceau-les-Mines road) 10km NW of Cluny, has a little, early Romanesque church that belonged to a Cluniac priory. The base of the font is thought to be Roman. At **St-Vincent-des-Prés**, 6km W, the Romanesque church has a nave with massive columns. Mazillé, on D17 about 8km SW, is described on the way from Paray-le-Monial to Mâcon in Route 22.

None of the various ways from Cluny to Mâcon takes in all the things worth seeing in the region. The simplest and shortest route (24km), by D980 and then N79, is also the least interesting. A better variant follows D980 to (5km) the junction with N79 but then almost immediately branches left on the signposted Route Touristique. This passes beneath (5km) **Berzé-le-Châtel**, where the medieval castle (access to terraces only) was the seat of the first barony of the Mâconnais and guarded the southern approach to Cluny from its hilltop site. On the rocky outcrop of **Berzé-la-Ville** (510 people), 2km beyond, the Cluniac 'obedience' or estate which the Order acquired in 1093 was a favourite retreat of Hugues de Semur, the prime mover of Cluny III. The little chapel built at his direction towards the end of his life is decorated with Romanesque ******wall paintings unique in Burgundy and rivalled in France only at the abbey church of St-Savin near Poitiers. They may or may not have been complete by Hugues' death in 1109. Though all the interior was originally decorated, the paintings in the nave decayed almost beyond trace while those in the choir and apse were discovered beneath a protecting layer of whitewash in 1887. To ensure their preservation the scholar Joan Evans bought the chapel after World War II and presented it to the Academy of Mâcon. The semi-dome of the apse is dominated by Christ in Majesty, seated in a mandorla flanked by apostles and saints. His right hand is raised in blessing while his left proffers a parchment scroll—presumably the Law—to St Peter, the patron saint of Cluny. The hand of God holding the crown above Christ's head is one of several touches betraying Byzantine influence. More saints fill the wall surfaces below, while the arcatures flanking the windows carry elaborately detailed scenes of martyrdom. On the N side the healer St Blaise is shown curing a sick animal and being beheaded. On the S side three superbly malevolent torturers roast St Vincent of Saragossa on a gridiron (like St Lawrence); his relics had been preserved in the cathedral at Mâcon since the 6C.

Several places near Berzé-la-Ville are connected with Lamartine. The 17C château (not open) at **Monceau**, beyond La Roche-Vineuse 3.5km E, was one of his favourite Mâconnais properties and, with St-Point (described below), the only one he managed to keep after the financial disasters of his later life. His childhood home (not open but marked with a plaque) in the centre of **Milly-Lamartine**, on the other side of N79 2km S of Berzé-la-Ville, went the way of his other family properties. He was a close friend of François Dumont, *curé* of the little church at **Bussières**, just to the SE of Milly, and a frequent visitor to the château (open) on the rocky outcrop at **Pierreclos** (760 people), to the S, a medieval building refurbished in the 16C. D45 leads SW from Pierreclos to the Col de Grand Vent, described below.

It would be very foolish to pass through the southern Mâconnais without seeing the frescoes at Berzé-la-Ville, but in other respects the most interesting route from Cluny to Mâcon goes further S to wind through the hills and vineyards on the fringes of the Beaujolais. Follow D980 S from Cluny but branch right on the little D22, which crosses N79 and follows the valley of the Valouze to (11.5km) **St-Point**. Lamartine and his English wife, Marianne Birch, are buried in the mausoleum near the handsome Romanesque church tower. They lie in the shadow of the medieval château (open) given to them by Lamartine's father on their marriage in 1820. Extravagantly enlarged and fiercely protected from the financial disasters of his last years, it was with Monceau (see above) his favourite property in the Mâconnais, the country home where he entertained Victor Hugo, Liszt and other famous guests. His study and many souvenirs are preserved.

D22 continues along the valley to (5km) **Tramayes** (880 people), a useful jumping-off point for some of the best and grandest scenery in the southern Mâconnais. D45 climbs E to the *Col de Grand-Vent**, shortly after which (at 5.5km) D31 branches right to drop down into (3km) the valley of the Petite Grosne. D185 heads N towards the outskirts of Serrières and at 1km D31 branches right to climb the other side of the valley. After another 4.5km D54 branches left for (2km) **Solutré**, the name of both the village and the *rock whose distinctive silhouette—like the crest of a breaking wave, say those given to romantic similes—rises above the Pouilly-Fuissé vineyards. Only the ugly smear of Mâcon in the distance spoils the view.

The Solutré rock was a centre of prehistoric culture from about 30,000 BC, roughly the same date when Cro-Magnon man was making his appearance at Les Eyzies in the Dordogne. To archaeologists it is particularly important as the type site for the Solutrean phase of Upper Palaeolithic culture which flourished from about 20,000 BC to about 16,000 BC, distinguished by its bifacially worked 'laurel leaf' flints (compare the Volgu hoard in the Musée Denon at Chalon). The absence of human skeletons from the site confirms that it was not a permanent settlement but a camp where hunters ambushed horses passing beneath the rock on their seasonal migration. The chief evidence of this slaughter is the 'Charnel House' covering about 2 acres at the foot of the rock: a thick magma or layer mixing clay and the bones of about 100,000 animals. The condition of the bones does not support the popular theory that the horses were actually stampeded to their death from the top of the rock. The **Musée Départemental de la Préhistoire**, opened in 1987, provides a clear and lively introduction to Solutré and its context in prehistoric culture, with finds, a video and an audio-visual display (English commentary available).

Beyond the rock D54 continues through vineyards towards (8km) Mâcon.

MÂCON (37,280 Mâconnais; Tourist Information) looks across the Saône from the Mâconnais to the Bresse. Originally an Aedui settlement, it grew into the Roman Matisco and later into the capital of the medieval county, seized from the French crown by Jean sans Peur in 1417 though two treaties under his successor Philippe le Bon were needed to legitimise the duchy's hold on it. Mâcon today is the *préfecture* of Saône-et-Loire. It remains a centre of the wine trade, but otherwise has nothing to compare with the attractions of the Mâconnais and surprisingly little to show for its history, apart from continual reminders that it was Lamartine's home town. The industry that has trebled Mâcon's population since the War has been further encouraged by the TGV line, strengthening its link with the Lyonnais. Mâcon is twinned with Crewe and Nantwich in England.

The **Pont St-Laurent**, a much altered 15–16C bridge which survived the retreat of the German armies in 1944, effectively divides the town centre into northern and southern quarters. To the N the towers of old **St-Vincent** make a distinctive landmark. Largely demolished in 1799, the Romanesque cathedral had flourished as the shrine of St Vincent of Saragossa, patron saint of *vignerons* and hence locally among the most popular of all saints. The ruined narthex keeps a tympanum of the Last Judgement, badly mutilated but still showing its curious division into five horizontal registers and, at the bottom left, a delightful vignette of three people sheltering in the safety of the Heavenly City. St Michael fights a demon on a capital below.

The nearby **Musée des Ursulines**, in the 17C buildings of a former convent for noble ladies, contains *faïence*, ceramics and local archaeology (reorganised and somewhat reduced since the opening of the museum at Solutré). Its great strength is the collection of *French painting, which begins with 16C portraits and continues with work by Charles Le Brun, Nicolas de Largillière, Philippe de Champaigne, Jean-Baptiste Lallemand (imaginary seaport in the manner of Claude), Greuze (portrait of Monsignor de Valras), Antoine Vestier, originally from Avallon (the Mlle Roland of his charming portrait is not a relative of the Girondin leader but a daughter of the Parisian sculptor), Fantin-Latour, Corot (landscape), Félix Ziem of Chalon and Monet (small Dutch scene).

At the Revolution the convent buildings became a prison where Lamartine's royalist father was held. He was still able to communicate with his wife since the outhouses of the family home stood on the opposite side of the Rue des Ursulines. It was in one of these, now demolished, that the poet was born in 1790. The main house itself is around the corner in the Rue Bauderon-de-Senecé, marked with a plaque. Another plaque marks the 18C **Hôtel d'Ozenay** in the nearby Rue Lamartine, which Lamartine's father bought in 1804. It was the poet's Mâcon home until his marriage in 1820 and part of his inheritance, though debts eventually forced him to sell it.

At the N end of the Rue Lamartine stands the cathedral of **St-Vincent**, sullen neo-classical replacement of the ruined Romanesque church. Its first dedications—St-Napoléon (!) and, in deference to Louis XVIII, St-Louis—reflect the turbulence of the years 1812–1815 when it was built. Lamartine's funeral service was held here, though he was buried at St-Point (visited earlier in this route). The cathedral looks across the square to the dome of the **Hôtel-Dieu** built to Jacques-Germain Soufflot's design in 1761. Now a psychiatric hospital, it still keeps the pharmacy with its original medicine jars and cabinets (open by arrangement with the Musée des Ursulines).

The Quai Lamartine, S of the Pont St-Laurent, hosts Mâcon's market on Saturday mornings. It has a statue of Lamartine by Falguières. The **Hôtel Senecé**, on the nearby Rue Sigorgne, contains souvenirs, documents and Henri Decaisne's fine portrait of the poet as the embodiment of Romantic sensitivity, together with a collection of tapestries, paintings and furniture that includes a Renaissance cabinet attributed to Hugues Sambin of Dijon. The building itself is a handsome early 18C *hôtel particulier*, later headquarters for the Mâcon Academy of which Lamartine was several times president. The **Maison de Bois-Doré**, on the corner of the Rue Dombey and the Place aux Herbes nearby, is a half-timbered house with elaborate carving. The church of **St-Pierre**, further S, is a painfully correct Romanesque pastiche built by Berthier, a pupil of Viollet-le-Duc, in the 1860s. It faces the **Hôtel de Ville**, originally built for an 18C president of the Burgundian *parlement* but ill served by later alterations, and the **Office de Tourisme**. The neighbouring **Résidence Soufflot** occupies the 18C buildings of Soufflot's former Hospice de la Charité. It includes a striking chapel (open by arrangement with the Office de Tourisme) and, to the right of the front door, a curious revolving entrance that allowed foundlings to be left anonymously during the night.

9 The Saône Plain and the Bresse: Dijon to Mâcon via Louhans and Bourg-en-Bresse (Brou)

Directions and distances. Total distance 167km (104 miles). D996 from **Dijon** to (23km) Cîteaux. D996, (36km) D973 to (39km) Seurre. D973, (44km) N73, (47km) D996, (73km) N78 to (83km) **Louhans**. D996 to (133km) **Bourg-en-Bresse** (for **Brou**). N79 to (167km) **Mâcon**.

Connections with other routes. Dijon is described in Route 5, Mâcon in Route 8. The upper reach of the Saône at Pontailler is described in Route 1. Cîteaux lies E of Clos de Vougeot and Nuits-St-Georges (Route 6). Cuisery, St-Trivier-de-Courtes and Romenay are E of Tournus (Route 8).

This route tours the eastern fringe of Burgundy, between the range of hills that runs down from Dijon to Mâcon and the foothills of the Jura, whose crest marks the Swiss border. In this flat countryside the determining landmarks are the rivers, which divide it into two regions: the **Saône Plain** in the N and the *****Bresse**, south of the Saône's tributary the Doubs. This spreading *pays* includes the 'Bresse bourguignonne', with its centre at Louhans, and, outside the modern definition of Burgundy, the 'Bresse burgienne', belonging to the department of Ain and centred on its *préfecture* at Bourg-en-Bresse.

These modern labels reflect the complex history of a region which lay on the border of Burgundy proper, and even of France, for centuries after the treaty partitioning Charlemagne's empire in 843 used the Saône and its northern tributary the Vingeanne (see Route 1) as the boundary between France and Lotharingia, the so-called Middle Kingdom. The country between Dijon and the two rivers became a stronghold of the Capetian dukes, but the territory beyond developed into the separate entity of Franche-Comté: the 'free county' as opposed to the duchy of Burgundy. The Capetian dukes tried but failed to join the county with the duchy, and it was left to Philippe le Hardi to make the union secure by his marriage to Marguerite de Flandre in 1369. After the death of Charles le Téméraire in 1477 Franche-Comté passed via his daughter Marie de Bourgogne to the Austrian Habsburgs and then the Spanish Habsburgs, a fate that made it a frequent battleground of the Thirty Years' War. It was not united with France until the Treaty of Nijmegen which ended the Dutch War in 1678. The Bresse burgienne had meanwhile passed from its local *seigneurs* at Bâgé-le-Châtel to the dukes of the Savoie until it was captured for France in 1601 by Henri IV, who moved its capital to Bourg.

The Burgundian historian Gaston Roupnel has described the Saône Plain as 'a rich country, populated, happy, with a clear sky and peaceful waters, fat and bright'. He might also have added that, like so many areas which armies have hotly contested in the past, it is also rather dull. The plain has lost its main historical landmarks—the Capetian castle of Rouvres and the original buildings of Cîteaux—and is now merely a flat expanse given over to market gardening and crops. The old frontier towns on the Saône smack of the industry that the river later attracted, though they make favourite spots for fishermen and have a distinctive local dish in *pôchouse*, a *bouilla-baisse* made with freshwater fish and white wine.

No more immediately appealing to the eye, the Bresse proves altogether more interesting, not least in the subtle gradations of a landscape no longer completely flat but gently undulating, with substantial patches of woodland and a network of small ponds and streams. Like the Saône Plain, it is largely agricultural, producing milk, pork, wheat and maize but best known for its blue cheese and its chickens, with their white feathers, red crests and bluish legs. The Bresse rears about a million of these birds a year, their quality guarded by an *appellation d'origine contrôlée* which requires that they be fed on the traditional diet of white cornmeal, wheat and milk and that each bird should enjoy at least 10 square metres of living space.

Chickens are not the only distinctive feature of a region which is stubbornly protective of its traditions, as the Écomusée at Pierre-de-Bresse and its branches vividly show. The Bresse is rich in domestic buildings which, lacking the limestone and granite found elsewhere in Burgundy, depend on brick, tile and timber to create an unmistakably local look. The farmhouses have brick-nogged walls below shallow pantile roofs whose eaves overhang to make awnings or galleries where maize was dried. The 'Saracen chimneys' in a fanciful variety of rounded, square or conical shapes, like miniature brick Romanesque church towers, originated in the Middle Ages, though most surviving ones are 17C. The neighbourhood of St-Trivier-de-Courtes has a particularly good group.

The route below is very much a journey of convenience, following the straight main roads which cut through the centre of the region from Dijon to Louhans and Bourg-en-Bresse. Most of the real atmosphere of the countryside is to be found on the detours that lead W and E towards the distant outlines of the Côte and the Jura.

D996 is the most convenient of several main roads which head S or SE from **Dijon** towards the Saône. Beyond (10km) Saulon-la-Rue minor roads branch E through Saulon-la-Chapelle and across D968 to (9km) **Rouvres-en-Plaine** (800 people), a spreading village which was once a centre of the Capetian duchy. Philippe de Rouvres, the last duke, died from the plague here in 1361. The castle was destroyed in the Thirty Years War and the chief relic of Rouvres' former greatness is the late 13–14C church, originally founded by Alix de Vergy, widow of Eudes III, in 1233. It contains several reminders of the ducal connections that continued into the Valois era, most notably the statues of the Virgin Mary, John the Baptist and St John the Evangelist on the altarpiece in the N chapel; the first two are attributed to Juan de la Huerta, the sculptor who worked on Jean sans Peur's tomb at Dijon. The 16C stalls come from Dijon's St-Michel, and the curious 15C statue of John the Baptist in the S transept from the school of Mussy-sur-Seine. The church also owns a richly decorated 12C or 13C reliquary cross. **Longecourt-en-Plaine** (1020 people), on D968 7km S of Rouvres, has a château (open) with a handsome Italianate façade added in the mid 18C.

D996 continues beyond Saulon-la-Rue to (11km) **Cîteaux**, another place of former greatness, site of the abbey which pioneered the Cistercian Order. Cistercians resettled here in the 19C and Cîteaux has again become the Order's chief house but its buildings are largely 18–20C. An audio-visual display introduces its early history. In 1098 St Robert left the abbey he had established at Molesmes to found a new house which would better observe the original Benedictine rule, and by 1100 he had settled in the isolated, swampy forest of Cistercium. (The name may come from *cistelli*, the reeds that abounded in the fields, or *cisternae*, the cisterns needed for drainage.) When he obeyed his superiors' call to return to Molesmes he left behind St Alberic and St Stephen Harding from Sherborne to continue his experiment. Revised as the Cistercian constitution, their principles received papal confirmation in 1119. Quite as important was the arrival in 1113 of the 23-year-old St Bernard with about 30 followers, including four of his brothers. He left Cîteaux only two years later to found its daughter house (the third of four) at Clairvaux, where he became the driving force of an Order which challenged, invigorated and, by the end of his life, dominated the Church of his day. Cîteaux itself was the mausoleum of the Capetian dukes, as the Chartreuse de Champmol was of their Valois successors. It became a prison after the Revolution and was virtually rebuilt in the 19C, though the Louvre preserves the tomb of Philippe Pot of La Rochepot from the original abbey church.

D996, which runs through the forest, and D973 lead to (16km) **Seurre** (2730 people), where two branches of the Saône meet. The 16C Maison Bossuet, one of several old buildings, houses the Syndicat d'Initiative and an Écomusée of the Saône.

Seurre is one of the more pleasant towns on this rather dull stretch of the river, though **Verdun-sur-le-Doubs** (1070 people; Tourist Information), where the Dheune and the Doubs meet the Saône 18km SW, is a favourite spot for fishing. The former Hôtel de Ville contains a museum of wheat and bread, a branch of the Écomusée at Pierre-de-Bresse. **St-Jean-de-Losne** (1340 people; Tourist Information), 15km NE of Seurre at the head of the Canal de Bourgogne and near the head of the Canal du Rhône au Rhin, withstood a siege by the Imperial armies during the Thirty Years War, when the Saône still marked the French frontier. **Auxonne** ('Aussonne'; 6780 Auxonnais; Tourist Information) is a fortified frontier town 18km beyond St-Jean-de-Losne. As a young lieutenant in the artillery, Napoléon was stationed here in 1788–1789 and again in 1791. The Musée Bonaparte in a 15C tower of the castle by the river has souvenirs, together with other items of local history. The big, heavily restored Gothic church of Notre-Dame stands on the Place d'Armes near the market hall, originally part of the 17C arsenal built by Vauban, and the house where Claude Noisot of Fixin (Route 6) was born. Pontailler-sur-Saône, 16km further, is passed on Route 1.

D973 continues S from Seurre to join (5km) N73, which in turn soon joins (3km) D996 at the Doubs, marking the northern boundary of the Bresse. From **Frontenard**, 3km S, D73 leads E past the 17C château (not open) at **Terrans** to (10km) the little market and industrial centre of **Pierre-de-Bresse** (1980 people). Its late 17C •château, the stateliest display of brick in the region, now houses the Écomusée de la Bresse bourguignonne. A big rectangular moat encloses both the outbuildings and the château proper, behind a separate arm of the moat spanned by its own little bridge. The superbly restrained main façade has an open ground-floor arcade with the arms of the Thyard family, who built the château, on the central pediment. Apart from the wrought-iron main staircase, the interior lacks most of its original decor. The museum displays make up for the loss by giving an excellent introduction to the history and character of the Bresse. Sections devoted to crafts and economic activities (furniture-making, poultry farming, fishing) present an unsentimental view of the past and an informative view of the present. The Écomusée has branches at Verdun-sur-le-Doubs, Perrigny, St-Germain-du-Bois, Louhans, Sagy, Rancy, Cuiseaux and Varennes-St-Sauveur.

D996 leads S from Frontenard to (13km) **Mervans** (1230 people). At the hamlet of **Perrigny**, beyond St-Martin-en-Bresse 10.5km W, the former school is a branch of the Écomusée devoted to the forests and woodworking traditions of the Bresse. **Montcoy**, 2.5km further W, has a fine brick-built 17–18C château (not open). **St-Germain-du-Bois** (1860 people), 6.5km SE of Mervans, is a little town (1950 people) with old houses and another branch of the Écomusée, with farm machinery.

Beyond Mervans D996 joins N78 for (20km) **LOUHANS** (6140 Louhannais; Tourist Information), whose position where main roads meet has made it the commercial and market centre of the Bresse bourguignonne. Bresse chickens dominate the livestock at the Monday morning markets. The town's main feature is the *Grande Rue, where the arcades of the 15–16C houses unite an otherwise casual medley of stone, brick and timber in a splendid streetscape. To its S stands the church of **St-Pierre**, with a polychrome roof recalling Dijon and the Côte. The former **Hôtel de Ville** near by is a charming 18C building. A right turn by the river at the E end of the Grande Rue quickly leads to the handsome Baroque *Hôtel-Dieu (open), which preserves its original pharmacy with 16C *faïence*. A left turn along the Rue des Dôdanes leads to the former offices of the local newspaper, closed in 1984 but preserved with their lintoype machinery and open as a branch of the Écomusée. The municipal museum above it has regional paintings.

Montcony, on D23 10km NE of Louhans, has a lovely brick 13C castle (not open) and a memorial to the RAF men who died here in 1942. The watermill at **Sagy** (1160 people), 8.5km SE, is a branch of the Écomusée and the starting point for a tour of other mills in the area. **Cuiseaux** (1780 people), on the edge of the Jura 19km SE of Louhans, is a handsome little town (1820 people; Tourist Information) with fragments of its walls and an interesting old centre. The outbuildings of the 17C Château des Princes d'Orange contain a branch of the Écomusée devoted to vineyards and wine. Édouard Vuillard (1868–1940) was born here. **Rancy** (590 people), 11.5km SW of Louhans on the way to Tournus (Route 8), has a branch of the Écomusée devoted to chair-making. **Cuisery** (1510 people), 9.5km beyond, has a Flamboyant parish church and Romanesque chapel.

From Louhans D996 leads to (7.5km) **Ste-Croix** (520 people), where the 15C church has good glass. The wife of the musketeer d'Artagnan, whose family owned the château, was buried here. At (10.5km) **Varennes-St-Sauveur** (1040 people) the 17C tile factory is a branch of the Écomusée.

St-Trivier-de-Courtes, a handsome little town 12km W on the way to Tournus (Route 8), is rich in traditional farmhouses with Saracen chimneys: the Ferme de la Servette, the Ferme de Grandval, the Ferme de Molardoury, the Ferme du Tremblay and, at **Courtes** to the E, the Ferme de la Forêt (now a farm museum). In nearby villages, see the Ferme du Grand Colombier at **Vernoux**; the Ferme de Malmont at **Curciat-Dongalon**; the Ferme de Bourbon at **St-Nizier-le-Bouchoux**; the Ferme de la Touvière at **Servignat**; the Ferme de Locelle and the Ferme de Montalibord at **Vescours**. **Romenay** (1570 people), 5km N of St-Trivier, is a pleasant little place with a centre bounded by two 14C gateways. It has a local museum and a poultry museum.

D996 continues from Varennes to (16km) **Marboz**. The Ferme du Sougey at **Montrevel-en-Bresse**, 9.5km W, has a Saracen chimney. **St-Étienne-du-**

Bois (1850 people; Tourist Information), 9.5km SE of Marboz, has a farm museum in the reconstructed 17C Ferme des Mangettes. D996 continues to (16km) Bourg-en-Bresse.

BOURG-EN-BRESSE (43,680 Burgiens or Bressans; Tourist Information) has been the *préfecture* of Ain since the department was created at the Revolution and the capital of the Bresse since 1601. Its centre has little of interest apart from a few old streets in the quarter round the 16–17C **Notre-Dame**. Classical motifs predominate on the W façade, while the Gothic interior has elaborate lierne vaulting. The furnishings include a Baroque pulpit and splendid *choir stalls of c 1530, which combine biblical scenes and saints' legends on the panels with earthy comedy on the misericords. They are apparently by Pierre Mochet of Geneva, though it is tempting to believe that Pierre Terrasson, who carved the stalls at Brou, also had a hand in them.

The **church (Caisse Nationale) at **Brou**, now a suburb about 1km SE of the town centre, was built by Marguerite d'Autriche in the early 16C. It stands as the last, posthumous monument to the culture of the Valois dukes, looking back across the Bresse towards the duchy which had died with Charles le Téméraire in 1477. A latter-day Chartreuse de Champmol, its Flamboyant Gothic marks the last phase of the court style established by Claus Sluter, preserving his delicacy of detail but abandoning his monumental clarity of design for a profusion of ornament that to some signifies joyous ripeness, to others over-ripe decline.

Marguerite d'Autriche (1480–1530) was descended from Charles le Téméraire by his daughter Marie de Bourgogne, wife of the Emperor Maximilian of Habsburg. When she was two Maximilian contracted with Louis XI of France to marry Marguerite to the Dauphin, the future Charles VIII, offering Franche-Comté and Artois as her dowry. After this arrangement failed, she was married first to Don Juan of Aragon and then to Philibert le Beau, duc de Savoie. His death in 1504 left her a widow for the second time at the age of only 24, and less interested in remarriage than in power. Declining the hand of Henry VII of England, she assumed the regency of the Netherlands and Franche-Comté when her daughter Joanna of Castile went mad, directed the education of her nephew, the future Emperor Charles V, and encouraged the invasion of Burgundy ending with the unsuccessful siege of Dijon by German, Swiss and Franc-Comtois troops in 1513. A determined, independent woman, she earned her claim to the motto 'Fortune, infortune, fort une', one of several possible translations being 'Through good times and bad, one woman is strong'. It appears throughout her church, together with marguerites (a rebus few medieval noblewomen of that name could resist) and the interlaced initials P and M, for Philibert and Marguerite. They are a reminder that she conceived the building as a memorial to her husband and as fulfilment of a vow made by her mother-in-law Marguerite de Bourbon (who had died in 1483) after the recovery of her husband Philippe de Bresse from a hunting accident. At Brou, therefore, the Valois taste for public splendour is partly softened by family affection.

Work began in 1506 to replace the Romanesque buildings of the Benedictine priory that stood on the site. The new monastic quarters were finished by 1508 and the church by 1532, just two years too late for Marguerite d'Autriche to see it complete. The long list of designers and craftsmen she employed shows both her Burgundian roots and her international connections. Jehan Perréal of Amboise, the original architect, was replaced by Loys van Boghem from Flanders in 1512. The tombs begun by

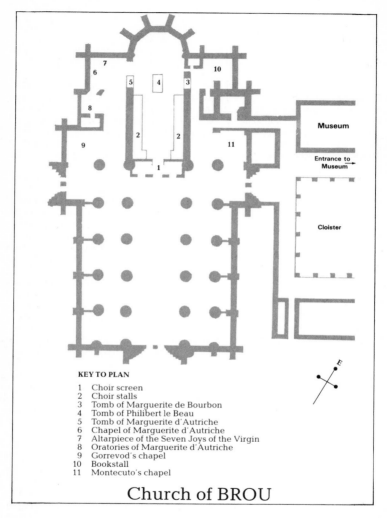

KEY TO PLAN

1 Choir screen
2 Choir stalls
3 Tomb of Marguerite de Bourbon
4 Tomb of Philibert le Beau
5 Tomb of Marguerite d'Autriche
6 Chapel of Marguerite d'Autriche
7 Altarpiece of the Seven Joys of the Virgin
8 Oratories of Marguerite d'Autriche
9 Gorrevod's chapel
10 Bookstall
11 Montecuto's chapel

Church of BROU

Perréal and Michel Colombe (who made the tomb of François, duc de Bretagne, at Nantes) were completed by Jan van Room from Brussels and the German sculptor Conrad Meyt. Van Room designed the choir stalls and a local craftsman, Pierre Terrasson (or Tarrasson) carved them.

The outside of the church lacks dramatic impact, partly through the absence of W or central towers to relieve its square proportions, and the hastily finished W façade suffers by comparison to the much finer sculptural detail inside. The tympanum over the doorway shows Marguerite d'Autriche and Philibert being presented by their patron saints to a suffering Christ. The saint on the central pier below is Nicholas of Tolentino, to whom the church is dedicated; Philibert died on his feast day. The figure of St Andrew on the balustrade above is a replica of an original destroyed in the 19C; his saltire cross was a device of the Valois dukes.

The broad nave, with aisles flanked by side-chapels, and the transepts show the pale Jura stone at its loveliest. The clustered columns, tall windows and lierne vaulting are Flamboyant at its most effectively restrained. Only the balustrades and roof bosses anticipate the rich elaboration of the E end. This begins, rather too abruptly, with Van Boghem's choir screen, each of its three arches divided into triple ogee curves and all its available surfaces transformed by filigree carving.

The three tombs in the choir remind the visitor of the church's chief purpose as a family mausoleum. Philibert lies in the middle, flanked to the S by Marguerite de Bourbon and to the N by Marguerite d'Autriche herself. Their poses emphasise the relationships that bind them: Marguerite de Bourbon turns her face toward her son and he glances across to his wife, 'his sagging features in quest of a final word of advice', an unkind critic has suggested. Otherwise, the three tombs differ in their style and magnificence. Marguerite de Bourbon's is the simplest and most traditional, her effigy lying on a black marble slab recessed into the wall. Note the row of *pleurants* below. Philibert appears twice, in all his worldly splendour on the marble slab and below it as a corpse, a newly fashionable *memento mori* apparently introduced into the design by Van Room. The slab is supported by open arches whose niches contain not *pleurants* but demure female Virtues in the Flemish style; the one with braided hair in the middle of the N side is particularly elegant. Marguerite d'Autriche also appears in life and death effigies. Conrad Meyt's figure of her corpse with its long wavy hair is a refined and sympathetic study in striking contrast to the rather mechanical riot of ornament on the canopy above, a last brazen assertion of worldly status.

Though the tombs dominate the choir, they do not completely overshadow its other furnishings. Pierre Terrasson's choir stalls make one of the best sets in France. The Old Testament episodes on the S side begin at the W end with the creation of Eve; the New Testament episodes on the N begin with the Nativity. Note particularly the splendid Samson carrying off the gates of Gaza and the Adoration of the Magi. The misericords show lively grotesque and realistic touches.

The glass in the apse, made by Lyonnais craftsmen from designs inspired by Dürer, shows Marguerite and Philibert watching the risen Christ appear to Mary Magdalen. They are portrayed again in the glass of the chapel on the N side of the choir, incorporated into designs adapted from Dürer and Titian. The nearby altarpiece is a profusely anecdotal treatment of the Seven Joys of the Virgin. This chapel and its neighbouring two-storey oratory were reserved for Marguerite d'Autriche's private use. The chapel beyond, connecting with the N transept, was reserved for Laurent de Gorrevod, governor of the Bresse, who appears with his wife in the stained glass watching Christ appear to Doubting Thomas. The chapel on the S side of the choir now contains the bookstall, while the southern partner to Gorrevod's chapel was reserved for Marguerite d'Autriche's confessor.

The ***Musée de Brou** is entered from the Grand Cloister, the middle of the three quadrangles E of the church. Its first floor makes a handsome setting for furniture from the Bresse and Lyonnais, 18C *faïence* from Meillonnas (NE of the town) and a rich collection of paintings. Bernard van Orley's portrait of Marguerite d'Autriche (her Habsburg features even more pronounced than on her tomb effigies) and a triptych of the life of

St Jerome she commissioned for her church are outstanding in a group of Flemish and Dutch work which also includes Jan 'Velvet' Bruegel's 'Stork Hunt'. The wide-ranging French collection includes Nicolas de Largillière, Jean-Baptiste Lallemand, Isabey, Gustave Moreau, Millet, Gustave Doré (an interesting group dominated by the stomach-churning 'Dante and Virgil') and Utrillo (view of Pérouges, S of Bourg-en-Bresse).

A40 heads W from Bourg-en-Bresse but N79 is a more interesting way of completing the journey to (34km) Mâcon. The Ferme des Planons N of (22km) **St-Cyr-sur-Menthon** is a traditional farmhouse with Saracen chimney. 5km beyond D28 leads N from N79 to (1.5km) **St-André**, where the Romanesque church built by the Tournus monks has a fine tower and capitals in the choir, and (0.5km) **Bâgé-le-Châtel**, seat of the medieval *seigneurs* who made it the original capital of the Bresse. **Mâcon** is described at the end of the previous route.

10 The Serein Valley: Joigny to Chablis and Semur or Avallon

Directions and distances. Total distance 112km (70 miles) to Semur, 101km (63 miles) to Avallon. D943 from **Joigny** to (10km) Migennes. D91 to (27km) junction with N77 for **Pontigny** (1.5km S). D91 to (41km) **Chablis**. D45, (61km) D86 to (65km) **Noyers-sur-Serein** and (80km) l'Isle-sur-Serein. For Semur: D86, (81km) D11 to (96km) Toutry, D954 to (100km) **Époisses** and (112km) **Semur**. For Avallon: D86, (81km) D11, (87km) D957 to (89km) **Montréal** and (101km) **Avallon**.

Connections with other routes. Auxerre (Route 11) makes an alternative starting point, using D84 via Seignelay to Hauterive on D91. From Joigny to Migennes via St-Cydroine, see Route 3. For Semur, see Route 4, which continues the journey to Dijon. For Avallon, see Route 11, which continues the journey to Vézelay; Route 12 continues from Avallon to Saulieu and Autun.

The **Serein Valley** offers a quiet alternative to the D905 and the Armançon valley if you are heading from Sens and Joigny towards Dijon (Routes 3 and 4) or to the N6 if you are heading for Avallon and Vézelay (Route 11). Never wide and often no more than a shallow stream, the river flows into the Yonne S of Joigny after an unhurried course that waters the Chablis vineyards and runs through a winding, wooded valley S of Noyers.

Hauterive, 18km SE of Joigny via the unlovely Migennes, is a convenient place to join the wide, rather bare countryside that marks the final stage of the river. At **Seignelay** (1540 Seignelois; Tourist Information), on the opposite bank 3km S, the 17C market hall on wooden pillars and the big church tower make an unexpectedly handsome group. 9km E of Hauterive D91 meets N77 about 1.5km N of where the Route Nationale cruelly slices through **Pontigny** (830 people). The *church, though stripped of its monastic buildings, ranks almost with Fontenay among the region's Cistercian architecture. Founded in 1114, the abbey was the second of the four daughters of Cîteaux, preceded by La Ferté (1113) and followed by Clairvaux and Morimond (1115). It quickly grew to power under its first abbot, Hugues de Mâcon, and founded daughter houses of its own. Three controversial archbishops of Canterbury were among its friends. Thomas à Becket began his Burgundian exile at Pontigny in 1164, though Henry II's threat to expel the Cistercians from his domains forced him the archbishop to move to Sens in 1166. Stephen Langton made it his refuge after King John refused to acknowledge his appointment, returning to England in 1213 for the campaign that resulted in Magna Carta. Edmund Rich (St Edmund of Abingdon, or St Edme), who retired to Pontigny worn out by his quarrels with Henry III, was buried in its church in 1242. His tomb became a shrine for pilgrims. Suppressed at the Revolution, Pontigny flowered again in the years before World War II when the philosopher Paul Desjardins made it the setting for the Décades which brought together figures like Gide, Malraux, Mauriac, Maurois, Thomas Mann and T.S. Eliot.

The church was begun about 1140, though a second building campaign in about 1185–1205 substituted an apse with ambulatory and radiating chapels for the original rectangular E end. Seen from the flat surrounding fields, its squat bulk is emphasised by the lack of towers; flying buttresses crouch round the chevet. Inside, the pointed arches and quadripartite vaulting of the nave mark another step in the development, from Vézelay via Fontenay, of the Cistercian style that Kenneth Conant has called 'Burgundian half-Gothic' and Robert Branner 'rib-vaulted Romanesque'. The clerestory (not used at Fontenay) and the white stone add light and space to the severe effect. The clustered columns of the choir, though slightly more elaborate, still harmonise with the earlier work. That is more than can be said for the Baroque and later additions, particularly the tomb of St Edme behind the altar, though the choir stalls could be wholeheartedly admired in another context.

Beyond its junction with N77 the D91 follows a straight, tree-lined course to (4km) **Ligny-le-Châtel** (1120 people), where the church has a big Renaissance choir dwarfing the Romanesque nave. Ligny marks the northern edge of the **Chablis vineyards** and as the road continues S via (3.5km) **Maligny** (610 people), with its château (not open), the country changes to gently rolling hills neatly planted with rows of vines: a landscape as dry and clean as the wine it produces. First systematically cultivated by the monks of Pontigny and Chablis, the vineyards have been threatened and reduced over the years by the phylloxera epidemic (a root-eating parasite), the depression following World War I and the ever present danger of spring frost this far north. They now spread almost to the Auxerrois vineyards in the W and the recently revived Tonnerrois vineyards in the E, and as far S as Poilly. Chablis is made only from the Chardonnay grape, locally called the Beaunois. Nineteen communes qualify for the *appellation* though only seven vineyards, together covering about 125 of the total 7000 acres, carry the *Grand Cru* label: Bougros, Les Preuses, Vaudésir, Blanchots, Grenouilles, Valmur and Les Clos. They lie immediately NE of (6.5km) **Chablis** itself, a little town (2570 Chablisiens; Tourist Information) with no real landmarks but all the tourists, restaurants, and *dégustation* and *vente* signs one would expect of a wine centre. There are some pleasantly shabby old streets, like the Rue des Moulins, by the river and round the church of St-Martin. The saint's relics were briefly kept in the previous church on the site on their way from Tours to the safety of Auxerre during the Norman invasions of the 9C. The horseshoes fixed to the door of the early 13C S porch are said to be ex-votos. The 18C Porte Noël stands near the Rue des Juifs, with the Renaissance façade of La Synagogue. The vineyards stretching away from either bank of the Serein are well worth exploring: take the drive E to (5km) **Fleys** and back via **Béru** or SW to **Courgis** and **Préhy** on the way to the separate *vignoble* of (13km) **Chitry**.

D45 leads to the southern fringe of the Chablis vineyards at (10km) **Poilly-sur-Serein**, with a late Gothic church, though wine and the wine trade have left their mark further S on (14km) ***Noyers-sur-Serein** (760 people), a picturesque old town tucked into a loop of the river. The name is pronounced 'Noyère'. Its fortifications are marked by two gates, the Porte Tonnerre in the N and the Porte Peinte in the S, and a chain of round towers, particularly well preserved on the tree-lined promenade by the river. They enclose a little network of narrow cobbled streets and squares, sometimes with names that remember the sources of the town's prosperity from the 15C to the 18C. Many old houses survive, some with ground-floor arcades, steep gables and richly carved half-timbering. Note particularly the charming Place de la Petite-Étape-aux-Vins and, in the Place du Grenier-à-Sel, the Renaissance bailiff's house with its Greek motto, 'Kamato' ('through suffering'). The Hôtel de Ville near the Porte Peinte has an 18C façade with wrought-iron balconies. Beyond the neighbouring Place du Marché-au-Blé is the late Gothic church, tall and heavily buttressed, with a bas-relief effigy on the wall by the S door. The museum contains naïve art in the manner of Douanier Rousseau.

A detour from Noyers leads SE via (5km) **Jouancy**, with a strikingly placed château, to (8km further) **Châtel-Gérard** and the forests that cover the limestone country between the Serein and Armançon valleys. The **Prieuré de Vausse** (open), 3km E, is a ruined Cistercian foundation of 1220 which now stands among farm buildings. It keeps a charming Romanesque cloister, smaller and simpler than the one at Fontenay. From Châtel-Gérard you can join the main route again by heading SW to (16km) **Thizy**, with the remains of a medieval château (not open) next to its church; 1km beyond is the junction of D11 and D957 S of l'Isle-sur-Serein.

The main route from Noyers follows D86 along a pleasantly wooded stretch of the river. **Civry-sur-Serein**, a quiet farming village to the left at 12km, has a handsome *lavoir* and a church with a 13C porch supported by a little double-columned arcade. **Coutarnoux**, in a quarrying region on the opposite bank, provided the stone for the choir at Vézelay. Beyond (3km) **l'Isle-sur-Serein** (530 people) D86 swings right to head directly for Avallon. Even if that is your goal it is worth taking the D11 3km further to the junction with D957. **Montréal**, a little hill village 2km W, was once Mont Royal, a residence of the notorious Merovingian queen Brunehaut (or Brunhild) and her grandson Thierry. Two medieval gates and some old houses survive, while the early Gothic church restored by Viollet-le-Duc contains one of the best sets of *choir stalls in Burgundy. The Rigolley brothers from Nuits-sous-Ravières near Ancy-le-Franc carved them in the 1520s. Note particularly, among the panels, the Annunciation and Christ in Joseph's workshop and, among the groups on top of the bench ends, the two men drinking wine and the two lions fighting over a bone. Near by is a 15C Nottingham alabaster altarpiece, now lacking several panels.

D957 continues W from Montréal to (14km) **Avallon**. The route to Semur follows the Serein a little longer by taking D11 via (6km) Guillon to join D954 near the Autoroute and (3km) Toutry. D954 heads E across the fertile plateau between the Serein and the Armançon to (4km) **Époisses** (790 people; Tourist Information), known for its cheese. The little town is dominated by its *château, on the site of another residence of Brunehaut and Thierry but dating largely from the 15C onwards. The moat and wall (note the *échaugette*) enclose an outer courtyard large enough to accommodate the village in time of trouble; its buildings include the 13C church and a 15C dovecot with holes for 3000 birds reached by a revolving ladder.

The château itself, inside the inner defences, lost half the buildings around its courtyard at the Revolution. The four big towers of the remaining segment mix medieval work and 17–18C rebuilding. The interior (open less often than the exterior and outbuildings) contains souvenirs of famous guests, including Madame de Sévigné. She lived at the château of **Bourbilly** (open), in a secluded little stretch of the Serein valley 10km SE of Époisses, previously the home of her grandmother Jeanne de Chantal, canonised for her work founding the Order of the Visitation. The original building was rebuilt in 19C Gothic. For Moutiers-St-Jean, 10km NE of Époisses, see Route 3. Beyond Époisses D954 continues to (12km) **Semur** (Route 4).

11 The Yonne, the Cure and the Cousin: Joigny to Auxerre, Avallon and Vézelay

Directions and distances. Total distance 95.5km (59 miles). N6 from **Joigny** to (27km) **Auxerre** and (79km) **Avallon**. D427 to (84.5km) Pontaubert. D957 to (95.5km) **Vézelay**.

Connections with other routes. This route continues the journey along N6 from Sens to Joigny in Route 3 and is in turn continued around the edge of the Morvan by Route 12, from Avallon to Saulieu and Autun. Route 13 describes the Morvan, for which Avallon and Vézelay make convenient starting points. Route 10 follows an alternative way from Joigny to Avallon along the Serein valley. Route 18 starts along N6 from Auxerre but branches S to Nevers.

N6, continuing along the Yonne valley from **Joigny**, runs near the route of the Roman Via Agrippa through Burgundy. The way to (27km) Auxerre is unremarkable except for (17.5km) **Appoigny** (2760 people; Tourist Information), where the big 13C collegiate church has gargoyles outside and a Renaissance choir screen inside.

*AUXERRE (38,820 Auxerrois; Tourist Information), now the *préfecture* of Yonne, developed from a settlement of the Senones into the Gallo-Roman Autissiodorum on the Via Agrippa. St Germanus, the city's fifth bishop, helped to make it an ecclesiastical and scholastic centre. After he died in 448 his reputation assured that the tradition continued, notably at the powerful abbey of St-Germain, where the crypt preserving his relics still survives: the most important pre-Romanesque work in Burgundy and the most impressive sight in a city unusually rich in reminders of its history.

Churches dominate first impressions of Auxerre, with the towers and spires of St-Pierre, the cathedral of St-Étienne and St-Germain rising above the calm waters of the Yonne. The view from the **Pont Paul-Bert** in the S is particularly satisfying. The quay between the bridge and its northern partners, the **Pont Jean-Moreau** and **Pont de la Tournelle**, has convenient parking places (otherwise not always easy to find) and deserves exploring in its own right. Near the footbridge about halfway up stands the **Syndicat d'Initiative**, also the headquarters of the Comité Départemental du Tourisme for Yonne. The Place St-Nicolas, in the shadow of St-Germain further N, is a charming little spot with a fountain in the centre and a coloured statue of the saint on one of the surrounding houses. In the neighbouring Place du Coche-d'Eau the 16C half-timbered house which serves as the administrative centre for the local museums also has temporary exhibitions.

There are several ways of reaching the centre from the river but the Pont Paul-Bert makes the best starting point for a fairly comprehensive walking tour. The Rue du Pont leads to the church of **St-Pierre-en-Vallée**, with an extravagantly ornate 17C gateway and façade and a Flamboyant tower. The route along the Rue Joubert and the Rue Fécauderie passes some interesting old houses and side streets (like the Rue Sous-Murs). There are more good buildings on the little square with the 18C **Hôtel de Ville** and a coloured wooden statue of the Auxerre poet Marie Noël (1883–1967) by François Brochet (see the Chapelle des Visitandines below). The Flamboyant **Tour de l'Horloge** with its tall spire and gilded clock, spanning the street to the W, stands on the site of the main gate to the Gallo-Roman city. A plaque remembers 'Cadet Roussel' (Guillaume Roussel, 1743–1807), the fervent Revolutionary whose extravagances and misfortunes were made famous in a popular song. The writer Restif de la Bretonne, born at nearby Sacy, worked as apprentice to a nearby printer in the 1750s.

Before going to the cathedral it is worth exploring the network of streets and squares W and N of the Place de l'Hôtel-de-Ville. From the end of the Rue de l'Horloge the Rue de la Draperie leads to the Place Charles-Surugue, with a fountain and a gaily coloured statue of Cadet Roussel by François Brochet. Close by rise the spire and handsome Romanesque tower of **St-Eusèbe**. On the Place Robillard, next to the Place Charles-Lepère, the stone-built 14–15C house at No 5, known as the **Hôtel du Cerf-Volant**, is the oldest domestic building to have survived in Auxerre. The Rue d'Egleny leads W to the **Musée Leblanc-Duvernoy**, a little 18C *hôtel particulier* which makes a pleasant setting for the collections of a local amateur. They include four early 18C Beauvais tapestries from a series reflecting the fashion for chinoiserie, 16–19C paintings, and *pottery ranging from Greek ceramics to grès from the Puisaye and local Revolutionary *faïence* ('Nous sommes invincibles'). The **Musée de l'Histoire Naturelle** on the Boulevard Vauban, further W, is part of a centre for nature conservation dedicated to Paul Bert (1833–1886), the physiologist and politician of the Third Republic who gave his name to the bridge at the start of the walking tour. The museum includes a display of his work together with interesting specimens of local palaeontology (a bear from the caves at Arcy-sur-Cure, dinosaur, ichthyosaurus). From the Place Charles-Lepère the Rue de Paris winds N past the handsome Renaissance **Hôtel dit 'de Crôle'** on the way to the **Chapelle des Visitandines**, a little neo-classical building of 1714 which now houses work by François Brochet, the local sculptor responsible for the statues of Marie Noël by the Hôtel de Ville and Cadet Roussel in the Place Charles-Surugue.

From the big Place des Cordeliers, N of the Hôtel de Ville, the Rue Fourier quickly leads to the square dominated by the cathedral of *St-Étienne*. Of the early churches to stand on the site the only survival, albeit an important one, is the crypt of the Romanesque church dedicated in 1057. Above ground the cathedral belongs to the building campaign started by Guillaume de Seignelay in 1215 but, thanks in part to the Hundred Years War, not finished for several centuries. Since the work progressed from E to W, the obvious route round the church involves a journey backwards in time, beginning with the Flamboyant work on the upper stages of the W façade. Its rose window and rich sculpture help make up for the absence of a S tower to balance the N tower. The 13–14C doorways below suffered the attentions of the Huguenots who mutilated St-Étienne in the 1560s but keep

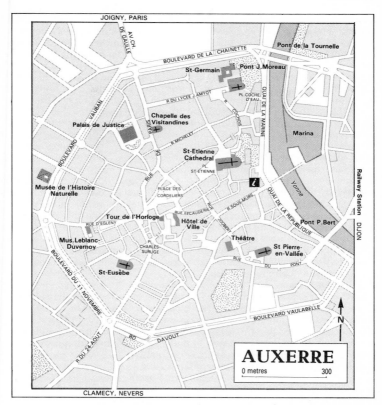

JOIGNY, PARIS

BOULEVARD DE LA CHAINETTE

Pont de la Tournelle

St-Germain

Pont J.Moreau

AV. CH. DE GAULLE

R DU LYCEE J AMYOT

PL COCHE D'EAU

QUAI DE LA MARINE

Chapelle des Visitandines

Marina

Palais de Justice

R MICHELET

RUE DE PARIS

R COCHOIS

St-Etienne Cathedral

PL ST-ÉTIENNE

BOULEVARD VAUBAN

Musée de l'Histoire Naturelle

PLACE DES CORDELIERS

QUAI DE LA RÉPUBLIQUE

Yonne

Railway Station

RUE DE L'EGLENY

RUE E.CAUDERIE

R. SOUS-MURS

Tour de l'Horloge

Hôtel de Ville

Pont P.Bert

DIJON

Mus. Leblanc-Duvernoy

PL CHARLES SURUGE

Théâtre

St Pierre-en-Vallée

BOULEVARD DU 11 NOVEMBRE

St-Eusèbe

RUE DU PONT

R.DU 24 AOUT

BD DAVOUT

BOULEVARD VAULABELLE

N

AUXERRE

0 metres   300

CLAMECY, NEVERS

some fragments of their delicate carving. The central tympanum showed Christ in Judgement; note the medallions with New Testament episodes and classical subjects (Hercules, Eros). The bases of the piers flanking the N doorway show episodes from the Old Testament: the Creation, Adam and Eve, the Fall and a delightful Noah's Ark. The tympanum of the S doorway, oldest of the three, has scenes from the childhood of Christ and the life of John the Baptist.

Inside, the building achieves surprising unity given the time that lapsed between the 14C nave, vaulted in the 15C, and the pure Gothic of the early 13C choir. Variations in the triforium and clerestory mark the change of style. Like the W end, the transepts have rose windows. The N transept contains a 20C statue of Jeanne d'Arc, who prayed in the cathedral on her way to present herself to Charles VII at Chinon in 1429 and returned via Auxerre at the head of the army accompanying the king to his coronation at Rheims. The lovely blue and red medallions of the 13C glass in the ambulatory invite comparison with Sens and St-Julien-du-Sault: note, among the biblical subjects, the scenes from Genesis (N side) and, among the saints' legends, St Eustace (S side near E end). The choir has a monument to the humanist and translator of Petrarch, Jacques Amyot (1513–1593), who also had the misfortune to be bishop during the Huguenot troubles. A chapel on the S side of the ambulatory now contains the cathedral treasury, with ivories, 12–13C *champlevé* enamels from Limoges and 13–16C Books of Hours. Near by is the entrance to the big Romanesque crypt built between 1023 and 1035. Its three-bayed nave leads to a semicircular apse with an ambulatory and an apsidal chapel which has two important wall paintings: a late 11C Christ mounted on a white horse and surrounded by angels on horseback (an unusual, if not unique, design obviously inspired by the Book of Revelation) and a 13C Christ in Majesty.

The Rue de l'Étang-St-Vigile and the rather more interesting Rue Cochois both lead N from the cathedral to **St-Germain**, where the abbey buildings now form part of a cultural centre and museum designed, when reorganisation is complete, to bring together the city's previously dispersed collections of art and archaeology.

Born at Auxerre in about 378 and appointed its bishop in 418, Germanus became a major figure in the early Church, preparing St Patrick for his mission to Ireland and himself twice visiting Britain to combat the Pelagian heresy, using the first occasion to pay respects at the shrine of St Alban. When he died at Ravenna in 448 devoted women followers, duly canonised in their turn, brought his body back for burial in the small oratory chapel he had built. His shrine formed the nucleus of the abbey founded between 493 and 545 by Clothilde, wife of Clovis, the first king of the Franks converted to Christianity. Later centuries saw it grow both in size and reputation as a centre of learning.

Today the Romanesque Tour St-Jean near the entrance stands isolated from the rest of the church by the demolition of the western bays of the nave in the 19C; the site has recently been excavated to reveal the foundations. The guided tour begins in the surviving eastern fragment of the church, where the late 12C–early 13C Gothic choir has a handsome apsidal chapel. The tour continues to the **crypt, a labyrinthine system of underground chapels where successive Merovingian, Carolingian and Gothic work create an astonishing palimpsest of architectural history. At its core, on the site of the original oratory chapel, is the confessio for Germanus' relics, enlarged first by Clothilde and then again, to its present form, by Conrad, uncle of Charles le Chauve, between 841 and 859. The little three-bayed nave, flanked by aisles on either side, has a barrel vault supported by oak beams. The capitals on its columns are reused Gallo-Roman work from Arles. The sarcophagus, raised from the cavity below in the 17C, is apparently a sham designed to throw predatory invaders off the scent. The rectangular ambulatory and chapels that enclose the confessio are of particular interest, not just for the tombs of Merovingian bishops but for the 9C wall paintings on the N side, the oldest to have survived in France, showing the trial and martyrdom of St Stephen. The wall paintings in the ambulatory and chapel on the S side, of bishops and the Adoration of the Magi, are apparently somewhat later. Conrad's rotunda beyond the E end was replaced in 1277 by two decagonal Gothic chapels built one above the other to form, with the apsidal chapel of the choir, a three-tier structure set into the slope of the hillside.

The museum being installed in the largely 17C cloisters and monastic buildings is an ambitious project. The *Gallo-Roman gallery in the monks' dormitory has a lively and informative display of local finds including stelae, architectural fragments and statues, a fine Minerva among them. The gallery of prehistory on the floor above has items from the Palaeolithic period onwards, notably Iron Age finds from the Hallstatt necropolis at Gurgy and the La Tène settlements at Cravant and Beaumont. The medieval collection will be housed in rooms leading off the cloister, scheduled to open after 1994. It includes Merovingian coffins and buckles; a 9C Byzantine cloth said to have been used as a shroud for St Germanus' relics; sculptural fragments from St-Germain itself; and a fine 15C altarpiece in painted wood. An adjoining wing of the building, scheduled to open in 1993, will display fine art. Ranging from the 15C onwards, the collection is strongest in French portraits, landscapes and sculpture of the 17–18C (Charles Le Brun, Antoine Coysevox, François Girardon, Antoine Coypel).

The little Place St-Nicolas and neighbouring Place du Coche-d'Eau are by the quay below St-Germain.

S of Auxerre the N6 and the Yonne, now flanked by the Canal du Nivernais, run through the pleasant countryside of the **Auxerrois**, once among the great wine-producing regions of France but now overshadowed in size as well as reputation by neighbouring Chablis. Its vineyards produce reds from the Pinot Noir and the local César, whites from the Chardonnay, Sauvignon and Aligoté, and rosé. The sparkling Crémant de Bourgogne, here made from a traditional local grape, the Sacy, has grown increasingly popular.

Escolives-Ste-Camille (510 people), to the right of the main road at 11km, has a charming Romanesque church with an open porch, an octagonal tower and two crypts, the lower sheltering the relics of Camilla, one of the women who brought Germanus' body back from Ravenna to Auxerre in 448. The Vauclusian spring on the outskirts of the village was a centre of settlement from Neolithic times. Conveniently close to the Via Agrippa, it became the Gallo-Roman Scoliva and later a Merovingian cemetery. The exhibition of finds from the site (Caisse Nationale) includes an impressive Gallo-Roman monument reused as foundations for the baths built in the 3C. **Coulanges-la-Vineuse** (880 people), 3km SW, is a pleasant little village that hardly makes an appropriate setting for the big neo-classical church (1742) by Servandoni, the Italian architect who built the W façade of St-Sulpice in Paris and worked with the Palladian Roger Morris in London. There is a good viewpoint W of Coulanges, while D85 runs E to rejoin N6.

D38 climbs the other bank of the Yonne to (3km) **Irancy**, birthplace of Jacques-Germain Soufflot (1731–1781), who built the Panthéon in Paris. Its church is now a curious patchwork, with an 18C choir and Renaissance buttresses, partly ruined, flanking the S side of its late 12C nave. Irancy is known both for its wines (red and rosé) and its cherries. The mixture of orchards and vineyards makes a lovely sight, particularly in spring, on the road winding up the hillside beyond the village. A left turn leads to (5km) **St-Bris-le-Vineux** (1020 people), an interesting little town with old streets and a handsome partly Renaissance church. Chitry lies NE near the Chablis vineyards (Route 10). At **Bailly**, by the river 2.5km SW of St-Bris, the underground quarries now serve as *caves* (open) for making Crémant de Bourgogne by the Champagne method.

N6 continues to **Cravant** (790 people), 19km from Auxerre, where the Cure flows into the Yonne. At the battle here in 1423 Anglo-Burgundian troops defending the fringes of Philippe le Bon's duchy defeated an army of Scottish mercenaries in the pay of Charles VII. The little town keeps a few fragments of its fortifications and a church with a Renaissance tower and choir whose radiating chapels make a virtuoso display of different vaulting patterns.

At Cravant N6 quits the Yonne (which Route 18 follows on the way to Nevers) for the valley of the Cure. The road passes limestone crests on the way to (5km) **Vermenton** (1110 people; Tourist Information). The statue-columns on the mutilated Romanesque doorway of the church have lost their heads but not their delicate drapery. Restif de la Bretonne (1734–1806) was born at the village of **Sacy**, about 9km E. 2km S of Vermenton a little side-road leads from N6 down to the river where the remains of the Cistercian abbey of **Régny**, notably its handsome Gothic refectory, are incorporated into farm buildings.

Arcy-sur-Cure (500 people; Tourist Information) is a pleasant little place astride the river 6km S of Vermenton. The W bank near by has several well-publicised but disappointing sights. The **Manoir de Chastenay** (open) is a largely Renaissance building which contains interesting 14C painted panels. Only one room is shown and the guided tour dwells at length on alchemical and esoteric symbolism detected in the ornamental motifs around the front door. The cave systems that riddle the hillside further S sheltered animals and humans from the Palaeolithic era onwards. The finds preserved in Auxerre are more interesting than the illuminated stalactites and stalagmites in the commercialised **Grottes d'Arcy** (open). Beyond lies the Gallo-Roman camp of Cora on the Via Agrippa.

After Arcy-sur-Cure N6 passes (5km) **Voutenay-sur-Cure**, near the entrance to the lovely little **Vau de Bouche**, and (4km) the heights commanded by the modern chapel of Notre-Dame-d'Orient and its 19C predecessor. D951, 1km beyond, follows the Cure on a quick route to Vézelay but it is better to stay on N6 and approach Vézelay via (10km) Avallon.

*AVALLON (8620 Avallonnais; Tourist Information) is a charming place, an old town on a granite spur whose southern tip overlooks the Cousin valley. The original Celtic settlement became the Gallo-Roman Aballo on the Via Agrippa. It was first fortified in the 9–10C, a wise precaution for a town which Saracens and Normans had already pillaged, but not enough to defend it from the marauding bands of soldiers known as *écorcheurs* and the battles between Philippe le Bon and Charles VII in the Hundred Years War. Avallon today keeps large sections of its walls, which enclose a centre with old buildings and the Romanesque church of St-Lazare.

The Promenade des Terreaux and neighbouring Place Vauban, with a statue of the Marquis, mark the N end of the old town. The main gate stood at the head of the Grande Rue Aristide-Briand, now pedestrianised. Among the buildings it passes on its route S are the 18C **Hôtel de Ville**, on the corner of the Place du Général-de-Gaulle, and the 16–17C former **Hôtel des Princes-de-Condé**, now a school. It is worth turning right before the clock-tower on the little Rue Masquée, with 15C houses. A left turn on the Rue Maison-Dieu at the end leads to the 16C provost's house, with scallop-shell decoration on its dormer windows. From here the Rue du Collège returns to the main street via the **Musée de l'Avallonnais** in the 17C buildings of the former college. The best items in a very mixed bag are the archaeological finds, particularly the statues from the 1C Gallo-Roman temple at Montmarte near Vault-de-Lugny (see below) and the early 3C mosaic from near Chastellux-sur-Cure (Route 13). Note also the head from a statue-column at St-Lazare; the paintings by Antoine Vestier, a native of the town (see also the Musée des Ursulines at Mâcon); and the paintings and engravings by Rouault.

The tall, spired 15C **Tour de l'Horloge** leads into the cobbled square with the half-timbered house that contains the **Syndicat d'Initiative** and, to the left of the church, a 15C house with a typical Burgundian feature in the staircase turret over its front door. The collegiate church of ***St-Lazare** was largely rebuilt in the first half of the 12C to accommodate the pilgrims attracted by the relics, supposedly of Lazarus, it had acquired a century earlier. Its W façade has suffered badly from the fall of the N tower in the 17C, the loss of the central tympanum (which showed Christ in Majesty) and the mutilation of the S tympanum (the Adoration of the Magi with, apparently, the Harrowing of Hell and the Resurrection on the lintel). A hint of its ancient glory survives in the richly carved arches, particularly the *roman fleuri* of the S doorway, and the one surviving statue-column, an Île-de-France touch in a building that otherwise pays local tribute to Cluny and Vézelay. The nave, following the slope of the hillside, has acanthus-leaf capitals below pointed arches and a vault which tries uncertainly to marry the groin vault and the dome. The choir with its semi-domed apse dates from the earliest phase of rebuilding.

The Rue Bocquillot continues past the 15C salt warehouse, on the right, to the 18C pilasters which mark the site of the Petite Porte. The terrace beyond gives a lovely panorama of the Cousin valley, and pleasant walks follow the walls overlooking the ravines to the W and E. On the W side a tree-lined promenade leads to the well-preserved **Tour des Vaudois** and eventually to the remains of the **Porte Auxerroise** and its bastion (note the *échaugette*) at the W end of the Promenade des Terreaux. Another *échaugette*, on the corner bastion, begins the walk on the E side; it continues via the **Tour de l'Escharguet** and the 15C **Tour Beurdelaine** and its bastion. The Rue du Bel-Air leads back into the main street.

Rising above terraced gardens which cling to the sides of the ravine, the walls of Avallon make a lovely sight from a distance. There is a particularly good view from the **Parc des Chaumes**, to the E, and some tantalising glimpses from the nearby Rue de Lormes as it runs along the bottom of the ravine.

The Lormes road lies on the best way from Avallon to (16.5km) Vézelay, which begins by ignoring the obvious route along D957 and heads S to the rocky little *Vallée du Cousin, where D427 goes W to join D957 at (5.5km) **Pontaubert**. The Templars built its dignified Romanesque church. **Vault-de-Lugny**, 2km NW, has a château (not open) preserving its medieval moat and keep, and a church with 16C wall paintings of the Passion. The site of the Montmarte temple (see the Musée de l'Avallonnais above) lies to its W.

D957 leads to (7km) **Fontette** and a distant view of Vézelay on its wooded hill. The prospect should not make you overlook the village near its foot, **St-Père-sous-Vézelay**, where the church of *Notre-Dame is a lovely little Gothic foil to La Madeleine on the hill above. The 13C tower and W façade with its triangular pediment are so richly ornamented with statues that the big 14C narthex adds clutter, handsome though it is in its own right. It shelters mutilated carvings of Girart de Roussillon and his wife Berthe in reminder that St-Père was the original site of the Vézelay community. Inside, the delicate 13C nave is made light by the pale stone and the triforium between the arcade and clerestory; the 15C columns of the choir do not mar the unity of the effect. Note the painted roof bosses. The museum next door contains finds from the Fontaines Salées, or salt springs, worked from about 6000 BC onwards, notably funeral urns, ex-votos and a hollowed-out tree trunk used in the piping system. The springs themselves, with remains of Gallo-Roman thermal baths as well as the necropolis and salt workings from the Iron Age Hallstatt culture, lie on the road to Pierre-Perthuis, on an interesting way into the Morvan (Route 13).

VÉZELAY (570 Vézeliens; Tourist Information) is a little village of narrow streets climbing steeply up to **La Madeleine**, the high-water mark of

Burgundian Romanesque and the greatest building in Burgundy. Among the pleasant old houses on the most direct way to the church are No 20 in the Rue St-Pierre, where Romain Rolland spent the last years of his life, and the former abbey guest house near the end of the Rue St-Étienne. Longer, less crowded routes follow the old town walls to the top of the hill. The northern circuit passes the 15–16C **Porte Neuve**, best-preserved of the town gates, and a side-road leading down to the cross that marks where St Bernard preached his outdoor sermon advocating the disastrous Second Crusade in 1146. The nearby chapel of **Ste-Croix**, built soon afterwards, keeps a few details inside to suggest it is by the masons who added the narthex to La Madeleine. Its popular name, La Cordelle, refers to the Franciscan community—the first in France—that installed itself here in 1217 and returned in 1946. Both routes round the walls lead to the terrace beyond the E end of La Madeleine, with a wide view over the Cure valley and the Morvan.

Whichever way you reach it, La Madeleine comes first as a disappointment. It may never have been particularly attractive outside, and now it is ugly. An incomplete tower leaves the W façade lop-sided, while the main doorway boasts only a bad 19C copy of the tympanum (the mutilated original is on the grass by the cloister). The flying buttresses that flank the nave are glumly functional. There is barely a hint of what lies inside, for no other building takes to such an extreme the Romanesque tendency of avoiding exterior drama for an interior drama of light and space, a spiritual world separate from the ordinary world though entered from it.

In sober fact, the history of Vézelay shows it thoroughly implicated in the strife and corruption of the ordinary world. The community originated in the religious house Girart de Roussillon and his wife Berthe founded at St-Père between 855 and 859. A Norman attack in 887 drove the monks, who had soon replaced the original nuns, up the hill to the former Celtic oppidum of Vercellas or Vercelai. Here they remained, subject to the Benedictine rule but resisting the clerical authority of the bishops of Autun over their church and the secular authority of the counts of Nevers over their lands. From the early 11C they claimed to hold the relics of Mary Magdalen, changing the dedication of their church from Notre-Dame to Ste-Madeleine in 1050 and working hard to promote the legend that she had fled from Palestine to Provence with Lazarus, Martha and two other Marys, the wife of Cleophas and the mother of James. Patron saint of penitent sinners, protectress of the weak and the oppressed, Mary Magdalen held a popular appeal that made Vézelay one of the most important shrines of its day. The guidebook for Compostela pilgrims by Aymery Picaud, chaplain of nearby Asquins, sung the praises of La Madeleine loud enough to establish it also as a major assembly point on the route to Santiago. St Bernard's sermon in 1146 forged a link with the Crusades, strengthened when Richard Coeur de Lion and Philippe Auguste of France met at Vézelay for the Third Crusade in 1190 and when St Louis (Louis IX) paid the last of several visits in order to pray for St Mary Magdalen's help shortly before his final crusade in 1270. Vézelay's political importance made it the obvious place for the exiled Thomas à Becket to deliver his sermon threatening Henry II with excommunication in 1166.

The papacy acknowledged the Vézelay relics in 1058 and reaffirmed their authenticity in 1103, official support that emboldened later abbots to claim they had the bodies of Martha and Lazarus as well. But St-Maximin of Provence never gave up its rival claim to Mary Magdalen, revived by the convenient rediscovery of relics there in 1279. The papal bull of 1295 ruling

La Madeleine, Vézelay

in Provence's favour spelled the end of Vézelay's short but spectacular period of glory.

One result was to confine the building of the church to a brief span that coincided largely with the flowering of Cluniac Romanesque and with the years when Vézelay, never faithful in its allegiance, came under the influence of Cluny. The popularity of Mary Magdalen's relics also assured that the church was designed not just for monastic use but as a great spectacle to greet pilgrims who made their way up the hill. Abbot Artaud began to replace the Carolingian church with a new choir and ambulatory about 1096, but his ruthless imposition of taxes to pay for the work made the Vézeliens rise up and murder him in 1105. His successor Renaud, a great-nephew of Hugues of Cluny, met with a different check when the Carolingian nave burnt down in 1120 (killing over 1000 people, claimed a chronicler in an age notoriously fond of exaggerating numbers). A medallion over the third arch on the S side of the present nave records the disaster, together with the promise that 'Though blackened with smoke now, I shall later become beautiful'. This new nave was apparently complete by 1140, and the narthex added to the W end during the next two decades. A new Gothic choir begun about 1185 marked the last phase of rebuilding.

Ambitiously conceived and carried out only in the face of recurrent disaster, the church then sank into decline. The canons regular who replaced the Benedictines in 1537 enjoyed no better relations with the local community than their predecessors, if only because of the rise of Protestantism. Vézelay—the birthplace of Calvin's follower Théodore de Bèze in 1519—had become the seat of a Calvinist community by the middle of the century. The Huguenots attacked the church in 1568 and again the following year. The Revolutionaries suppressed the chapter, mutilated the statues and tympanum on the W façade and demolished virtually all the surviving abbey buildings. Fire struck the church again in 1819 and it was little more than a shell when Prosper Mérimée, Inspector of the Commission on Historic Monuments, gave the job of restoring it to the young Viollet-le-Duc in 1840.

His work, stretching over twenty years and failing only to rescue the W façade, made Vézelay live again. Its renewal attracted admiring visitors from Proust, Claudel and Éluard onwards and has made the village the home (if sometimes only briefly or for the summer) of artists and intellectuals: not just Romain Rolland but the architects Jean Badovici and Le Corbusier, the painter Fernand Léger, the art collectors Yvonne and Christian Dervos, and the writers Georges Bataille, Maurice Clavel, Max-Pol Fouchet and Jules Roy (author of the excellent 'Vézelay, ou l'amour fou').

A detailed tour should start at the central doorway of the three leading from the narthex into the nave. The tympanum does not show the Last Judgement: that appears on the W doorway outside. The theme here is Pentecost, the Word and Spirit spreading throughout the world from the central figure of Christ in Majesty (marked 1 on the accompanying diagram). He is not the severe judge of Gislebertus' tympanum at Autun, but a dynamic figure, his robes a great vortex from which the Pentecostal wind blows, ruffling the hems of garments throughout the design. His huge hands reach far beyond the edge of the mandorla, over the Apostles (2) grouped in threes on either side. St Peter, on Christ's right hand, holds not just the customary key but also a book, as the other Apostles do: tangible embodiment of their mission in spreading the Word. The water and foliage above their heads (3 and 4) must surely be the River and Tree of Life from the last chapter of the Book of Revelation which promise 'the healing of nations'.

In the first of the inset panels two figures, now headless but presumably Apostles or Evangelists, sit writing (5). They begin a sequence depicting the nations of the world—known, half-known and fabulous—whom the Word can reach: Jews (6), Cappadocians looking like Siamese twins (7), Arabs and Cynocephali, or people with dogs' heads (8); and then, more doubtfully, Ethiopians with big noses (9), Phrygians (10), Byzantines (11) and Armenians (12). The theme continues on the lintel below. Its left-hand panel (13) shows what look like Scythians, holding bows and arrows, and Romans or possibly Jews leading a sacrificial animal. The right-hand panel (14) has a bizarre cavalcade of giants, pygmies—one using a ladder to

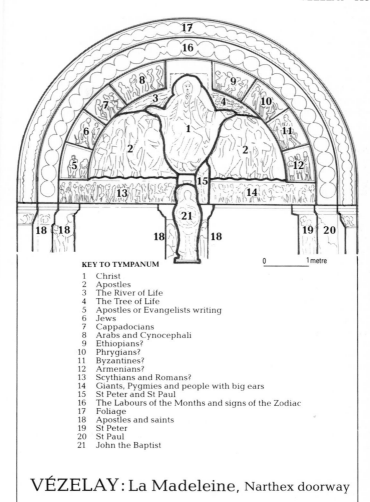

KEY TO TYMPANUM

1 Christ
2 Apostles
3 The River of Life
4 The Tree of Life
5 Apostles or Evangelists writing
6 Jews
7 Cappadocians
8 Arabs and Cynocephali
9 Ethiopians?
10 Phrygians?
11 Byzantines?
12 Armenians?
13 Scythians and Romans?
14 Giants, Pygmies and people with big ears
15 St Peter and St Paul
16 The Labours of the Months and signs of the Zodiac
17 Foliage
18 Apostles and saints
19 St Peter
20 St Paul
21 John the Baptist

0 _____ 1 metre

VÉZELAY: La Madeleine, Narthex doorway

mount his horse—and people with big ears. Though they stand where the damned do in a Last Judgement, they are not contemptible grotesques: the people with big ears make a touching family group, and all the monsters head confidently towards the centre of the lintel where St Peter and St Paul (15) wait near the feet of Christ to gather them into the universal Church.

The arch above (16) is filled with medallions showing the Labours of the Months and the signs of the Zodiac, except for the cryptic trio of a dog, an acrobat and a siren immediately above Christ's head. They are all contorted into circles, and it has been suggested they represent man's eternal folly in contrast to the eternity promised by Christ on the tympanum. The outer arch (17) has foliage. Among the Apostles and saints (18) on the capitals below the lintel St Peter and St Paul appear yet again, in conversation with each other (19 and 20). On the central pillar John the Baptist (21) holds a mutilated Paschal Lamb on a salver, an emblem appropriate to Pentecost, or Passover, and to the saint sent to announce the Lamb of God to mankind.

The smaller doorways on either side are devoted to scenes from the life of Christ. The doorway to the right shows the Incarnation, with the Annunciation and Nativity on its lower register and the Adoration of the Magi above. The doorway to the left shows the Resurrection, with the encounter on the road to Emmaus below an Ascension in which the delicately wind-blown robes echo the central tympanum.

The vista from the narthex down the nave to the radiant whiteness of the apse is among the most breathtaking any European church can boast. The effect owes a good deal just to the stone, for at Vézelay ambition and the sense of drama began in the daring choice of building materials. The builders of the nave went to the quarry at nearby Tharoiseau or at Mailly-la-Ville on the Yonne for a limestone marvellously responsive to light, the slightest change bringing out its rosy tint, buff patches and brown speckles, and accentuating the brown and white banding on the arches of the central vault—a Moorish touch that made Proust find La Madeleine a lovely Christian mosque. For the choir they chose a pure white limestone from Coutarnoux, near l'Isle-sur-Serein. It says much for eclecticism of the church that it can so effortlessly embrace such different stones, just as it can reconcile the delicate Île-de-France Gothic of the choir with the Romanesque of the nave.

Eclecticism, indeed, is the keynote of a church whose main doorway accepts and celebrates the world's variety. The sculptural detail there and on the capitals announces the presence of the Cluny atelier, but for the elevation of the nave the builders ignored Cluny III, the model for Paray-le-Monial and Autun cathedral, and followed instead the example of Anzy-le-Duc in the Brionnais. (It is probably no accident that Renaud came from Semur-en-Brionnais, or that the Vézelay narthex is developed from the narthex at Perrecy-les-Forges, which is clearly the work of Brionnais masons.) Engaged columns replace fluted pilasters. Above the round arches of the arcade, the false triforium has been suppressed in favour of a tall clerestory. The transverse arches of the central vault are not pointed but rounded, and the bays they divide have quadripartite groin-vaulting not barrel-vaulting. These are the ingredients from which Kenneth Conant has traced the Cistercian Gothic pioneered at Fontenay and Pontigny.

Yet in La Madeleine the effect is utterly unlike the severity of Cistercian architecture. If nothing else, there are the capitals: well over 100 in nave and narthex together, some simply showing foliage but a large proportion of them historiated. The accompanying ground-plan gives details. Seven copies and one new design in the nave, as well as most of the smaller capitals on the tribune of the narthex, date from Viollet-le-Duc's restoration; the mutilated originals are preserved in the monks' dormitory above the chapter house. A few capitals (38, 42 and some foliage designs) are reused older work of a slightly different size; their subjects turn up again elsewhere in the nave, just as subjects from the nave are repeated later in the narthex. Experts have distinguished the hands of five different masons in the nave: the master of the tympanum can be identified among them, though Gislebertus of Autun, whom there is good reason to place at Vézelay, remains elusive.

The life of Christ, so movingly portrayed at Saulieu and by Gislebertus at

Autun, is strikingly absent (as if, says Raymond Oursel, the great figure on the tympanum was enough). More surprising is the fact that Mary Magdalen appears only once, in the narthex (13), though she was often the subject of 13C glass in Burgundy (at Semur, for example). Otherwise, even a brief introduction to the most striking capitals on the S and N sides of the nave reveals a wide range of subjects. The rape of Ganymede (16) and the education of Achilles (21) may reflect the classical learning of Pierre le Vénérable, regent of the monastery school at Vézelay before he became abbot of Cluny in 1122, in whose theology some find a source for the compassionate theme of the tympanum. Near by is the 'Mystic Mill' (23), apparently by the master of the tympanum, showing two men at work with a corn mill. The nickname urges an allegorical reading: Moses pours the corn of the Old Law into a mill representing Christ, and St Paul collects the refined flour of the New Law. This, certainly, is what Suger meant by the similar design he prepared for one of his window medallions at St-Denis; Renaissance artists would later substitute a winepress for the mill. Here, the mill is indeed marked with a cross and the man holding the bag is half-bald, the identifying feature of St Paul conventional in medieval art. Yet the stress on allegory falsifies the character of Romanesque carving and fails to dwell on the beautifully naturalistic observation of the two calm, self-absorbed workmen, with the receding chins and beards characteristic of Burgundian Romanesque sculpture. The parable of Dives and Lazarus (24), one of surprisingly few New Testament subjects, is treated with compact force: devils wrench out the soul of the dying Rich Man, while on one side of him the Poor Man's soul is transported to Heaven as a new-born baby in a mandorla and, on the other, gathered to Abraham's bosom.

Saints' legends and the Old Testament are the most frequent sources: note, on the S side of the nave, St Martin protecting himself with the sign of the cross from the tree which a pagan is chopping down (30) and a charming Daniel in the Lions' Den (31), the later of the two capitals to treat the subject. The masons' knowledge extends to St Eugenia or Eugénie (49), who entered a monastery disguised as a man but answered a charge of sexual assault by baring her breasts; her relics are preserved at Varzy (Route 18) on the Compostela route towards Nevers and La Charité. Notice, too, a preoccupation with the hermits St Antony and St Paul, claimed as pioneers of western monasticism: they twice share a meal together (46 and, in the narthex, 2), while elsewhere St Antony watches lions digging St Paul's grave (51, a 19C copy).

This portrait of man at harmony with animals hints at the same vision of nature expressed in the image of Daniel sitting secure inside his mandorla flanked by very meek lions and, indeed, in the fond, appreciative observation of animals and plants throughout La Madeleine. Yet such tenderness is only one aspect of a sensibility which also finds the world thronged with devils, monsters and beasts that attack men at every turn, ever present spiritual danger embodied as immediate, physical threat. The two views of nature confront each other directly in the superb basilisk and grasshopper (50). This capital stands near a group of Old Testament subjects, perhaps the most clearly defined group in the church and certainly the most savage, preoccupied with retributive violence and, particularly, beheading: David ordering the execution of Agag for the murder of Saul (48); the Exterminating Angel killing Pharoah's son (52); Moses and the Golden Calf, with a splendid devil coming out of the idol's mouth (53); the death of Absalom (56); David and Goliath (58); and Moses killing the Egyptian slavedriver (59).

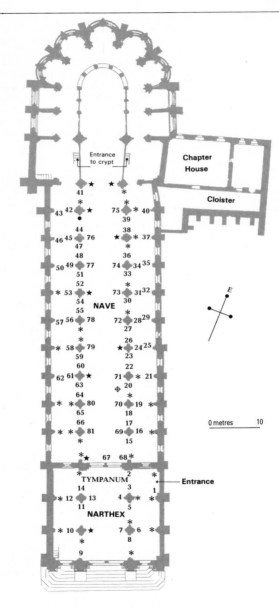

VÉZELAY : La Madeleine

KEY TO PLAN

- * foliage
- • 19C copy of foliage
- ★ foliage at upper level
- ⊕ medallion on arcade commemorating fire

Narthex

1 Beheading of John the Baptist (see also 11)
2 The hermits St Antony and St Paul sharing a meal (see also 46)
3 Temptation of St Benedict (see also 36)
4 Death of Cain (see also 26)
5 St Peter and St Paul
6 Isaac blessing Jacob (see also 34)
7 (upper level) 19C copy of a dragon and woman (Satan and the Church from Revelation?)
8 Joseph and Potiphar's wife (see also 74)
9 Two men eating grapes
10 Samson wrestling the lion
11 John the Baptist (see also 1)
12 Nathan rebuking David for his adultery with Bathsheba
13 St Mary Magdalen and (?) the Princess of Provence
14 St Benedict restoring a child to life

Nave: lower level of arcade and aisles

15 Humans fighting monsters
16 Ganymede raped by Zeus in the guise of an eagle
17 Unfinished 19C copy of animals playing music
18 Duel
19 Lust and despair
20 Conversion of St Eustace (or St Hubert)
21 Education of Achilles by Chiron the centaur
22 Libra (scales) and Gemini (twins)
23 The 'Mystic Mill'
24 Death of Lazarus and Dives
25 Not satisfactorily identified: council meeting?
26 Death of Cain (see also 4)
27 Not satisfactorily identified: Four Winds? Beekeepers?
28 David subduing a lion
29 Teachers and students?
30 St Martin stopping a tree falling with the sign of the Cross
31 Daniel in the Lions' Den (see also 38)
32 Profane music
33 Jacob wrestling with the Angel
34 Isaac blessing Jacob (see also 6)
35 Unidentified
36 Temptation of St Benedict (see also 3)
37 The Four Rivers of Paradise
38 Daniel in the Lions' Den (see also 31)
39 Lions
40 19C copy of animals worshipping the Cross (?)

41 St Peter freed from prison by the Angel
42 Adam and Eve (see also 79)
43 19C copy of the angel Raphael defeating the devil Asmodeus
44 19C copy of Temptation of St Antony
45 Vision of St Antony
46 The hermits St Antony and St Paul sharing a meal (see also 2)
47 Birds and grapes
48 David ordering the execution of Agag for killing Saul
49 Legend of St Eugenia
50 Basilisk and grasshopper
51 19C copy of St Antony watching lions dig the grave of his fellow hermit St Paul
52 The Exterminating Angel killing Pharaoh's son
53 Moses and the Golden Calf
54 Demons fighting
55 Elephants
56 Death of Absalom
57 Dives' feast
58 David and Goliath
59 Moses killing the Egyptian slavedriver
60 Summer and winter?
61 Lions
62 Birds
63 19C capital by Viollet-le-Duc of Judith and Holophernes
64 Avarice and Calumny being punished
65 Not satisfactorily identified: games?
66 Wisdom and Folly

Nave: upper level

67 Lions fighting
68 Bears and human among foliage
69 Judas hanging himself
70 Absalom killing his brother Amnon
71 Noah building the Ark
72 Martyrdom of St Andocius of Saulieu?
73 Not satisfactorily identified: Joseph before Pharaoh? Ebedmelech winning Jeremiah's freedom from King Zedekiah?
74 Joseph and Potiphar's wife (see also 8)
75 Samson and Delilah
76 Unidentified
77 Warrior fighting a dragon
78 Cain and Abel offering sacrifices
79 Adam and Eve (see also 42)
80 Herodias asking Herod for the head of John the Baptist
81 Pelicans

Beneath the Gothic choir that represents the last phase in the building lies the crypt, originally built in the 9C though refurbished after fire damage in the 12C. It still houses the relics on which the fortunes, indeed the very existence, of the church were based.

12 Round the edge of the Morvan: Avallon to Saulieu and Autun

Directions and distances. Total distance 80km (50 miles). N6 from **Avallon** to (39km) **Saulieu**. D980 to (80km) **Autun**.

Connections with other routes. Avallon is described in Route 11, along N6 from Joigny via Auxerre; it can also be reached by Route 10 along the Serein valley from Joigny. Of the many ways into the heart of the Morvan (Route 13) from this route, Avallon itself, Rouvray and Saulieu are particularly convenient. Saulieu is also the starting point of Route 14 and Autun of Route 15, both going to Chalon or Beaune.

From **Avallon** N6 follows the Via Agrippa around the edge of the Morvan to (39km) Saulieu. At 14.5km it slices through **Ste-Magnance**, a village which takes its name from Magnentia, one of the women followers who brought St Germanus' body back from Ravenna to Auxerre in 448 but herself died on the journey. The church contains her beautifully carved 12C *tomb. One of its panels depicts the sleeping pilgrim to whom she appeared in the 7C, rescuing him from a poisonous snake and prompting him to discover the whereabouts of her remains. 3km further, N6 bypasses the pleasant village of **Rouvray**, which offers a useful way into the Morvan via St-Léger-Vauban (Route 13). 4.5km beyond Rouvray D70 branches left on a switchback route through the Auxois via Précy-sous-Thil to Vitteaux (Route 4). **La Roche-en-Brénil** (890 people), 5km further along N6, has a 17–18C château (not open) on the site of its medieval predecessor. Curious rock formations sometimes identified as menhirs dot the countryside in this corner of the Morvan, known locally as **La Suisse Morvandelle**.

SAULIEU (2900 Sédélociens; Tourist Information) was the Gallo-Roman Sidolocum, or Siduolocum, on the Via Agrippa and later a staging post on the Paris–Lyon coach road. Its reputation for food was well established by the 18C and restaurants still line the Rue d'Argentine, as the N6 is called on its way through the town. The most famous is the Côte d'Or, where the master chef Alexandre Dumaine entertained Pétain, de Gaulle and Lattre de Tassigny (though not at the same time).

Despite the mutilations it has suffered, **St-Andoche keeps capitals that rank with the best Romanesque work in Burgundy. It commemorates Andochios (Andoche) and Thyrsos (Thyrse), missionaries from the East martyred in about 177 with Felix (Félix), a local inhabitant who had sheltered them. Their relics were attracting pilgrims by the 5C and an abbey had been founded on the site by the 8C. It later became a dependency of the bishop of Autun and so lay within Cluny's sphere of influence when the Carolingian basilica was replaced during the first half of the 12C. The common assertion that the new Romanesque church was ready for consecration in 1119 springs from a misreading of the medieval sources: work probably did not begin until about 1125 and may have continued until about 1150. The E end was burnt by the English during the Hundred Years

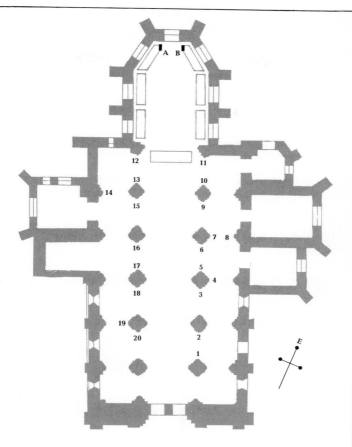

KEY TO PLAN

0 metres   10

Capitals

1   Winged serpents
2   The risen Christ appearing
    to Mary Magdalen
3   Judas hanging himself
4   Eagles
5   Acanthus leaves and
    grotesque heads
6   The Flight into Egypt
7   Fighting cocks
8   Acanthus leaves and
    monsters' heads
9   Pastoral scene
10   Owls and acanthus leaves
11   Fern leaves

12   Fern leaves
13   Wolf and acanthus leaves
14   Centaur
15   Doves and acanthus leaves
16   Fighting boars
17   Alder tree
18   The First Temptation
     of Christ
19   Bees on flowers
20   Balaam

Bench ends

A   Flight into Egypt
B   Annunciation

SAULIEU : St-Andoche

'Balaam and his Ass': a capital in St-Andoche, Saulieu

War and, with the transepts, rebuilt in the 18C. At the W end, where the N
tower had already been given an 18C Italianate dome, a pupil of Viollet-
le-Duc replaced the doorway and its tympanum with a lifeless but
apparently faithful copy in 1869.

These unhappy changes have left the nave untouched, with an elevation
and a superb set of capitals announcing the presence of the Cluny atelier.
Even the simplest subjects among the more than 50 carvings show workmanship of the highest order. Note, for example, the owls in the S arcade
(marked 10 on the accompanying ground plan), the lucid designs of fern
leaves at the entrance to the choir (11 and 12) and the alder tree in the N

arcade (17). Note, too, the witty invention of the pastoral scene (9) in which a shepherd makes music for two dancing goats, watched by a wolf and a bear. Inevitably it is the five biblical scenes that most absorb attention: the risen Christ appearing to Mary Magdalen (2), Judas hanging himself (3), the Flight into Egypt (6), the First Temptation of Christ (18) and the false prophet Balaam and his ass being waylaid by the angel (20). They are clearly by the same hand, and though the subjects are not systematically chosen, all appear again in St-Lazare at Autun. No additional evidence survives to shed light on the link between the two churches—even the dating of St-Andoche is conjectural—and to show whether the Master of Saulieu was pupil, colleague or merely contemporary of Gislebertus. His suicide of Judas lacks the unfettered savagery and his risen Christ the expressive delicacy of Gislebertus' treatment. Such effects lie outside his range, though not the subtlety of design that makes his Temptation of Christ echo both the customary portrayal of the Temptation of Eve and, more immediately, the alder tree on the opposite face of the same pillar. His métier is the homely tenderness that informs his two undoubted masterpieces, the Flight into Egypt and Balaam. In the first, the ass which carries a stylised infant Christ on its back and picks its way across a stylised design of ornamental rocks is itself a triumph of affectionately realistic observation. So too is the ass on which Balaam sits, the speaking centre of a drama that beautifully combines wonderment with humour.

Among the later furnishings of the church, the 14C carved stalls that survive in the 18C choir deserve attention. The Flight into Egypt appears, with an Annunciation, on the panels at the E end.

The **Musée** in the 17C house next to the church has a rather dowdy collection which nevertheless includes some interesting Gallo-Roman stelae and ex-votos; fragments of Romanesque work from St-Andoche; and a room devoted to the sculptor François Pompon (1855–1933), a native of Saulieu, whose deceptively simple animal studies are also well represented in the Musée des Beaux-Arts at Dijon. His grave lies in the churchyard of **St-Saturnin** to the S. Pompon made the bronze bull which stands near the Place de Charles-de-Gaulle at the N end of the Rue d'Argentine, a fitting emblem for a lively market town which holds a Charolais festival each August.

Route 14 follows N6 from Saulieu via Arnay-le-Duc to Chalon or Beaune. The present route heads due S, where D980 continues the course of the Via Agrippa to Autun. The little **Ternin Valley** to the W makes a pleasant alternative for the first 17km of the way. At 4km it passes the **Lac de Chamboux**, newest (1985) and smallest (185 acres) of the Morvan reservoirs, and, just before rejoining D980, the turning for **Ménessaire**, where the largely 17C château (open) has medieval corner towers and a polychrome roof. The name of **Pierre-Écrite**, 10km S of Saulieu on D980, refers to the weather-beaten Roman stele which stands under a tree in the main street of the village. A nearby plaque marks the former coaching inn where Napoléon stopped on his way back from Elba to Paris in March 1815. The name of (14km) **Lucenay-l'Évêque** remembers that it was once a staging post for the bishops of Autun on their journeys to Sens. The rest of the way to Autun (another 17km) is uneventful.

*AUTUN (17,910 Autunois; Tourist Information) stands on the flank of a hill watered by the Arroux, a site chosen by the Romans to replace Bibracte, the Aedui capital on Mont Beuvray in the fastness of the Morvan to the W. The Emperor Augustus founded it in the late 1C BC—hence its original name, Augustodunum Aeduorum—and planned the 6km circuit of walls

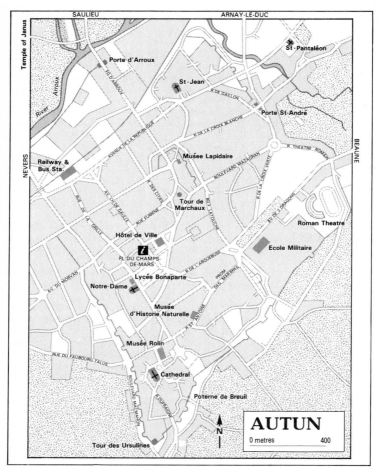

that enclosed it a hundred years later, pierced by monumental gates at the four main points of the compass. The third largest city in Gaul after Augusta Treverorum (Trier) and Nemausus (Nîmes), Augustodonum grew at the height of its power to a population of perhaps 80,000. A city of learning rather than a military or administrative centre, it was known particularly for the schools of rhetoric which helped win it a reputation as 'soror et aemula Romae', the sister and rival of Rome herself. From 270 onwards it suffered the civil disturbances and barbarian invasions that went with the decline of Roman power. The Frankish victory over Gondomar, king of the Burgundiones, at Autun in 534 marked the end of the first kingdom of Burgundy, and the collapse of Merovingian power in the 8C left the city at the mercy of the Saracens. By the Middle Ages its population had shrunk to only a tenth of its former size. By this time, too, the city had divided into a lower and upper town: the commercial Quartier Marchaux in the N and, in the S angle of the fortifications, the citadel with the cathedral that was its chief remaining claim to greatness.

Autun has never regained its ancient importance, or even its ancient size, but keeps some fine Gallo-Roman remains and a Romanesque cathedral, St-Lazare, whose sculpture is one of the great glories of Burgundy. Many tourists simply head straight for St-Lazare and the nearby Musée Rolin. Those who want to take a more leisurely approach to a city which requires but rewards patience can start by driving round the outskirts where the surviving gates and walls of Augustodunum stand.

Following the course of the Via Agrippa, the road from Saulieu leads directly to the **Porte d'Arroux**, the old Porta Senonica or Sens Gate, with two arches for vehicles and two for foot passengers still straddling the roadway and pavements. Its upper gallery has pilasters with Corinthian capitals that provided local inspiration for the purity of the Cluniac work in the cathedral. Beyond the other side of the Arroux to the W is the so-called **Temple de Janus**, the surviving corner of a square tower which was indeed a temple but apparently dedicated to Mars rather than Janus. Beyond the gate the Faubourg d'Arroux continues to the Avenue de la République, where a left turn leads to the chain of roads which mark the course of the walls down the E side of the town. The first landmark is the heavily restored **Porte St-André**, the Porta Lingonensis or Langres Gate, built to the same plan as the Porte d'Arroux but without the same delicate upper gallery. The martyrdom of St Symphorian is supposed to have taken place here in the 2C or 3C. The gate was originally flanked by round towers, one of which survives as the core of the chapel of **St-André**, now a Protestant church, which contains fragments of late 12C–early 13C wall paintings of the Labours of the Months. To the S lie the rebuilt remains of the **Roman Theatre** which was among the largest in Gaul, capable of holding 12,000 spectators. A historical spectacle, 'Il était une fois Augustodunum', is staged here each summer. Among the local buildings for which stone was pillaged from the theatre is the nearby 17C **Lycée Militaire**, with its polychrome tile roof.

Fragments of the walls line the way down to the S tip of the old town. Before this is reached, the Rue du Faubourg-St-Pancrace leads SE to (about 1km) the **Pierre de Couhard**, a 1C funeral monument or cenotaph, now eroded to an irregular pyramid, built well outside the Gallo-Roman city. Not particularly expressive in itself, it commands a splendid view, the first on this tour so far to show how well the Romans chose the site for their city. The spire of the cathedral rises above the walls which still mark a sharp division between the city and open farmland. Though only a few minutes' drive from the centre, the hamlet of Couhard is an agreeably rural spot with a little river leading to a waterfall.

At the S tip of the walls stands the **Tour des Ursulines**, a 12C tower on a Roman base, named after the nunnery it housed from the 17C. A particularly impressive stretch of the walls, reused in the Middle Ages, lines the neighbouring Boulevard MacMahon. It encloses the network of pleasant old streets that makes up the cathedral quarter, entered from the W by the Rue Cocand and from the E by the handsome Rue Dufraigne or the picturesque little **Poterne de Breuil**. All lead eventually to the Place St-Louis, with its charming Renaissance fountain. Law Courts and the Bishop's Palace flank the E side.

The cathedral of * *St-Lazare** was begun by Bishop Étienne de Bâgé in about 1120 to house the relics of Lazarus acquired from Marseille some forty years earlier. It rose next to the old cathedral of St-Nazaire (founded in the 5C) and usurped its functions by degrees until St-Nazaire was eventually demolished in the 18C. St-Lazare was consecrated in 1130 and the relics installed beneath its high altar in 1146, though neither date marked the end of building work. It officially became the cathedral in 1195. Externally, it lost most of its Romanesque look with Cardinal-Bishop Rolin's Flamboyant additions in the 1470s: the central tower and spire which make so prominent a landmark, the upper level of the choir, and the side-chapels flanking the nave. In the 1860s Viollet-le-Duc supervised rebuilding of the W towers in a scholarly imitation of Paray-le-Monial.

Étienne was an ally and disciple of Cluny, so his church was close to the source of Burgundy's great Romanesque achievements. Given the changes St-Lazare has suffered, it is lucky that so much original work survives, either in the cathedral itself or as fragments in the nearby Musée Rolin. Most of the sculpture is by one man: Gislebertus, who apparently came to Autun in 1130–1140 from Cluny by way of Vézelay. His signature boldly interrupts the mottoes running along the upper edge of the lintel over the W doorway: 'GISLEBERTVS HOC FECIT'.

This is where a visit should start. Gislebertus' tympanum treats its subject, the Last Judgement, with an ambition and dramatic detail that makes it, in Malraux's phrase, 'an epic of Western Christendom'. The centre of the composition is Christ in Majesty (marked 1 on the accompanying diagram): a huge, static figure with palms outstretched beyond the edges of a mandorla supported by four angels (2). His head, knocked off when the sculpture was plastered over in 1766 after Voltaire's jibes against its crudity, was identified and replaced in 1948 by the cleric and scholar Denis Grivot. The aloof stare and severe pose, utterly unlike the dynamic figure in swirling robes on the Vézelay tympanum, set the cue for the theme of Judgement announced by the sun and moon on either side of his halo (3) and the four angels blowing trumpets at the edges of the tympanum (4), like the four angels standing at the corners of the earth in the Book of Revelation. The text on the rim of the mandorla spells it out: 'OMNIA DISPONO SOLVS MERITOSQUE CORONO QVOS SCELVS EXERCET ME JVDICE POENA COERCET' ('I alone dispose of all things and crown the just. As judge I punish those whom crime leads').

On the lintel below, another angel (5) segregates the dead rising from their tombs into the saved (6) and the damned (7). The saved, symbolically placed on Christ's right, gesture and aspire upwards, while the damned bend or look down, deformed by misery. Together, they make a richly particularised cavalcade of medieval life. Note among the saved (from the spectator's left to right) the two bishops with their crosiers, the angel tenderly shepherding three children, and the pilgrims wearing the Jerusalem cross and the cockleshell of St James on their wallets. The disorderly parade of the damned includes a miser clutching his money bag, a poor fellow with his head gripped by huge talons and a woman with serpents attacking her breasts. (Lust is female in medieval art: note also the capital inside labelled 25.) The last but one figure on the right, holding what looks like a barrel marked with the Cross, has been variously identified as a drunkard or a Jew with Eucharistic Host and knife, a touch that would be in keeping with medieval anti-Semitism.

The motto on the edge of the lintel above the saved reads: 'QVISQVE RESVRGET ITA QVEM NON TRAHIT IMPIA VITA ET LVCEBIT EI SINE FINE LVCERNA DIEI' ('Thus he who does not lead an impious life shall rise again, and the light of day shall shine for him without end'). The

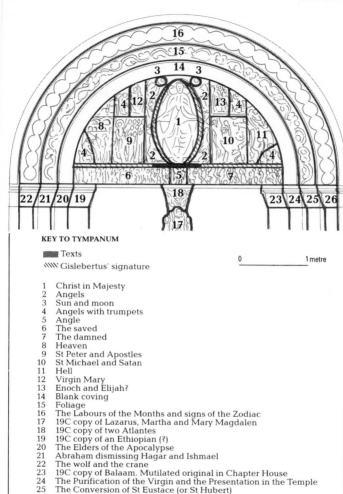

KEY TO TYMPANUM

▨ Texts
〰〰 Gislebertus' signature

0   1 metre

1   Christ in Majesty
2   Angels
3   Sun and moon
4   Angels with trumpets
5   Angle
6   The saved
7   The damned
8   Heaven
9   St Peter and Apostles
10   St Michael and Satan
11   Hell
12   Virgin Mary
13   Enoch and Elijah?
14   Blank coving
15   Foliage
16   The Labours of the Months and signs of the Zodiac
17   19C copy of Lazarus, Martha and Mary Magdalen
18   19C copy of two Atlantes
19   19C copy of an Ethiopian (?)
20   The Elders of the Apocalypse
21   Abraham dismissing Hagar and Ishmael
22   The wolf and the crane
23   19C copy of Balaam. Mutilated original in Chapter House
24   The Purification of the Virgin and the Presentation in the Temple
25   The Conversion of St Eustace (or St Hubert)
26   St Jerome

AUTUN : St-Lazare, West doorway

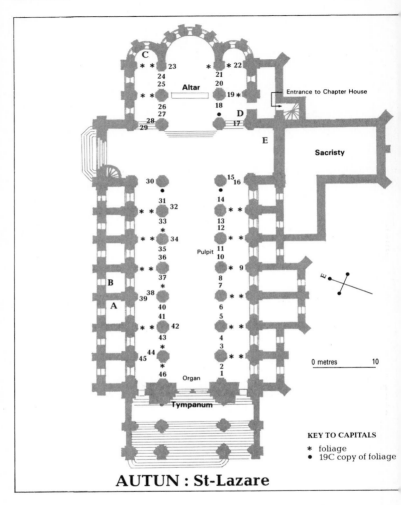

AUTUN : St-Lazare

KEY TO CAPITALS

* foliage
● 19C copy of foliage

promise is fulfilled on the tympanum immediately above, where the souls of the saved enter the narrow gate of Heaven (8). As usual in medieval art, they are portrayed as new-born babies. Note, too, that Heaven is represented by Romanesque arches with miniature carved capitals: capitals appear on capitals several times inside the church, a typically witty detail. St Peter, with his key, stands flanked by the other Apostles (9). Their place in the design may symbolise their power to intercede with Christ on behalf of man; their size, larger than ordinary humans but smaller than Christ, certainly expresses their spiritual rank.

The statuesque calm of this scene, emphasised by the elongated figures of the Apostles, contrasts with the turmoil on the corresponding register to

KEY TO PLAN

1   Devil with fork
2   Man fighting a griffin
3   St Vincent's body guarded from wild animals by birds
4   Nebuchadnezzar's Dream?
5   Simon Magus falling
6   Simon Magus trying to fly
7   The Fourth Tone of Music
8   Christ washing the Apostles' feet. Not by Gislebertus
9   Moses and the Golden Calf
10 Samson wrestling the lion. Not by Gislebertus
11 St Stephen being stoned to death
12 Samson pulling down the temple
13 Noah's Ark on Mount Ararat
14 19C copy of Charity, with chalice, above Greed and Patience (or Hope)
    and Anger (or Despair).   Original in Chapter House
15 19C copy of God asking Cain, 'Where is Abel thy brother?'. Original in
    Chapter House
16 19C copy of Judas hanging himself. Original in Chapter House
17 19C copy of a fight with a basilisk. Original in Chapter House
18 19C copy of a bird with three heads. Original in Chapter House
19 19C copy of a man riding a bird. Original in Chapter House
20 The Emperor Constantine triumphing over a pagan?
21 The first Temptation of Christ. Restored in stucco
22 Faun and siren
23 The Four Rivers of Paradise. Restored in stucco
24 The risen Christ appearing on the road to Emmaus? Restored in stucco
25 Lust. Restored in stucco
26 19C copy of the Flight into Egypt. Original in Chapter House
27 Original position of the Dream of the Magi, now in Chapter House
28 Original position of the Magi before Herod, now in Chapter House
29 19C copy of the Adoration of the Magi. Original in Chapter House
30 19C copy of the presentation of the Church, with bishop Etienne.
    Original in Chapter House
31 19C copy of the Death of Cain. Original in Chapter House
32 (upper level) The Annunciation to St Joseph
33 The Tree of Jesse
34 (upper level) Ball players?
35 The risen Christ appearing to Mary Magdalen
36 Daniel in the Lions' Den
37 The second Temptation of Christ
38 The Conversion and Baptism of St Paul
39 Cockfight
40 St Peter freed from prison by the angel
41 The three Hebrews in the fiery furnace
42 (upper level) Lions fighting
43 The Annunciation to St Anne
44 Abraham preparing to sacrifice Isaac
45 The Nativity
46 Devil and snake

A Ingres' Martyrdom of St Symphorian; **B** Tree of Jesse window;
C Statue of Virgin and Child; **D** Jeannin monument; **E** Flamboyant doorway

Christ's left (10). The motto on the lintel edge below reads: 'TERREAT HIC TERROR QVOS TERREVS ALLIGAT ERROR NAM FORE SIC VERVM NOTAT HIC HORROR SPECIERVM' ('Here let fear strike those whom earthly error binds, for the horror of these images proclaims their future fate'). St Michael and Satan weigh souls in the balance; a three-headed serpent twines round Satan's leg, while an assisting devil carries a toad. In the corner the damned are stuffed into the jaws and flaming cauldron of Hell (11).

Above these scenes of salvation and damnation sit, respectively, the Virgin Mary (12) and two figures usually identified as the prophets Enoch and Elijah (13), who like the Virgin entered Heaven without dying.

'The Dream of the Magi': one of Gislebertus' capitals in St-Lazare, Autun

The blank inner arch above the tympanum (14) was originally decorated. The next (15) is carved with foliage, the outer arch (16) with medallions showing the signs of the Zodiac and the Labours of the Months, a delicately realised sequence of rural vignettes. At the apex sits a new-born baby representing the New Year.

The sculpture beneath the lintel is much less interesting. The figures of Lazarus with his sisters Martha and Mary Magdalen on the central pillar (17) and several of the capitals are 19C copies. But note among the original capitals the wolf and the crane from Aesop's fable (22) and St Jerome taking the thorn from the lion's paw (26).

Inside, the nave keeps the elevation that makes St-Lazare, like Paray-le-Monial, a direct descendant of Cluny III: three storeys, with a pointed arcade below a round-arched false triforium and clerestory; fluted pilasters; and a pointed barrel vault. Scholars cite the Roman Porte d'Arroux as a local source for the pilasters and triforium. As at Cluny, the aisles are groin vaulted. Only the clutter of side-chapels and the altered upper storeys of the choir mar the restrained purity that makes an ideal foil for the capitals. There are about 100 in all (the accompanying ground-plan gives details) and they repay close attention though, thanks to the side-chapels, the cathedral is often too dark to encourage browsing. If it is, start in the chapter house (reached from the S choir aisle), where some of the best originals are displayed at eye-level and in good light. Viollet-le-Duc removed them and put 19C copies in their place when he strengthened the pillars round the transept crossing.

Experts like Grivot and Zarnecki detect the hand of an earlier school of masons in the now largely mutilated capitals at the lower level of the apse, and they do not doubt that assistants helped carve many of the foliage capitals which make up more than half the total. But the historiated capitals are apparently from Gislebertus' chisel in all but two cases (8 and 10 on the plan). Nevertheless, the attempt to find iconographic unity quickly sinks into generalities that might be expected to hold true of more or less any sizeable body of medieval art. Some capitals portray, with relish, the monsters and fabulous beasts whose appearance in churches so outraged St Bernard. A few attempt allegory or abstract representation, though not very successfully: the Fourth Tone of Music (7), thought to be copied from Cluny, and the Four Rivers of Paradise (23) are among the few mundane carvings in the building. But most are narrative. They draw on biblical episodes, apocryphal stories added to the Bible and saints' legends, the common stock of medieval knowledge that also nourished the sculptors at Vézelay and particularly at Saulieu, where the choice of subjects is suggestively close to Gislebertus'. Their original audience, versed in both the stories and the narrative conventions for depicting them, would have identified most of the capitals without difficulty. They did not need to be told that the balding man in a barrel is St Paul being baptised (38). Such things now need explanation, like the legend that the body of the marytred St Vincent was protected by birds against the animals of the forest (3); or the career of the false magician Simon Magus, whose failure to fly is watched by a compassionate St Peter and St Paul and a gleeful Devil (5); or the rabbinical legend that, after murdering Abel, Cain was shot in mistake for an animal by the blind archer Lamech, directed by Tubalcain (chapter house). The Nativity scene (45) follows the popular account in the Gospel of the Pseudo-Matthew, as scholars now call it, and shows the Virgin Mary lying in bed while the infant Christ is given a bath by the midwives Zelemie and Salome. The medieval audience would also presumably have noted that when Gislebertus tackles Daniel in the lions' den (36), a favourite subject with Romanesque sculptors, he follows the legend that Habakkuk was flown in by an angel with a bucket of alternative food for the lions. One would like to know what they would have made of details that now puzzle: why, in the Second Temptation of Christ (37), it is the Devil who perches on the gable of the temple, and why, as Abraham prepares to sacrifice his son Isaac (44), the angel carries the ram rather than pointing to it in a nearby thicket.

Yet Gislebertus' fluency with narrative, his confidence in design and his eye for detail assure that a great deal remains easily approachable: the dynamic grouping of the executioners stoning St Stephen (11); the ingenious simplification of buildings and objects in Samson destroying the Temple (12) and Noah's Ark on Mount Ararat (13); and the expressive gesture of the risen Christ ('Noli me tangere') appearing to Mary Magdalen (35).

The capitals in the chapter house show Gislebertus at his best. Judas' suicide, more convincingly savage than its counterpart at Saulieu, echoes the infernal scenes on the tympanum and the fate of Simon Magus in the nave. It contrasts with a tender Christmas group that includes a Flight into Egypt (yet another subject also chosen by the Saulieu Master) and an Adoration of the Magi which adds a sleepy Joseph to the corner of the scene. The masterpiece is probably the Dream of the Magi. Still wearing their crowns, the three kings lie side by side beneath a richly embroidered coverlet, one just woken by the touch of the angel's finger. This is not the artistic naïvety that some scholars still insist on finding in Romanesque sculpture: this is narrative compression of the highest order, and superb design too, instantly effective in its power to explain and its power to move.

Only a few of the later additions to St-Lazare need noticing. The side-chapels off the N aisle of the nave contain a painting by Ingres (1834) of the martyrdom of St Symphorian at the Porte St-André and an early 16C Tree of Jesse window. The chapel on the N side of the choir has a statue of the Virgin and Child by Juan de la Huerta (see Musée Rolin). Near the entrance to the chapter house on the S side of the choir are the kneeling statues of Pierre Jeannin and his wife. (Later one of Henri IV's ambassadors, Jeannin was the president of the Dijon *parlement* who intervened to prevent the St Bartholomew's Day Massacre of Protestants in 1572 spreading to Burgundy. His heart is buried at Chagny.) The S transept has a good Flamboyant doorway.

On the little Rue des Bancs, leading N from the Place St-Louis, the ****Musée Rolin** has an excellent collection of finds from the Gallo-Roman city, Romanesque sculpture from St-Lazare (including work by Gislebertus), and later medieval art. It is well arranged in the pleasant setting of the 19C Hôtel Lacomme and the wing that survives from the *hôtel* built for himself by Nicolas Rolin (1376–1461), Philippe le Bon's chancellor and founder of the Hôtel-Dieu at Beaune.

The Gallo-Roman display on the ground floor of the Hôtel Lacomme conveys a more vividly detailed picture of Augustodunum than any of the Gallo-Roman buildings that still stand in modern Autun. It embraces small everyday objects, funeral monuments, statuettes of both Roman and Celtic deities and several large mosaic fragments. Note particularly the helmet in the shape of a human face surrounded by bay leaves and the bronze three-horned bull.

The Romanesque sculpture is across the courtyard on the ground floor of the Hôtel Rolin. Gislebertus' great 'Temptation of Eve', a portrait of awakening sexuality that strikes an unexpected note in Romanesque art, formed part of the lintel for St-Lazare's N doorway. The lintel was broken up in 1766, when taste also demanded that the W tympanum be plastered over; the other fragments to survive give little idea of the general design. Its near contemporary, the shrine for Lazarus' relics, is better documented, and magnificently represented by the monk Martin's sculptures of Martha, Mary Magdalen and a pensive, attenuated St Andrew. Among other, smaller items is a curious 11–12C head of Christ from the abbey of St-Martin, associated with St Odo.

Upstairs, later medieval art includes a 15C Virgin and Child in painted stone, a very human mother with a swaddled child, popularly known as the 'Virgin of Autun'. It stands near the finest of several paintings, the 'Nativity of Cardinal Rolin' (c 1480) by the Master of Moulins, now usually identified as Jean Hey, in which the donor and his dog figure memorably. It makes an interesting comparison with van Eyck's 'Virgin and Child with Chancellor Rolin' in the Louvre. Jean Rolin, Chancellor Nicolas' son, followed a worldly career in church politics that made him bishop of Autun as well as cardinal; it was he who made the Flamboyant alterations to the cathedral. He is portrayed again in one of three fragments from a painted Entombment and in a statue attributed to Antoine Le Moiturier. A marble St Catherine is one of several items attributed to Juan de la Huerta, who with Le Moiturier carved Jean sans Peur's tomb in the Beaux-Arts at Dijon.

The rest of the collection looks rather pale by comparison. It includes: finds from Bulliot's excavation of Bibracte (Mont Beuvray); carved angels by Jean Dubois; an armoire in the manner of Hugues Sambin; paintings by Sébastien Bourdon, Nicolas Bertin and Horace Vernet; statuettes caricaturing his 19C contemporaries by Jean-Pierre Dantan; and a group of 20C paintings by Maurice Denis.

The **Musée d'Histoire Naturelle**, around the corner from the Musée Rolin on the Rue St-Antoine, has regional collections of geology, palaeontology and fauna; the specimens of European birds include a Great Auk.

The Place du Champ-de-Mars, N of the Musée Rolin by the Petite and Grande Rue Chauchien and the Rue St-Saulge, marks the centre of modern Autun, linking the upper and lower town. The market is held here on Wednesdays and Fridays. On the W side gilded wrought-iron gates guard the entrance to the **Lycée Bonaparte**, founded as a Jesuit college in 1709, though the Jesuits had been expelled before the arrival of Napoléon and his brothers in 1779. Napoléon spent only a few months here, but returned to Autun on his way back from Elba to Paris in March 1815. Burgundians who attended the school include Bussy-Rabutin and Lazare Carnot. The chapel of **Notre-Dame** has an 18C interior. The 19C shopping arcade off the Rue du Général-André-Demetz on the S side of the square has been handsomely restored. The 19C **Hôtel de Ville** on the N side houses a library with Carolingian manuscripts, illuminated manuscripts and early printed books.

The Avenue Charles-de-Gaulle and the Rue Eumène lead N and E to the old and still pleasantly unfashionable Quartier Marchaux, with a 15C tower near the meeting of the Petite Rue and the Grande Rue Marchaux. The chapel and cemetery of the St-Nicolas hospital house the curious **Musée Lapidaire**, an annexe to the Musée Rolin, with a collection of Gallo-Roman capitals, statuary, stelae, pavements and architectural fragments laid out in an effect depressingly like a builders' yard. One post-Roman curiosity is the boat made from a single piece of timber, once thought to be prehistoric but now known to be 15C. The chapel, which embodies two stages of Romanesque work, still has traces of a fresco of Christ in the semi-domed apse. Fragments of the medieval walls which enclosed the quarter, well inside the Roman fortifications, survive on the boulevard beyond the E end.

13 The Morvan

The *Morvan is the stone in the midst of all: a great plateau of granite and forest rising up in the centre of a region where rolling limestone hills and rich farmland are otherwise the norm. Never an administrative unit in its own right—it straddles all four departments of modern Burgundy—the Morvan has a powerful geographical and cultural identity of its own.

An outlier of the igneous and metamorphic rock that makes up the Massif Central, it forms a roughly shaped rectangle about 30km broad and 60km long, rarely level and growing steadily higher in the S to reach its major summits at Haut-Folin (901m), Mont Preneley (855m) and Mont Beuvray (821m). Here, too, the forests that cover more than half the surface of the Morvan grow densest and pine plantations darken the landscape. These woods and hills are a nursing ground for streams and rivers which create waterfalls (like the Saut de Gouloux) or force their way through ravines (like the Gorges de la Canche) before flowing down from the tableland as major arteries for the rest of Burgundy. The Yonne, the Cure and the Cousin all rise in the Morvan. They head N while others, like the Canche and the Ternin, go S.

The lakes that now dot their course are all artificial reservoirs. The oldest, Lac des Settons, was created in the 19C to help *flottage*, the floating of timber from the forests to Clamecy, a gathering point for the rest of the journey downriver to Paris. The other five reservoirs, which range in size from Lac de Pannesière (1285 acres) to the little Lac de Chamboux (185 acres), date from the 1930s onwards and are designed to control seasonal fluctuations in the rivers or supply water to neighouring areas. Several have hydro-electric plants. The growth of tourism has also made them, particularly Lac des Settons, popular centres for outdoor activities and water sports. Tourist literature, however, is unwise in promoting the lakes among the natural beauties of the Morvan, for even the careful landscaping does not take away their artificial look and has succeeded only occasionally in placing them among striking configurations of hills.

Where its mountains are wildest and its forests thickest the Morvan has a dark, secretive atmosphere that well suits the Celtic provenance of its name: the black mountain. Elsewhere, the deciduous trees among the conifers, particularly the lovely oaks and beeches, and the shades of buff, pink, grey and blue in the rock also give it a quiet beauty captured by the subdued palette of Corot. Yet nowhere does the soil offer an easy means of livelihood: the Morvan has always been poor and sparsely populated, despite the efforts of enlightened landowners like the Marquis de Vauban to help its economy. Traditionally the women went to Paris as wet-nurses or took babies into their homes, while the men worked in the forests or left the plateau for seasonal labour in the vineyards of the Côte. They gained a reputation for being set apart, like the country in which they lived: neither good wind nor good people come from the Morvan, ran a saying popular among other Burgundians (who also like to say that it rains every day in the Morvan). The region's independence was amply proved during the Second World War, when the forests gave shelter to Maquis groups and Nazi reprisals made local Oradours of Montsauche, Dun-les-Places and Planchez. The memory of these events is kept fresh by the Musée de la Résistance at St-Brisson and the many monuments, sometimes almost hidden in the depths of the woods.

Despite agricultural techniques which reclaim farmland from forest and despite the intensive exploitation of pine plantations, the Morvan today is no more prosperous than it has ever been and its ageing, dwindling population averages less than 30 people per square kilometre. Château-Chinon, its largest centre if we exclude Saulieu as being too marginal to the region to count, still has under 3000 inhabitants even with the new industries François Mitterand attracted during his mayoralty. The combination of poverty and granite gives many towns and villages a pinched look, and many houses are now *maisons secondaires*. Encouraged by the creation of the Parc Naturel Régional du Morvan in 1970, tourism plays an increasing role in the economy of a region which has obvious attractions for the outdoor visitor. The information centre in the Maison du Parc at St-Brisson supplies details of the full range of activities, which include bird-watching, canoeing, horseriding and cycling. There are many short local walks and two long-distance paths, the 'Tour du Morvan par les Grands Lacs' and GR (Grande Randonnée) 13 from Vézelay to Autun, described in the excellent 'Topoguides' series. IGN map 306 covers the park at a scale of 1:100,000 (1cm to 1km).

The road system that feeds the rest of Burgundy goes round, not through, the Morvan. Its only major road is the D978 which cuts across the southern half, via Château-Chinon, on the way from Nevers to Autun. Otherwise the Morvan depends on a maze of side-roads, many of them not for the faint-hearted, which wind and intertwine in patterns defying even the local signposts. Firm and detailed directions for routes are little use. The accounts of the northern and southern halves of the Morvan that follow concentrate on the main highlights and suggest a few of many possible itineraries for touring a region where, anyway, part of the pleasure comes from getting lost.

North Morvan

An easy but not comprehensive tour would be sure to take in Quarré-les-Tombes, St-Brisson, Lac des Settons, Ouroux-en-Morvan and Lac de Pannesière on the way down to Château-Chinon. Quarré-les-Tombes itself can be reached by various routes from 'gateways' on the northern fringe of the Morvan: Vézelay (Route 11) via Pierre-Perthuis and Chastellux-sur-Cure; Avallon (Route 11) via Chastellux; or Rouvray on the N6 (Route 12) via St-Léger-Vauban. Shorter routes would start in the E from Saulieu (Route 12) or in the W from Lormes (near Corbigny in Route 18) and head for St-Brisson.

Pierre-Perthuis, about 7km S of Vézelay via St-Père-sous-Vézelay and the Fontaines Salées by D958, is a picturesque little place still within sight of the hill where La Madeleine stands. An 18C hump-backed bridge and its 19C successor span the Cure. The church was originally the chapel of its castle, from which a few other remnants survive. The village takes its name from La Roche Percée, a natural stone arch eroded from the hillside on the opposite bank. To its SE the Cure is dammed by the **Barrage de Malassis**, with a hydro-electric plant. **Bazoches**, 6km further S on D958, proudly remembers its connection with the Marquis de Vauban (born at St-Léger-de-Vauban), who bought the château (not open) and was buried in the church. His heart was removed to a place of honour in Les Invalides at Napoléon's direction.

Chastellux-sur-Cure is hidden away by the river about 10km SE of Pierre-Perthuis and 14km S of Avallon by D944. 19C restoration does not prevent the medieval castle (not open) from looking marvellously dramatic on its hilltop. It is still the home of the family which produced Claude de Beauvoir, the chamberlain of Jean sans Peur who led the Anglo-Burgundian army to victory at the Battle of Cravant in 1423. The village of **St-André-en-Morvan** to the W was painted by Corot in 1842 (the landscape now hangs in the Louvre). About 2km SE of Chastellux the Cure and its tributary the Chalaux were dammed in the 1930s to form the **Lac du Crescent** (408 acres), with a hydro-electric plant. The side-roads which encircle both arms of the reservoir continue to Quarré-les-Tombes, about 10km E.

St-Léger-Vauban lies 8km SW of Rouvray and the N6 by D4, which becomes D55 after it crosses the departmental boundary. The village changed its name from St-Léger-de-Foucheret to honour its most famous son, Sébastien Le Prestre, marquis de Vauban (1633–1707). After a career as the most distinguished military engineer of his day Vauban returned to Bazoches in the Morvan, where his interest in the depressed local economy

and, particularly, his attack on the crippling effects of taxation earned him
the displeasure of Louis XIV but also the admiration of later reformers and
the permanent respect of his fellow Morvandiaux. He is remembered by
an exhibition in the Maison Vauban. The church of his baptism has modern
additions in the carved doors (by Marc Hénard) and the ceramic tiled floor
of the choir (by Hénard and Serge Jamet). There are memorials to Père
Muard, the 19C founder of the **Abbaye de la Pierre-qui-Vire**, a Benedictine
community hidden away in the forest 4km S and named after a local rocking
stone. It deserves a visit for the setting and the chance to buy its two famous
products: an excellent farm cheese and the Zodiaque press books on art
and architecture, which include Raymond Oursel's 'Bourgogne romane'.
D55 continues from St-Léger to (5.5km) Quarré-les-Tombes.

The name of **Quarré-les-Tombes** (740 people) refers to the hundred or so
Merovingian sarcophagi which lie round its church, survivors of a much
larger number. Historians still debate whether they belonged to a cemetery
or a storage depot in the locality. Though small and grim-looking, the town
serves as a market centre—and something of a centre for restaurants—in
this part of the Morvan. The **Lac de St-Agnan** (351 acres) lies on the Cousin
about 8km SE. Created in 1969, it is the newest of the Morvan reservoirs
except for the little Lac de Chamboux near Saulieu.

D10, D211 and D6 lead SE from Quarré-les-Tombes to (18km) St-Brisson.
The **Forêt au Duc*, spreading W from the D10 towards the Cure, was once
the personal hunting ground of the Valois dukes. It has ancient oaks and
beeches. A little one-way Route Forestière leads through its southern half
to the **Rocher de la Pérouse**, worth the climb for its view over the Cure
valley. **Dun-les-Places** (470 people), a few kilometres S of the rock but most
easily reached by D211 and D6, is one of the Morvan's Oradours. A
monument near the big granite church commemorates the 27 people shot
by the Germans on 26 June 1944 in reprisal for aid given to the Maquis
groups which the region sheltered. The **Forêt de Breuil-Chenue**, beside
D6 on the last leg of the journey to St-Brisson, has a wild deer enclosure.

At **St-Brisson** the Maison du Parc, an early 19C manor house set in
pleasant grounds by the Étang Taureau, serves as the Information Centre
for the Morvan as well as home for a research centre and temporary
exhibitions. The **Musée de la Résistance* uses documents, propagandist
literature, mementoes and photographs to create a detailed, often moving
account of wartime life in a region still proud of its *maquisards* and still
scarred by Nazi atrocities.

D977 bis leads SW from to (11km) Montsauche. After about 5km it passes
near the **Saut de Gouloux**, a waterfall on a little tributary of the Cure.
Montsauche (or Montsauche-les-Settons; 710 people; Tourist Information)
is a high-lying town with a post-war look. On 25 July 1944 German troops
cleared the inhabitants and burnt it to the ground in reprisal for an ambush
by the Maquis Bernard. The post office and police station were virtually
the only buildings left intact. **Planchez**, another high-lying place 9km S,
had suffered the same fate exactly a month before, on 25 June 1994. The
Lac des Settons, on the Cure about 4km SE of Montsauche, is the oldest of
the Morvan reservoirs, built to help *flottage* in the 19C, and now the most
popular with summer visitors.

Ouroux-en-Morvan (840 people; Tourist Information), about 8km SW of
Montsauche by D977 bis and D12, is a pleasant little town which has a good
view towards the **Lac de Pannesière**, another 8km further SE. The largest
of the Morvan reservoirs (1285 acres), it was created by damming the Yonne
in the 1940s. Side-roads lead from the dam and hydro-electric plant at its

NW corner round both the western and eastern shores towards Château-Chinon, about 20km S.

Lormes (1470 Lormois; Tourist Information), an alternative starting point for touring the north Morvan, is a dull town sandwiched between the Nivernais and the Morvan 13km NE of Corbigny (Route 18). The terrace outside the church of St-Alban commands a wide view across the Nivernais, though on his visit in the 1840s Corot chose to paint the church rather than the view. The **Mont de la Justice** (470m), about 1km NW, includes the Morvan in its panorama. The **Lac de Chaumeçon**, about 8km E of Lormes, is a reservoir (334 acres) formed by damming the Chalaux, a tributary of the Cure, in the 1930s. The best view is from the NW corner where D150 and D235 meet. Dun-les-Places is 8km E of the lake by D6. The Lac de Pannesière is 20km SE of Lormes by D944.

South Morvan

Château-Chinon, the 'capital' of the Morvan, makes an obvious starting point for tours through the wilder country of the south Morvan. Several of the sights most worth seeing lie to either side of the D978 on its way E to (37km) Autun in Route 12. The southern fringe of the Morvan, and particularly the splendid Mont Beuvray, can also be toured from Moulins-Engilbert or St-Honoré-les-Bains, again heading towards Autun. Route 19 sketches a long detour from Digoin via Gueugnon, Issy-l'Évêque and Luzy to reach the Morvan at Larochemillay.

Château-Chinon (2500 Châteauchinonnais; Tourist Information) lies at the end of the previous journey through the north Morvan and 19km E of Châtillon-en-Bazois in Route 18. A high-lying town, it has hilly streets and outskirts swollen by the industries François Mitterand succeeded in attracting during his long term as mayor, beginning in 1959. There is little of interest except its museums on the Rue du Château. The Musée du Costume, des Arts et Traditions Populaires is particularly strong in its displays of 18–20C clothes, while the Musée du Septannat is stocked with gifts from around the world received by Mitterand during his first term of office as President. The panoramic view from Le Calvaire (609m) to the N takes in the Nivernais as well as the Morvan summits of Haut-Folin and Mont Preneley.

The **Forêt de St-Prix**, SE of Château-Chinon, marks the highest and wildest part of the Morvan, though pine plantations have made incursions into its natural beauty. The best way to reach it is by the little D177 and D179 which run from **Arleuf** (860 people), on D978 9km E of Château-Chinon. They lead to a Route Forestière which meanders through the woods and climbs to the summit of **Haut-Folin** (901m), with a small ski resort. To the S lie **Mont Preneley** (855m) and the source of the Yonne, reached from the village of Anvers. The Route Forestière continues E of St-Prix to join D978 near the Gorges de la Canche (see below).

The equally rugged *****Forêt d'Anost** is best reached by following D177 and D88 N from Arleuf to (10km) **Anost** itself (750 people), a picturesquely placed little centre. D2 continues N to the panoramic viewpoint at the nearby **Notre-Dame de l'Aillant** (625m). Shortly beyond, a Route Forestière branches left, passing a wild boar enclosure (recently depopulated by disease) and a monument remembering that the woods sheltered the Maquis Socrate from May 1944 until Liberation.

On the rest of its way E from Arleuf to Autun D978 passes just N of (8.5km) the **Gorges de la Canche**, with a hydro-electric dam, and (7km beyond) **La Celle-en-Morvan** (520 people), with a monument to the dead of the Maquis Socrate.

Moulins-Engilbert (1710 people) lies beyond the western edge of the Morvan, 16km SW of Château-Chinon and 17km SE of Châtillon-en-Bazois (Route 18). It holds a large cattle market on Tuesday mornings. **Commagny**, 2km SW, has the Romanesque church of a Benedictine priory: note the carved capitals and interesting choir. Mont Beuvray is 23km E of Moulins-Engilbert by D18.

St-Honoré-les-Bains (750 St-Honoréens; Tourist Information), 11km S of Moulins-Engilbert by D985, has the faded atmosphere usually found in Burgundy's several little spa towns, though its thermal baths and recreational centres are still open. Louis Malle's film 'Souffle au coeur' was shot here. **Sémelay**, 8km S, has a Romanesque church with a large choir and some good monsters and animals on the capitals. SE of St-Honoré is the **Vieille Montagne** (556m) with a good view towards Mont Beuvray. D299 leads E past (7km) **Mont Genièvre** (637m) to join D277 and D18 for Mont Beuvray, another 18km E.

*Mont Beuvray is an isolated hill rising to a broad plateau (821m) with beech woods as beautiful as any in the Morvan and a view that commands the Autun basin. Naturally inviting settlement, it flourished from the 2C BC as Bibracte, the capital of the Aedui, whose control of the land between the Saône and the Loire made them the most powerful Gallic tribe in Burgundy. Their use of enamel in the jewellery found at Bibracte suggests that they were also the most technically advanced. Though their friendliness to the Romans helped Caesar gain his first foothold in Gaul, the Aedui later joined the rebellion headed by the Avernian chieftain Vercingetorix, chosen at Bibracte in 52 BC to lead the tribes. After his victory over Vercingetorix at Alesia, Caesar made Bibracte his winter quarters and described the oppidum in the 'Commentaries on the Gallic War' which he began here. Subsequently the Romans took the unusual step of moving the city down into the valley and founding Augustodunum, the modern Autun. The hilltop site is hence particularly interesting to archaeologists in being Gallic rather than Gallo-Roman. The viewpoint at La Chaume is marked by an orientation table, a plan and a monument to Jacques-Gabriel Bulliot, the 19C archaeologist whose pioneer work identifying and excavating Bibracte was prompted by lingering folk legends of the great city which had once stood on the hill. The line of the ramparts can be discovered in the neighbouring woods, together with the St-Martin chapel and later buildings that mark the site of Gallic temples. President Mitterand declared Bibracte a 'site national' in 1985. A new campaign of excavation begun in 1984 still continues, yielding finds from from the Fontaine St-Pierre lower down the hill. The base at Glux-en-Glenne organises summer afternoon tours, which leave from the car park at La Chaume, and the town hall of **St-Léger-sous-Beuvray** (540 people), 4km E, shelters a small exhibition. D61 continues from St-Léger to join N81 for Autun, where Bulliot's work is remembered in the Musée Rolin.

Larochemillay, 7km S of D18 on the way to Mont Beuvray, has an 18C château (not open) on the site of a medieval fortress guarding the Roche and making an impressive southern gateway to the Morvan from the lower countryside on the way from Luzy (Route 19), 12km further S.

14 Saulieu to Chalon or Beaune

Directions and distances. Total distance 85km (53 miles) to Chalon, 72km (45 miles) to Beaune. N6 from **Saulieu** to (28km) **Arnay-le-Duc** and (56km) junction with D973. For Chalon: N6 to (68km) **Chagny** and (85km) **Chalon-sur-Saône**. For Beaune: D973, (70km) N74 to (72km) **Beaune**.

Connections with other routes. Route 12 describes Saulieu, Route 6 Chagny and Beaune, Route 7 Chalon.

Beyond **Saulieu** N6 leaves the fringes of the Morvan for the valley of the Arroux and then the Côte. At 4.5km D977 bis heads left to (5.5km) **Thoisy-la-Berchière**, with the 15C château built by Cardinal Rolin in the 15C but heavily altered in the 19C (not open). In the countryside of the Auxois to the NE rise Mont-St-Jean and Croix St-Thomas, described in Route 4.

N6 continues to (23.5km) **Arnay-le-Duc** (2040 Arnétois; Tourist Information), a pleasant old town by the Arroux. It acquired the suffix to its name when Eudes IV, the Capetian duke, bought the lordship in 1342. The future Henri IV first bore arms at the battle fought here in 1570, when Amiral de Coligny's Protestants overwhelmed the Catholic forces. The 17C buildings of the former Hospice St-Pierre, on the N6 by the river, house the Syndicat d'Initiative and Maison Régionale des Arts de la Table with changing displays of furniture, silver, glassware and *faïence*, including two pieces by Bernard Palissy. Behind the E end of the largely Renaissance church stands the Tour de la Motte-Forte, a big 15C round tower which is all that survives of the feudal fortress destroyed in the Wars of Religion. It now contains an exhibition of local archaeology. An old archway leads into the Place de Bonaventure-des-Périers, named after the satirical poet born c 1510 at Arnay, with the handsome 18C Hôtel de Ville and a house with an *échaugette*. The 'new' 16–17C château beyond keeps some Flamboyant details, well restored.

W of Arnay the D17 crosses the Arroux on its way to (13km) the prominent **Signal de Bard** (554m). Beneath its western flank lies the village of **Bard-le-Régulier**, or Bar-le-Régulier, where the Romanesque church has an octagonal tower topped by an elegant dome. Note the broken arches on the openings of the upper storey. The choir contains superb late 14C *stalls. The subjects of the bench ends include an Annunciation, Visitation and Nativity of grave simplicity, a beautifully organised Last Supper and episodes from the legend of John the Evangelist (patron saint of the priory which built the church), shown in one scene having boiling oil poured over him. The columns of the upper stalls are supported by acrobats, animals and an angel. The little village of **Manlay**, S of the Signal, has been virtually rebuilt since German troops burnt it during the Occupation, a fate also suffered by several villages in the neighbouring Morvan.

Beyond Arnay-le-Duc N6 climbs from the valley of the Arroux towards the Hautes-Côtes, with several striking viewpoints. **Cussy-la-Colonne**, to the N at 17km, is named after the Roman column it preserves. Beyond **Ivry-en-Montagne**, S of the road, is the château of **Coraboeuf** (open) with the gateway tower, keep and other fragments of the 16C castle. The gardens and their 18C summer house exude a pleasant atmosphere of picturesque decay.

About 2km beyond Cussy and Ivry D17 branches left from N6 across the Hautes-Côtes to Beaune, passing near St-Romain. N6 continues another

9km to the big road junction W of Nolay, where D973 heads directly towards (16km) **Beaune**. (Route 6 describes a more interesting way from the junction through the Hautes-Côtes to Beaune via La Rochepot, St-Romain and Pommard.) Beyond the junction with D973, N6 passes St-Aubin, Gamay and the turning for Santenay, all described in Route 6, on the way to (12km) **Chagny** and (17km) **Chalon-sur-Saône**. The way from Chagny to Chalon through the vineyards of the Côte Chalonnaise described in Route 7 is far more interesting.

15 Autun to Chalon or Beaune

Directions and distances. Total distance 61km (38 miles) to Chalon, 48km (30 miles) to Beaune. D973 from **Autun** to (28km) **Nolay** and (32km) junction with N6. For Chalon: N6 to (44km) **Chagny** and (61km) **Chalon-sur-Saône**. For Beaune: D973, (46km) N74 to (48km) **Beaune**.

Connections with other routes. Route 12 describes Autun, Route 6 Nolay, Chagny and Beaune, Route 7 Chalon.

D973 runs E from **Autun**, connecting the Morvan and the Côte, like N6 in the previous route. **Curgy** (1040 people), N of the road at 7km, has a beautifully simple Romanesque *church built of granite, with a 12C fresco (recently restored) in the semi-domed apse showing Christ in Majesty surrounded by the four Evangelists. D326, 3km beyond, branches left for (4.5km) **Sully** (580 people), with one of the grandest and most dignified châteaux in Burgundy (access to outside only). Though it keeps an essentially medieval plan, with big square corner towers and a wide moat enclosing its central courtyard, it was built in the 16C by Nicolas Ribonnier for the Saulx-Tavanes family, leading supporters of the Catholic faction during the Wars of Religion. Its most handsome feature is the neo-classical *N façade added in the 18C, with a terrace and stairs leading down to the moat. The château was the birthplace of Maurice de Mac-Mahon (1808–1893), commander of the army which suppressed the Paris Commune in 1870 and afterwards a President of the Third Republic.

Just after the turning for Sully a Route Forestière loops S from D973 through the **Forêt des Battées** and rejoins the main road about 5km later. At 4km this charming little rabbit-hole of a road passes the former priory of **Val-St-Benoît**, where the Gothic church and domestic buildings are being restored by the community of nuns which installed itself here in 1982.

Épinac, N of D973 16km from Autun, is a glum little town (2570 people; Tourist Information) which developed around the coal mines opened in 1755 and finally closed in 1966. It keeps some fragments, notably two big towers, of the château once owned by Nicolas Rolin (not open).

D973 continues to (12km) **Nolay**, described in Route 6, and (4km) the junction with N6 also reached in the previous route. D973 heads directly towards (16km) **Beaune**. (Route 6 describes a more interesting way from the junction through the Hautes-Côtes to Beaune via La Rochepot, St-Romain and Pommard.) From the junction with D973, N6 continues past St-Aubin, Gamay and the turning for Santenay, all described in Route 6, on the way to (12km) **Chagny** and (17km) **Chalon-sur-Saône**. The way from Chagny to Chalon through the vineyards of the Côte Chalonnaise described in Route 7 is far more interesting.

16 The Puisaye: Joigny to Cosne-sur-Loire

Directions and distances.Total distance 97.5km (61 miles). From **Joigny** D943, (13km) D3 to (18km) La Ferté-Loupière. D3, (33.5km) D955 to (38.5km) **Toucy**. D955 to (54.5km) St-Sauveur-en-Puisaye. D85 to (65.5km) **St-Fargeau**. D18, which becomes D2 after it crosses the departmental boundary, to (78.5km) St-Amand-en-Puisaye. D955 to (97.5km) **Cosne**.

Connections with other routes. Route 3 describes Joigny. Auxerre, in Route 11, makes an alternative starting point for a journey going straight to Toucy. Route 17 describes Cosne before continuing along the Loire.

The ***Puisaye** lies between the Yonne and the Loire, its centre—marked by a trio of towns, St-Fargeau, St-Sauveur and St-Amand—straddling the boundary between the departments of Yonne and Nièvre, and its western fringe overflowing into the department of Loiret, outside Burgundy in the usual definition. Lacking formal administrative status or even coherence, the Puisaye has its own compact geographical identity. Looking back from Paris to her childhood in St-Sauveur, Colette remembered 'a countryside a little sad, darkened by the forests, a peaceable and poor village, a humid valley, a bluish hillside where not even goats can live'. This admirably evokes the character of her native *pays*, where ponds and forests, marshes and little rivers combine to create a quiet, almost secretive landscape that surprises visitors who associate Burgundy only with hilltop views, wide plateaux and open valleys. The local building materials, again surprising those who think Burgundy has only limestone and granite, are equally distinctive: a dark brown ironstone that resists smooth cutting or neat coursing, and a rose-red brick that turns grey or blue when fired longer. They can make handsome châteaux like Ratilly and St-Fargeau, but leave the churches to compensate by the richness of their wall paintings (at La Ferté-Loupière and Moutiers, for example).

Traditionally the Puisaye has ranked with the Châtillonnais and the Morvan among the poorest regions of Burgundy, a fate which may have have left its villages peaceable, as Colette suggests, but has usually made its towns grim and pinched. Apart from farming, the only sources of livelihood offered by the countryside were the forests and the clayey subsoil. The forests yielded charcoal and, of course, timber—already prized in the Middle Ages when Abbé Suger sent to the Puisaye for the beams of St-Denis. The clay from which the local bricks are made also nurtured a tradition of pottery making. The characteristic stoneware (*grès*) is heavy, rough in texture and warm brown in colour, though enamel glaze is sometimes used, notably for the blue ware from St-Vérain. St-Amand is now a centre for pottery studios, and good displays of traditional ware can be seen at Villiers-St-Benoît and Ratilly.

If nothing else, its proximity to Paris has guaranteed that the Puisaye should not have gone undiscovered. Weekend cottagers and tourists are now part of the local economy, though good hotels (indeed, in some corners, hotels of any sort) are surprisingly hard to find and the simpler forms of rural accommodation a much safer bet. Many visitors are attracted particularly by the opportunities for walking or riding the quiet countryside offers. Details of riding schools and footpath routes can be obtained from local Syndicats or the Maison de la Puisaye in St-Fargeau, the information centre for the region.

The quickest way from **Joigny** through the Puisaye, shorter (71km) but less interesting than the route proposed below, follows D955 to Toucy and D965 via St-Fargeau to join the Loire below Cosne. The little town of **Aillant-sur-Tholon** (1490 people; Tourist Information), at 13km on the first stage of the journey, has a church of 1864–1867 by Viollet-le-Duc. The museum of folk art at **Laduz**, 5km SW, contains paintings, sculptures, toys and tools illustrating everyday life in rural Burgundy.

It makes more sense to head SW from Joigny on D943, changing to D3 after crossing the A6 at 13km. The church at **La Ferté-Loupière** (540 people), 5km beyond, has late 15C–early 16C *paintings on the N wall of its nave. 'Les Trois Morts et les trois vifs' shows three skeletons confronting three young noblemen, a common moral warning that also appears locally at Villiers-St-Benoît and St-Fargeau. In the adjoining 'Danse macabre' a procession of people from all ranks are summoned by death: hermit, labourer, minstrel, bishop, duke, king, cardinal, emperor and pope.

Charny (1630 Charnycois; Tourist Information), 12km W of La Ferté-Loupière, is a glum little town that still has an old brick-nogged market hall suppported on stone columns. On the outskirts of **Prunoy**, 4km NE, stands the 18C château of Vienne, now a hotel, keeping a round tower from its medieval predecessor. You can continue the detour by following the valley of the Ouanne S from Charny on D950 to (12km) **Grandchamp**, a little village dominated by its late 16C château built on a terrace surrounded by moats; the chimneys and towers make a dramatic skyline (not open). Villiers-St-Benoît, 4.5km further, is described in the main route below.

D3 continues from La Ferté-Loupière up the valley of the Vrin. Beyond (5km) Sommecaise it passes near the château of **Bontin** (open by appointment), on the Les Ormes road, a late 17C building in brick, stone and roughcast, on the site of a house that belonged to Henri IV's minister Sully. After another 10.5km D3 joins D955 for (5km) **Toucy** (2590 Toucycois; Tourist Information), on the Ouanne, where the 13C church is fortified by the grim ironstone walls of the castle *enceinte*. The lexicographer Pierre Larousse (1817–1875) was born here.

Villiers-St-Benoît, 8.5km NW of Toucy, has an excellent *museum of regional art. It contains some outstanding items: a portrait by Nicolas de Largillière and a head, perhaps of St Michael, attributed to Antoine Le Moiturier, the sculptor who worked on Jean sans Peur's tomb in Dijon. Otherwise, the domestic atmosphere that still lingers on the ground floor of this typical late 18C–early 19C Puisaye house is quite as engaging as the individual objects on view. Upstairs, the large, informatively displayed collection of Yonne *faïence* and Puisaye *grès* includes some charming pieces, decorated with saints, birds, flowers, vignettes of rural life, mottoes, doggerel ('L'amour demande du vin,/ pour dissiper son chagrin') and Revolutionary slogans ('Vivre libre ou mourir'). The nearby church contains a fine 15C wall painting of 'Les Trois Morts et les trois vifs' (compare La Ferté-Loupière and St-Fargeau). The hamlet of **Les Vernes**, about 9km E of Toucy and just short of Pourrain, has a little museum of World War II organised by a former member of the Dutch Resistance, with military vehicles and Maquis souvenirs. **Fontenoy**, on a tributary of the Ouanne 10.5km S of Toucy, was the Fontanet where Charlemagne's three grandsons fought the battle in 841 that led to the division of his empire. **Tremblay**, on the hill W of Fontenoy, is a largely 17C château built by the family later allied by marriage to Madame du Deffand, hostess of a glittering salon in 18C Paris. Its outbuildings house an exhibition of contemporary art.

The pleasant D955, heading S from Toucy, passes a good view of the countryside after (5.5km) Fontaines. **St-Sauveur-en-Puisaye** (1010 San Salvatoriens; Tourist Information), 10.5km further, is a sleepy, crumbling little place where Colette's birthplace, on the street renamed in her honour, now looks ordinary enough beside her own evocation of 'a large solemn house, rather forbidding, with its shrill bell and its carriage-entrance with a huge bolt like an ancient dungeon, a house that smiled only on its garden side' ('La Maison de Claudine', translated as 'My Mother's House'). On the outskirts of town, the shell of a circular medieval keep survives near the château completed in the 17C.

With St-Fargeau and St-Amand, St-Sauveur marks the heart of the Puisaye. More or less all the roads linking the three little towns are worth exploring to get the flavour of the countryside but the D85 to St-Fargeau, fringed by ponds and the river Loing, makes a good beginning. After 2km it passes N of the little village of **Moutiers**. In the church, with its unexpectedly elaborate Romanesque porch, the drought of 1982 caused the whitewash to peel and so began to reveal *wall paintings that range from the mid 12C to the late 16C. The earliest work, on the N wall of the nave, shows two overlapping designs that include angels and a crucified Christ. The S wall has an ambitious painting of about 1300, with a procession above scenes from Genesis and, in the bottom register, the life of John the Baptist.

ST-FARGEAU (1880 Fargeaulais; Tourist Information), on the Loing 11km from St-Sauveur, was the old capital of the Puisaye and has become the centre of its tourist trade. With its slate-covered spire, the late 15C **Tour St-Nicolas** makes a distinctive landmark in the brick-built town. The ironstone church of **St-Férreol**, its W façade dominated by a rose window, contains a Pietà among its 15-16C furnishings. (Its 13C glass was removed in the 19C and can now be seen in the Musée d'Art et d'Histoire at Geneva.) The late 15C chapel of **Ste-Anne**, in the cemetery, contains wall paintings that include 'Les Trois Morts et les trois vifs', inviting comparison with those at La Ferté-Loupière and Villiers-St-Benoît.

The reason most visitors come to St-Fargeau is to see the *Château (open), particularly on the summer evenings when it serves as setting for the *spectacle*, one of the largest in France, dramatising its history from the Hundred Years War to World War II. The *spectacle* is one of several remedies used by the present owner to rescue a building which, even with daylight exposing the extent of its decay, still declares itself a virtuoso essay in the uses of the local brick and ranks among the best châteaux in Burgundy. Its plan—an irregular polygon with huge drum towers guarding the corners and main gateway—betrays its origin in the castle built in large part by Antoine de Chabannes, Jeanne d'Arc's companion in arms and Charles VII's favourite, between 1467 and 1488. The features that give St-Fargeau its distinctive character—the Oriental lanterns topping the conical roofs of the towers, and the cheerfully splendid main courtyard—are the work of Louis Le Vau, architect of Versailles. They belong to the restoration campaign with which 'La Grande Mademoiselle' (Anne-Marie-Louise d'Orléans, duchesse de Montpensier; 1627–1693) occupied herself during several spells of enforced exile from the court of her cousin Louis XIV. Her initials, AMLO, are emblazoned over the semicircular entrance staircase in the courtyard. The chapel contains the tomb of a subsequent owner, Louis-Michel Le Peletier, whose assassination in 1793 made him the first official martyr of the Revolution and originally earned him a place in the Panthéon. 19C alterations make much of the interior disappointing, though the main staircase and state rooms are being restored and two features are outstanding: the Tour Jacques-Coeur, a hollow tower with an interior courtyard for collecting rainwater, and the attic floor with its massive, intricately assembled roof timbers.

Bléneau (1590 Blenassiens; Tourist Information), on the Loing 12km NW of St-Fargeau, is a cheerless place. It gave its name to the nearby battle of 1652 at which Turenne defeated the Grand Condé and his Frondeurs, thus saving the young Louis XIV and his court, then lodged at Gien on the Loire. The country round Breteau, Champoulet, Dammarie-en-Puisaye and Batilly-en-Puisaye, over the Loiret border to the SW, is more rewarding.

The little D185, leading SE from St-Fargeau to the D955 between St-Sauveur and St-Amand, passes the Bourdon reservoir, created in 1904. At 8km the park (open) belonging to the manor house of **Boutissaint**, once a priory, is now a sensibly managed refuge for European animals, with deer, wild boar, European bison and Corsican mountain sheep kept in large enclosures or roaming free among the woods. After another 6km, beyond the D955, D185 passes *Ratilly* (open), a 13C castle with pepperpot towers flanking its entrance and guarding its corners, humbly built out of the local ironstone and, except for the gateway tower added in the 17C, roofed in red clay tiles. Guy de Vallery and his band of Breton *écorcheurs* made it their headquarters during the Hundred Years War, burning the priory at Moutiers among their other local adventures. In later centuries it became a Huguenot stronghold and a refuge for Jansenists. Now peaceful and completely charming, it houses a distinguished pottery studio founded by Jeanne and Norbert Pierlot and a permanent historical exhibition of *grès*, with concerts and temporary shows of modern art in summer. **Treigny** (930 people), 1km E, has a big Flamboyant church, while **Perreuse**, in open country 4km further E, is a pleasant village of old houses.

St-Amand-en-Puisaye (1360 Amandois; Tourist Information), built of the local brick and ironstone, lies 15km from St-Fargeau on D18 (which becomes D2 after it crosses the departmental boundary) and 13km from St-Sauveur. It is now a centre of pottery studios: almost a dozen are open to visitors. The Renaissance château (access to outside only) has a handsome façade. **St-Vérain**, a little outpost of the Puisaye 7km S, is known for its blue glazed ware. It keeps fragments of its 13C fortifications and an interesting 12–13C church.

D955 quickly makes the last leg of the journey to (19km) Cosne, though D957, joining the Loire lower down at (21km) Neuvy-sur-Loire, is a more pleasant road. **Cosne** is described in the next route.

17 The Loire Nivernaise: Cosne to La Charité-sur-Loire and Nevers

Directions and distances. Total distance 53km (33 miles). N7 from **Cosne** to (15km) Pouilly-sur-Loire, (28km) **La Charité-sur-Loire** and (53km) **Nevers**.

Connections with other routes. The previous route reached Cosne via the Puisaye from Joigny. Route 18 reaches Nevers from Auxerre. Route 19 continues along the Loire from Nevers to Paray-le-Monial.

This route and the two routes that follow explore the department of Nièvre, which corresponds to the *pays* traditionally known as the **Nivernais**. Once held by the Courtenay family, the original county was among the territory which the first Valois duke, Philippe le Hardi, gained by his marriage to Marguerite de Flandre in 1369, though he quickly bestowed it on a younger son. Passing into a junior branch of the Valois dynasty, it thus became a satellite of its powerful neighbour. After the fall of the Valois dukes, the Nivernais passed to the Clèves and then, promoted to the status of duchy in its own right, to the Gonzagas, a Mantuan family whose name was gallicised to Gonzague. Cardinal Mazarin bought it in 1659 and bequeathed it to his nephew Mancini, whose family held it until the Revolution transformed the duchy into the modern department.

Though the department voted to join the other three which make up the modern region, its history explains why it has always been regarded as off-Burgundy rather than Burgundy proper. So does its position, largely cut off by the Morvan from the major routes that unite the rest of the region. It is linked with Berry and the Bourbonnais by the Loire, for all the navigational problems caused by its wandering sandy course and its variable depth a natural artery for trade with Paris. The side-canal between Briare and Digoin (196km or 122 miles) linking the Canal du Centre and the Canal du Nivernais with the Briare Canal further encouraged the growth of coalmining, ironworking and steelworking which has left its unpicturesque mark on the valley.

The present route begins a journey along the Loire Nivernaise which Route 19 continues beyond Nevers. You can reach the starting point at Cosne by approaching Burgundy along the river from Orléans (D952) or from Paris and Montargis (N7), or by taking Route 16 through the Puisaye from Joigny. Route 18 takes Auxerre and the Yonne valley as the starting point for exploring the less industrialised hinterland of the Nivernais, a wooded region of gentle limestone hills divided by the tributary rivers— notably the Nièvre itself—which make their way S to swell the Loire.

Cosne-sur-Loire (12,640 Cosnois; Tourist Information), the second largest town in Nièvre, has been an industrial centre since its foundries began making anchors and cannon in the late 17C. The few sights worth seeing are near the Place de l'Hôtel-de-Ville, with the Syndicat d'Initiative and the Mairie. To the W, where the Nohain flows to meet the Loire, the Musée de la Loire is dedicated to the history of the river and its navigation. N of the square are the 15C church of St-Jacques, with lierne vaulting, and the Musée des Chapelains, with finds from the Gallo-Roman town, Condate. St-Agnan, to the S, has a Romanesque W doorway and apse. The nearby Rue des Forges preserves the entrance to the old Forges de la Chaussade, the naval ironworks bought by Louis XVI and moved to Guérigny (Route 18) in 1782. The Place des Marronniers, marked by a large 19C anchor, has a view of the river.

N7 runs directly from Cosne to (15km) Pouilly-sur-Loire but it is well worth making a detour SE on D33 to (17km) **Donzy** (1720 people; Tourist Information), on the edge of forests spreading over the Nivernais hills. Once capital of the powerful barony whose lords became counts of Nevers, the little town still has some handsome old houses. The 14C castle of **La Motte-Josserand** (open), 4km N, fell into the hands of two notorious *écorcheurs*, the 'Archpriest' Anatole de Cervole and Perrinet-Gressart, during the Hundred Years War. The ruined Cluniac priory at **Donzy-le-Pré**, about 1km SW of Donzy, keeps a mid 12C *tympanum over the narthex doorway. Isaiah and an angel kneel on either side of the canopy where the Virgin Mary sits enthroned, in richly flowing robes, with the infant Christ on her knee; note the hand of God above. At **Suilly-la-Tour**, 5km SW of Donzy-le-Pré, the big 16C Château des Granges (open) has an Italianate chapel. D28 continues through vineyards to (10km) Pouilly.

Pouilly-sur-Loire is an unremarkable little town (1710 people; Tourist Information) known for its white wines, particularly Pouilly Fumé (not to be confused with Pouilly-Fuissé from the southern Mâconnais). On the opposite bank of the river are the vineyards of Sancerre. N7 continues another 13km to La Charité.

LA CHARITÉ-SUR-LOIRE (5690 Charitois; Tourist Information) is a pleasant old town at a major crossing point on the Loire used by, among others, pilgrims on the way from Vézelay to Compostela. Its position on the border between French and Burgundian spheres of influence gave it an unwelcome strategic role during the Hundred Years War. A company of *écorcheurs* held La Charité in 1363–1364 though Jeanne d'Arc, fresh from her victory at St-Pierre-le-Moûtier, failed to capture it in 1429. But its historical importance stemmed from the Cluniac priory of ****Notre-Dame**, whose great Romanesque church is still the main reason for visiting the town.

Legend tells of a religious community established at Seyr, as La Charité was then called, by about 700 and of its destruction in the Saracen invasions soon afterwards. In 1056 Bernard de Chaillant gave the Cluniac monk Gérard the land on which Hugues de Semur, the abbot of Cluny, founded a priory, 'the oldest daughter of Cluny', in 1059. Contemporary reference to an earlier ruined church on the site has been confirmed by modern excavations revealing a Carolingian oratory beneath an early 11C church, St-Laurent, apparently the first provisional Cluniac building. The church of Notre-Dame itself was built in successive campaigns lasting from about 1059 until about 1135, transforming the original Benedictine plan into a building to rival Cluny III itself. Its W façade was an ambitious composition, anticipating Bourges cathedral, of two towers and five doorways. The nave, five aisles wide and ten bays long, led to a crossing dome surmounted by an octagonal tower and a choir with ambulatory and five radiating chapels.

This is the church which survives today, though only in a mutilated and fragmentary state. Its W end overlooks the little Place des Pêcheurs, flanked on the left by the priory's 15C gateway to which this tour of the buildings will eventually return. Of the original W façade only the N tower, the Tour Ste-Croix, still stands; the main doorway is 16C Flamboyant work. One of the two Romanesque doorways at the base of the tower keeps its tympanum showing Christ in a mandorla blessing the Cluniac foundation; the Annunciation, Visitation, Nativity and Adoration of the Shepherds appear on the lintel. A second tympanum, from the S tower, is preserved inside the building.

The façade no longer leads immediately into the church, since fire destroyed the six western bays of the nave in 1559 and the site has become the curious little Place Ste-Croix. Fragments of Romanesque work can still be made out on its N side (where the Syndicat d'Initiative has its summer office). Note particularly the cusps that decorate the arches of the false triforium, a stylistic signature, apparently betraying Arabic influence, which appears on the Tour Ste-Croix and again in the choir.

The remaining portion of the church was walled up and a new W entrance created in the 18C. The four bays of the nave are greatly altered but not so disastrously as to distract attention from the lovely transepts and E end, where the choir, ambulatory and radiating chapels survive intact except for the substitution of a cruciform apsidal chapel in the 14C. The three-storey

The 'Transfiguration' tympanum at Notre-Dame, La Charité-sur-Loire

elevation, rising to a pointed barrel vault, is persistently inventive in its details. Note the animal and foliage capitals (particularly on the main piers of the choir), the frieze of eight beasts running below the false triforium of the choir, and the pilasters and arches of the triforium itself. The second tympanum to survive from the W façade, rescued by Prosper Mérimée in the 1840s, is displayed in the S transept. Its theme is the Transfiguration, a feast day added to the Cluniac calendar in 1132 (compare Charlieu in the Brionnais, Route 20). Christ appears as lawgiver and teacher, holding a book and flanked by Moses, Elijah and kneeling Apostles. The Adoration of the Magi on the left-hand panel of the lintel makes a superbly handled group; the scene to the right shows the Presentation of Christ in the Temple or the Purification of the Virgin.

To begin a tour of the rest of the priory, take the door in the S transept which leads via the little vaulted Passage de la Madeleine to the Grande Rue. From No 45, higher up the street, another passage leads back to the Square des Bénédictins, with a lovely view of the chevet. On the excavation site to the right the stepped apse of the 11C St-Laurent can clearly be made out among the foundations of other monastic buildings. Two interesting walks lead from the opposite end of the square. One follows the 14C walls and ruined towers which marked the N boundary of the medieval *enceinte*; the towers of Notre-Dame with the river in the background make a fine view from several points along the way. The second walk turns left from the square and passes the remains of the priory cloister and 13C chapter house on the way to the Cour du Prieuré and the Cour du Château, with the 15C monks' storeroom and the Flamboyant doorway of the 15C prior's lodging. Both routes end in the handsome old Rue des Chapelains, with the priory gateway at its S end.

The Hôtel Adam in the park near its N end houses the **Musée Municipal**, with an interesting display of finds from the excavations and objects illustrating everyday life in the priory. Work from later periods includes sculptures by Rodin's pupil Alfredo Pina, who died at La Charité in 1966, and decorative art (Art Nouveau, Art Deco) from the period 1880–1930.

At **Champvoux**, 7km SE of La Charité, the Romanesque church has lost its nave but keeps its apsidal E end with some primitive, strongly carved capitals. N7 passes near Champvoux on its straight course from La Charité to (13km) the decayed spa town of **Pougues-les-Eaux** (2360 people; Tourist Information). Mont Givre, to its E, has a view over the valley. Parigny-les-Vaux, on the way E to Guérigny, is described in Route 18.

N7 continues to (12km) Nevers. An alternative route, approaching the city from the W, takes D8 from Pougues to (3km) **Garchizy** (3940 people), where the church has an octagonal Romanesque tower and capitals on its W doorway, and (3km) **Fourchambault** (5040 people), an ironworking centre developed in the 19C. D131 continues S to (5.5km) **Marzy** (3030 people), a pleasant little place with a heavily restored Romanesque church and a local museum containing Nivernais *faïence*. 2km S there is a dramatic view of the **Bec d'Allier**, the meeting of the Loire and the Allier (see also the Pont du Guétin later in this route). The centre of Nevers lies about 4km E of Marzy.

***NEVERS** (41,970 Nivernais; Tourist Information) developed from the Roman Noviodunum Aeduorum, on the edge of Aedui territory, into the capital of the county, later the duchy, of Nevers and finally into the *préfecture* of Nièvre. Yet none of the chief monuments to its long history, like the cathedral or ducal palace, is of the first rank. It takes patience to penetrate the city's bland but not quite stately façade, and to discover the real provincial character that still lurks in many old corners, together with some surprisingly rich parish churches and museums.

The Place Carnot marks the centre of the modern city, with the **Syndicat d'Initiative** on the corner of the nearby Rue du Rempart. None of the sights described on the walking tour that follows lies much more than a stone's throw away. The best starting point is to the W at the **Porte du Croux**, the most impressive survival of the defences built in the late 12C by Pierre de Courtenay, comte de Nevers, and refurbished in the late 14C. A good stretch of wall still stands to the S, flanked by pleasant gardens leading down to the **Tour Goguin** on the quay by the Loire. There is a good view of the bridge (1770–1832) which stands at an ancient crossing point on a pilgrims' route from Vézelay to Compostela.

The Porte du Croux houses the **Musée Archéologique** with, apart from Greek marbles, a local collection of Gallo-Roman and medieval items including a mosaic from Villars and *Romanesque sculpture from St-Sauveur (a fragment of which still stands on the Place Mossé by the river). The tympanum, on which Christ appears twice, and capitals showing the Parable of the Rich Man and St Peter curing the lame man are all apparently by the same highly sophisticated hand; cruder but still vigorous capitals show the jaws of Hell and a man being attacked by a bear.

The crumbling little Rue de la Porte-du-Croux leads towards the centre.

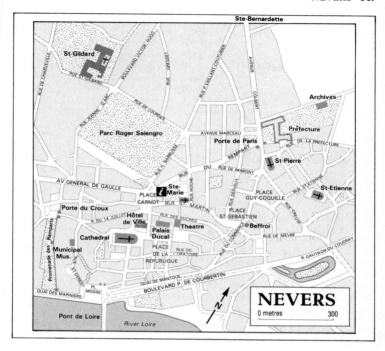

The *faïencerie* on the left, established in 1648, survives from the heyday of an industry introduced when the Gonzagues brought Italian craftsmen to Nevers in 1585. The city's studios employed 1800 people in the 17C. Their work can be seen in the **Musée Municipal** around the corner in the Rue St-Genest, partly housed in the pleasant surroundings of the 13C chapter house which belonged to Notre-Dame abbey. The ˙collection includes a statuette, 'La Vierge à la Pomme' (1636), in imitation of the Della Robbias and pieces showing the range of Italian, Persian, Chinese and Meissen styles copied by Nivernais potters. Also on display are curious scenes made from spun-glass figures, one of Pierre-François Palloy's models of the Bastille and work by local artists.

The left fork in the road beyond the junction of the Rue de la Porte-du-Croux with the Rue St-Genest leads into the Place Carnot, and the right, by a flight of steps, to the W end of the cathedral of **St-Cyr-et-Ste-Julitte**. At first sight you will probably wonder if it is the W end, since it has a Romanesque apse. The cathedral is unusual for a French church in having apses at both ends, the one to the E being heavily buttressed 14C Gothic work. Despite this oddity, the dominating feature is still the tall square tower, 14C below and, much more richly ornamented, early 16C above. Many of the statues are later replacements. The inside is as motley as the outside, satisfying only in details like the triforium of the 13C nave, with lively carved figures at the base of its columns, and the tall windows of the choir which combine triforium and clerestory. The W apse has a 12C wall painting of Christ with the emblems of the Evangelists and the Elders of the Apocalypse, and the crypt below contains a handsome late 15C–early 16C Entombment. Note also the 16C clock with *jaquemarts*, or striking jacks; the mutilated 15C stone altarpiece (in the second chapel on the S side of the nave); and the 15C Pietà (fourth chapel on N side).

Beyond the E end lie the **Hôtel de Ville** and, now serving as its annexe, the former **Palais Ducal**. The N side preserves the 14C corner towers of Jean de Clamecy's château but the rest was built by the Clèves and Gonzague families between 1464 and 1565. The S façade is particularly striking, its central turret decorated with bas-reliefs (recut in the 19C) of scenes from the legend of St Hubert and the swan emblem of the Clèves. The rooms inside have been largely modernised as offices but one corner tower has been reserved as a display area for temporary exhibitions, which extend over several floors effectively combining old and modern décor.

Next to the ducal palace stand the charming early 19C **Théâtre** and the **Petit Château**, now derelict, built in 1601–1637. The Rue des Récollets continues E past some good old buildings, notably the 18C gateway of the old convent, the 17C **Hôtel de Fontenay** and the house with a crow-stepped gable facing the end of the street. The backs of some of these buildings make a picturesque show in the Rue des Ouches as it returns to the Place Carnot.

S of the ducal palace the handsome tree-lined Place de la République leads down towards gardens overlooking the river. Several side-streets are worth exploring. The Rue de l'Oratoire, on the left, has the crumbling gateway of the **Chambre des Comptes** (1405) and the mutilated **Chapelle de l'Oratoire** (1679). The Rue Parcheminerie, on the right at the bottom, has half-timbered houses and an *échaugette*. Modern development spoils the view of the Loire from the gardens.

The last stage of the walking tour heads E from the Place Carnot to the lower town outside the medieval walls. The easiest route follows the Rue du Rempart. A more interesting way begins by taking the Rue St-Martin, where the Baroque Italianate *façade of the **Chapelle Ste-Marie** (1639) is a delightful surprise, though the building is now sadly derelict. The pedestrianised Rue du Commerce leads N past the partly 15C **Beffroi** to the church of St-Pierre. It was begun in 1612 but the handsome W façade was not finished until 1676. The Baroque interior has murals (now being restored) and, above the altar, a painting of St Michael attributed to the Le Nain brothers. At the end of the Rue du Rempart N of the church stands the **Porte de Paris**, an 18C triumphal arch replacing the medieval city gate, with verses by Voltaire praising Louis XV and his victory over the English at Fontenoy in 1745.

The neighbourhood off the Rue St-Étienne to the E is one of the most interesting old corners of Nevers, and it has the city's best building in *St-Étienne, a Cluniac priory church consecrated in 1097. The W façade has lost its narthex but the chevet keeps its beautiful cluster of radiating chapels. The severe, almost unadorned interior, with a three-storey nave and dome over the crossing, marries the styles of Cluny and the Auvergne into a commanding unity: 'a complete statement of mature Romanesque', as Kenneth Conant has called it.

Bernadette Soubirous (1844–1879), the visionary of Lourdes, spent most of her adult life as a sister in the convent of **St-Gildard**, N of the Place Carnot and the municipal park. Her tomb and a museum of relics are popular with pilgrims. The modern church of **Ste-Bernadette-du-Banlay** by Claude Parent (1966) lies about 1.5km N of the Porte du Paris by the Avenue Colbert.

Pont du Guétin

The industrial suburb of **Chaluzy**, about 2km E of the city centre, preserves the Romanesque chapel of St-Symphorien, with a curious tympanum.

The peninsula of flattish, sometimes wooded farmland between the Loire and the Allier S of Nevers is well worth exploring, particularly for its Romanesque churches. Most of the places to visit lie on either side of N7, the Moulins road. At 3.5km D976, the Bourges road, branches W from N7 to (5km) the **Pont du Guétin**, the aqueduct built in 1838 to carry the Loire Canal across the Allier. The Bec d'Allier is just to the N (see Marzy earlier in this route). N7 continues S past the racing circuit at (8.5km) **Magny-Cours** (1480 people) to (3.5km) Moiry. At **Mars-sur-Allier**, 4.5km W, the 12C church, once part of a Cluniac priory, has a primitive tympanum apparently of local workmanship. On the lower register Christ in Majesty is flanked by emblems of the Evangelists and six of the Apostles; on the upper register foliage emerges from the mouth of a Green Man. The church at **St-Parize-le-Châtel** (980 people), 3.5km E of Moiry, has a crypt with *capitals on its short, sturdy columns which make up for the naïvety of their design by the vigour of their details. These include: a centaur shooting a stag; an acrobat; a sciapod shading himself beneath his single massive foot; an owl; a tortoise; several Green Men; lions vomiting foliage; a pig and a monkey playing stringed instruments; a serpent; a demon whispering in the ear of a miser who clutches his money bags; a siren; and a man stirring a big cooking pot. **St-Pierre-le-Moûtier** (2090 people; Tourist Information), 7.5km S of Moiry on N7, is an interesting little town with old houses and fragments of its medieval walls. A statue proudly remembers that Jeanne d'Arc captured it in February 1429, her last victory before failing to take La Charité and falling into Burgundian hands at Compiègne. The 12–13C *church is a treasure-house of detail. The rich, though mutilated, tympanum of the N doorway shows Christ surrounded by the four Evangelists, with angels on the arch above; note the little cities on the capitals below. There are more good capitals inside, where the nave was made asymmetrical by the rebuilding of the N arcade. Note particularly the second column from the W in the S arcade, showing what is apparently the three ages of man on one face and musicians on another, and Daniel in the lions' den among the reused Romanesque capitals in the N arcade. The S transept contains a 14C tomb effigy and the choir a fine 16C Pietà.

18   The Nivernais: Auxerre to Nevers

Directions and distances. Total distance 151km (94 miles). From **Auxerre** N6, (16km) D100, (26km) D39 to (29km) Mailly-le-Château. D130, (32km) D100 to (39km) Châtel-Censoir. D21 to (49km) Coulanges-sur-Yonne. N151 to (58km) **Clamecy**. D951 to (66km) Dornecy. D985 to (88km) **Corbigny**. D977 bis, (120km) D977 to (122km) Prémery. D977 to (137km) Guérigny and (151km) **Nevers**.

Connections with other routes. Auxerre and places along N6 are described in Route 11. Several towns, notably Corbigny and Châtillon-en-Bazois, offer convenient ways into the Morvan (Route 13). Nevers is described near the end of Route 17, along the Loire Nivernaise from Cosne.

See the introduction to Route 17 for a general note on the Nivernais and Loire Nivernaise.

The quickest but not the best route from Auxerre to Coulanges-sur-Yonne (34km) follows N151. It passes (9km) **Gy-l'Evêque**, with a ruined church whose fine 13C wooden carving of Christ is now housed elsewhere in the village, and (14km) **Courson-les-Carrières** (720 people), a bleak place once, as its name announces, a centre of quarrying. The last stage of the journey runs through the **Forêt de Frétoy**.

A more interesting route from Auxerre to Coulangès follows the Yonne and the **Canal du Nivernais**. Its first stage through the Auxerrois vineyards that flank N6 is described in Route 11. At 16km, before Cravant, D100 branches right to follow the river and the canal through a pleasant stretch of country near the edge of the Morvan. **Prégilbert**, on the opposite bank at 6km, has a 13C church with a tall tower while neighbouring **Ste-Pallaye** has a simple Romanesque church dedicated to Palladia, one of the women followers who brought St Germanus' body back to Auxerre in 448 (compare Escolives-Ste-Camille in Route 11 and Ste-Magnance in Route 12). 4km later D39 branches away from the river to (3km) **Mailly-le-Château** (560 Mailly-Castellois), an old fortified village on a cliff overlooking the water. There is a view from the terrace near the church, whose primitive Gothic W façade has an unusual gallery with statues at the base of its columns. D130 crosses the river by a 15C bridge which still keeps its little chapel and rejoins D100 at 3km, where the *valley, hitherto gentle, is flanked by splendid cliffs. The **Rochers du Saussois**, opposite **Merry-sur-Yonne**, are a favourite with climbers. The railway yards that fill the valley make a grim introduction to **Châtel-Censoir** (600 people), 7km S, but the old centre on the hill above is much more pleasant. Despite Renaissance additions, the church has an 11C chancel with capitals showing foliage and fabulous animals. D21 leads past the little village of (5.5km) **Lucy-sur-Yonne**, with the handsome 15–16C château of Faulin (not open) on the edge of nearby woods.

Coulanges-sur-Yonne (580 people), 4.5km beyond, may be dull but the area round it is not. The best sight is **Druyes-les-Belles-Fontaines**, 11.5km W, and the best way to reach it is by taking D39 to Andryes and Ferrières. Approaching the village from the S, D148 gives a marvellous view of the *castle (open) on the hill above, now one of the most picturesque ruins in Burgundy. It was originally built in the 12C by the Courtenay family, counts of Auxerre and Nevers, and several times refurbished in the course of the Middle Ages. Here in 1216 Pierre de Courtenay accepted the Latin emperorship of Constantinople in preparation for the Fifth Crusade. Of the triangular outer *enceinte* little remains except the 14C gateway and the ruined bastions looking down into the village. Some of the houses on the little street belonged to the château which later replaced the castle but has vanished in its turn. A big 15C gateway tower, recently restored, leads into the shell of buildings round the inner courtyard, notable for the lack of a central keep and for its surprisingly small seigneurial apartments, whose Romanesque arches can still be made out, together with vestiges of the chapel. In the valley below stands the handsome Romanesque church, with some carved capitals in its choir. Near by is the source from which the village gets its name.

As it enters Nièvre and the Nivernais S of Coulanges the Yonne valley runs through striking scenery on the way to (9km) Clamecy, either by N151 or by D233 to Surgy and then D144 on the opposite bank.

CLAMECY (5280 Clamecyois; Tourist Information) stands on a promontory where the Beuvron flows into the Yonne. Until the early 1900s it relied on a timber trade first systematically developed in the 16C. Logs were floated from the Morvan forests down rivers dammed to control seasonal fluctuation and, on arriving at Clamecy, organised into convoys of rafts for the journey along the Yonne towards Paris. The *flotteurs* who once accounted for half the town's population played a crucial part in bringing the Revolution to Clamecy, the Nivernais and the Morvan. Their truculent spirit is celebrated in the novel 'Colas Breugnon' by Romain Rolland, born here in 1866. A statue of a typical *flotteur* stands on the **Pont de Bethléem** over the Yonne.

The centre to the W is dominated by the church of **St-Martin**, with its handsome Flamboyant *tower and W façade begun in 1497. The largely 13C interior has two striking curiosities in the false rood screen added by Viollet-le-Duc and the rectangular choir. The **Hôtel de Ville** opposite stands on the cellars of the castle built by the counts of Nevers. The best of the surrounding old streets is the Rue de la Monnaie, which branches from the Rue du Grand-Marché near the **Syndicat d'Initiative** and passes the half-timbered 15C **Maison du Tisserand** (Weaver's House) on its way round to the Rue Romain-Rolland, where the writer was born. Here also is the back entrance to the **Musée**, facing the Avenue de la République. The display about *flottage* is the most interesting feature of a diverse collection which also includes a disappointing clutch of Italian, Dutch and French paintings, a more adventurous exhibition of contemporary art, 17–19C *faïence* from Nevers and Clamecy, and editions and translations of Rolland's work.

The Pont de Bethléem and the neighbouring suburb of Bethléem on the E bank of the Yonne owe their name to the fact that the Bishop of Bethlehem, expelled by Saladin in 1223, installed his see here in the Hôpital de Panténor, a foundation willed to the bishropic by a Crusading count of Nevers. The bishop's successors remained at Clamecy until the Revolution. Only a fragment of their church remains, incorporated in the **Hôtel de la Boule d'Or**, though they have a substantial, if ugly, monument in the **Église de Bethléem** (1927), pseudo-Orientalism in reinforced concrete.

The quickest but not most interesting way from Clamecy to Prémery follows N151 to (16km) **Varzy** (1460 people; Tourist Information), in its distinctive ring of hills. It lay on the Compostela route from Vézelay to La Charité or Nevers. Pilgrims stopped to venerate the relics of St Eugenia (Eugénie) and St Regnobert, now preserved in the handsome Gothic church of St-Pierre, which also has a 16C altarpiece of the legend of St Eugenia (for which see Vézelay in Route 11). Near by are the old *lavoir* and the eclectic little museum, with Egyptian and Middle Eastern antiquities, medieval sculpture, Nevers *faïence* and old musical instruments. D977 continues from Varzy to (24km) Prémery.

A more interesting way to Prémery from Clamecy follows the river and the canal, taking D951 to (8km) Dornecy and then branching S on D985. Romain Rolland was buried at (2km) **Brèves**, once the site of a Merovingian cemetery of more than 200 tombs. 5km beyond D985 reaches the turning for (3km) **Tannay** (670 people; Tourist Information) on the opposite bank, which produces a white *vin de pays*. The 13C church, enlarged in the 15C, has a handsome nave with a bas-relief depicting the conversion of St Hubert (or St Eustace) at the W end. **Metz-le-Comte**, 2.5km E of D985, has an isolated little 12–13C church among vineyards on the top of the hill where a castle of the counts of Nevers once stood.

Corbigny (1800 people; Tourist Information), 8km further down D985, is a little market town with some pleasant riverside scenery where the Anguison flows towards its meeting with the Yonne. From the bridge there is a view of the 17–18C buildings of the former abbey of St-Léonard. Near by is the 16C Flamboyant church of St-Seine, with a lierne-vaulted nave and the altar and stalls from the abbey. **Cervon** (630 people), 6km SE, is a pleasant place with old houses and a church whose Romanesque work includes two tympana, the W one a particularly fine piece of work showing Christ flanked by emblems of the four Evangelists. Lormes is 13km NE of Corbigny: see the Morvan, Route 13.

The route to Prémery leaves the Canal du Nivernais and turns W. Before heading that way, it is worth following the canal S into the quiet countryside of the **Bazois**. At (8km) **Sardy-lès-Epiry** it parts company with the Yonne. On the way to the hamlet of **La Collancelle**, 6km SW, it runs through a deep wooded ravine before disappearing into a tunnel from which it emerges about 2km beyond, near the pleasant **Étang de Baye** and the **Étang de Vaux**. From Baye, 2km S, a perilously narrow road follows the bank, passing (2km) **Bazolles** and (6km) the little hill at **Mont-et-Marré**. **Châtillon-en-Bazois** (1160 Châtillonnais; Tourist Information), 4km beyond, is unremarkable except for the partly medieval château (open) on its outskirts. The church at **St-Saulge** (850 people), 14km NW of Châtillon, has superbly coloured 16C *stained glass in the nave. A ruined Romanesque church stands on the wooded hillside at the hamlet of **Jailly**, 4km W, its delicately sculpted W doorway isolated by the fall of part of the nave. Château-Chinon lies 19km E of Châtillon-en-Bazois by D978 and Moulins-Engilbert 17km SE by D978 and and D985: see the Morvan, Route 13. Avoiding Prémery,

D978 runs W from Châtillon directly to (21km) Nevers, passing (10km) **Rouy**, where the Romanesque church has a handsome choir.

D977 bis from Corbigny to Prémery soon passes (3.5km) **Chitry-les-Mines**, the name recalling its 15–16C silver mines. Jules Renard (1864–1910), author of 'Poil de Carotte', was brought up here and served as mayor. At (13.5km) **St-Révérien** the Romanesque *church, once part of a Cluniac priory, is one of the loveliest in the Nivernais. Its nave is only a 19C imitation of the original but the E end survives intact, with choir, ambulatory, radiating chapels and sculpted capitals that show a close connection with La Charité (Route 17). Among the subjects depicted, note the story of Jacob and the marvellously compact Last Judgement, both on the S side of the choir, as well as the foliage and fabulous beasts. The capital at the E end of the ambulatory showing two atlantes is signed 'Robertus me fecit'.

The woods of **Compierre**, about 2km NW, make a pleasant setting for the excavated *remains of a large 1–4C Gallo-Roman vicus, which include an unusual octagonal temple (open). About 7km further NW a church and a fragment of the 13C castle mark the summit of the **Butte de Montenoison** (417m), a splendid viewpoint over the surrounding country.

D977 bis continues from St-Révérien to (5km) **Moussy**, below Montenoison. A monument to 30 members of the Maquis Mariaux killed in August 1944 stands by the side of D256 in the woods to the SE.

8km later the road joins D977 and the river Nièvre on the way into (2km) **Prémery** (2380 people; Tourist Information), a little town that just manages to maintain its dignity in the shadow of its chemical factory. The bishops of Nevers made Prémery their summer residence and built the 14–17C château whose remains have been put to civic use. They also founded the handsome Gothic *church, built in the 1220s and 1230s. The N aisle of its nave contains a 15C Pietà and a statue of St John in the style of Claus Sluter. The college of canons included Canon Appelline (died 1466), spiritual adviser to Louis XI, whose house survives as the Maison du Saint.

D977 follows the wooded, broadening valley to (15km) **Guérigny** (2410 people; Tourist Information), a glum little industrial town which became the site of the Forges de la Chaussade, or naval ironworks, when they were moved from Cosne-sur-Loire in 1782. They closed in 1971 but their buildings now shelter an exhibition of industrial history. The villages of **Ourouër**, 9.5km SE, and **Parigny-les-Vaux** (940 people), 4km W, both have Romanesque churches. D977 continues to (14km) **Nevers**, described in the previous route.

19 The Loire Nivernaise continued: Nevers to Paray-le-Monial

Directions and distances. Total distance 112km (70 miles). N81 from **Nevers** to (34km) Decize. D979 to Bourbon-Lancy (bypassed at 69km) and (100km) Digoin. N79 to (112km) **Paray-le-Monial**.

Connections with other routes. This route continues Route 17, along the Loire Nivernaise from Cosne to Nevers. Route 18 reaches Nevers from Auxerre. A long detour leads from Digoin up to the Morvan (Route 13). Paray-le-Monial is the starting point for several journeys: through the Brionnais (Route 20), along the Canal du Centre via Le Creusot to Chalon (Route 21), and through the Charolais to Charolles and Mâcon (Route 22).

See the introduction to Route 17 for a general note on the Nivernais and Loire Nivernaise.

From **Nevers** N81 follows a stretch of the Loire and its canal long since given over to industry. **St-Éloi** (1810 people), at 5km, is named after Eligius, patron saint of smiths and metalworkers. See Route 17 for the Romanesque church in the outskirts of Nevers at Chaluzy to the N. There is another one at **Sauvigny-les-Bois** (1590 people) to the E. **Imphy** (4480 people), 7km further along N81, keeps its steelworks. **Chevenon** (720 people), on the opposite bank of the river, has a striking 14C castle (access to outside only). **Béard**, 10km beyond Imphy, has a disused but lovingly restored Romanesque *church with a fine crossing tower and dome.

N81 continues to (12km) **Decize** (6880 Decizois; Tourist Information), on the peninsula of rock where the Loire is joined by the Aron and the Canal du Nivernais on the last leg of its course from Auxerre. Descended from the Gallo-Roman Decetia and never as industrialised as its neighbours, the town still has fragments of its medieval walls and the château built by the counts of Nevers, together with the prominent 17C Couvent des Minimes. Beneath the church of St-Aré lies the heavily restored Merovingian crypt built for the tomb of the local bishop Arigius (died 558). Opposite the town hall stands a handsome 19C clock tower commemorating Guy Coquille (1523–1603), historian of the Nivernais and local celebrity. The Revolutionary leader Antoine de Saint-Just (1767–1794), also born at Decize, is not so prominently remembered.

La Machine (4190 people), 7.5km N among hills and forests with a long tradition of charcoal-burning and mining, is bluntly named after the equipment for coal extraction introduced in the 17C. Its collieries fuelled the naval ironworks of the Loire in the 18C and the Schneiders' factories in the 19C and 20C. They closed in 1974 and the mine headquarters now house a modest but well-organised museum which preserves the 19C manager's office together with displays of equipment (miners' lamps) and social history. Guided tours led by former miners leave from the museum for the pit at nearby Glenons, with pithead machinery and reconstructed galleries.

Beyond Decize D979 follows the Loire valley, growing flat and agricultural as it leaves the Nivernais. On a hill E of the road at 35km stands **Bourbon-Lancy** (6180 Bourbonnais; Tourist Information), a spa town with a carefully preserved old quarter that includes fragments of its walls, the 15C clock tower and some half-timbered houses, one of them containing a museum of military uniforms. The Romanesque church of St-Nazaire, once part of a Cluniac priory, is now a museum with local archaeology, medieval sculpture (tomb of a Compostela pilgrim) and work by the 19C artist Puvis de Chavannes. The **Signal de Mont** to the NE makes a good viewpoint (469m).

D979 continues past (6.5km) **St-Aubin-sur-Loire**, where the 18C château contains good tapestries and furnishings (open). The Arroux joins the Loire just before (24.5km) **Digoin** (10,030 Digoinais; Tourist Information). The little town also marks a major junction where the Loire Canal continues S as the Roanne canal while the Canal du Centre (explored in Route 21) heads E via Paray-le-Monial. The aqueduct (1834–1838) carrying the Canal du Centre over the Loire makes an impressive sight, though the scenery lacks the charm of the Pont du Guétin in Route 17. The nearby Syndicat d'Initiative occupies the same 18C building as the *Centre de Documentation devoted to the local ceramics industry, with a collection ranging from Gallo-Roman to contemporary work and an absorbing account of the history of manufacturing techniques. The 19C pseudo-Romanesque church of Notre-Dame-de-la-Providence in the centre of town is best avoided.

A long detour (56km in all) from Digoin to the Morvan begins by following D994 and the Arroux to (16km) the dull industrial town of **Gueugnon** (9700 people). D25 continues to (16.5km) **Issy-l'Évêque** (1010 people), with a late Romanesque church and, in the Tour de Luzy, a display of local history that includes finds from **Mont Dardon** to the SE, a site inhabited from the Neolithic era until the Middle Ages and an important oppidum contemporary with Bibracte. D25 changes its name to D27 on the way to (11.5km) **Luzy** (2420 people; Tourist Information) and (12km) Larochemillay, near Mont Beuvray (Bibracte) on the southern edge of the Morvan (Route 13).

At Digoin N79 quits the Loire and follows the Bourbince and the Canal du Centre to (12km) Paray-le-Monial.

Paray-le-Monial: Sacré-Coeur and the river Bourbince

PARAY-LE-MONIAL (9860 Parodiens; Tourist Information) is dominated by its stately Romanesque church beside the river Bourbince. Once Notre-Dame, it is now dedicated to Sacré-Coeur, a cult which originated at Paray and attracts pilgrims each June as well as devout visitors throughout the year.

**Sacré-Coeur belongs largely to the closing decades of the 11C and the opening years of the 12C. It was built by Hugues de Semur (St Hugh of Cluny) at the same time he was directing work at Cluny itself and so, of all the Romanesque buildings to survive in Burgundy, echoes Cluny III most closely. The only major exception is the W end overlooking the Bourbince, where the two-storey narthex and its flanking towers belonged to an earlier 11C church. The upper stages of the N tower are noticeably more elaborate than the rest of a façade that was always severe and made more so by fire in the 16C and restoration in the 19C. Simplicity is elsewhere the keynote of a building which relies on confident harmony of proportion rather than richness of sculptural detail. Though well worth attention in its own right, the Arabic decoration of the transept doors is less characteristic than the lucid geometry of the chevet, where choir, ambulatory and radiating chapels make a lovely pattern of semicircles in warm, honey-coloured stone and red pantiles. Above them rises the octagonal crossing tower, accurately reconstructed in the course of 19C restoration.

The same emphasis on proportion is apparent inside the church, where the carved capitals and the moulding of the arches play only a subsidiary role. Most observers have noted the recurrence of the figure three: three aisles, three bays, three storeys and so forth. In the nave, however, it may be partly accidental, for the hasty junction with the older W wall suggests that a plan for a longer nave and new W end was abandoned at a late stage in building, perhaps on the death of Hugues de Semur in 1109. But nowhere can the characteristic Cluniac elevation be seen to more impressive effect. Fluted pilasters flank the tall pointed arches of the ground-floor arcade, while in the false triforium and clerestory engaged columns enclose each group of three round arches. The central aisle has a pointed barrel vault, while the side-aisles are groin-vaulted. The rest of the building subtly varies these motifs. Note, for example, the engaged columns that unite all three storeys of the transepts. In the two-storeyed E end small double columns appear on the ambulatory walls, while the choir itself is supported by a tall, narrow arcade with round arches. The 14C fresco of Christ in Majesty on the semi-domed apse is one of the few later additions to a church that has quite wonderfully kept its original purity.

The 18C cloister S of Sacré-Coeur contains the ***Musée de la Faïence charolaise**, with the Molin collection of *faïence* from the workshops established at Charolles in the 1840s, notable in particular for the classic designs of Elisabeth Parmentier in the late 19C.

Sacré-Coeur's present dedication reflects the popularity of the cult of the Sacred Heart, which leaves its mark throughout Paray. It was originated by Marguerite-Marie Alacoque (1647–1690), a nun in the Convent of the Visitation. Between 1673 and 1675 she experienced four visions of Christ, who charged her to promote devotion to his heart as a symbol of his love for mankind. Her visions were greeted with hostility by the other nuns, as her attempts to establish a devotional cult were by Louis XIV. She was not beatified until 1864 nor canonised until 1920. The cult itself did not become popular until the years after the Franco-Prussian War, when the first pilgrimage to Paray-le-Monial in 1873 prompted the decision to dedicate France to the Sacred Heart and to build the hideous Sacré-Coeur in

Montmartre. The pilgrimage, now second only to Lourdes among French pilgrimages, takes place on the Friday following the Feast of Corpus Christi in June. The saint's feast day is on the Sunday following 16 October.

Even at other times of year the streets around the church are often full of visitors who arrive by coach to see the various sights connected with the saint. The **Chambre des Reliques**, opposite the E end, has a reconstruction of her cell while the neighbouring **Parc des Chapelains**, where the pilgrimage ends each year, boasts a diorama of her life. To the N is the **Chapelle de la Visitation**, a 17C building heavily revamped in the 19C, where the saint was granted her revelations and where her shrine now stands.

The **Musée du Hiéron** on the corner of the Rue de la Paix and the Rue Pasteur contains a masterpiece in the early 12C Romanesque *tympanum from the priory at Anzy-le-Duc, a splendid foretaste of what the Brionnais churches toured in the next route have to offer. Characteristic of the region in both its subject and its style, it shows Christ in a mandorla, supported by angels, with a Nativity watched by saints and the Evangelists on the lintel below. The rest of the collection, assembled by Baron de Sarachaga in the 19C, consists of paintings, altarpieces and liturgical objects treating the Eucharist; it includes an interesting 16C Eucharistic ark carved in bone and ivory, but the general effect is bizarre and depressing.

The Rue de la Paix leads W to the Place Guignaud. The square 16C **Tour St-Nicolas** is a relic of a vanished church, while the richly sculptured façade of the Renaissance **Hôtel de Ville** makes fine use of the same local stone of which Sacré-Coeur and the neighbouring churches of the Brionnais are built.

20 The Brionnais

Its combination of peaceful countryside and village churches makes the **Brionnais** one of the nicest corners of Burgundy. It is more or less literally a corner: a little adjunct to the Charolais on a triangle of land that forms the southern tip of Burgundy below Paray-le-Monial, far enough from the great centres of the region for its inhabitants to call themselves first Brionnais and then, secondly, Burgundians. As the crow flies (though of course the winding country roads never follow the crow's flight) the Brionnais is only about 32km long, from Paray to Charlieu at the southern tip of the triangle, and only about 28km across at its broadest point, just S of Paray.

In the W, where the Loire marks its boundary, the Brionnais can be flat and sometimes dull. In the E, where the Sornin flows near the foothills of the Beaujolais mountains, it grows hilly and thickly wooded. But the country is at its most characteristically charming in the heartland round St-Christophe: a friendly, cultivated, rather English landscape of gently rolling hills and green pasture neatly divided by hedges or the occasional dry stone wall and dotted with clumps of woodland. The Charolais that graze the fields and fill the cattle pens at St-Christophe's weekly market are the staple of Brionnais agriculture. Its ancient importance gave Semur-en-Brionnais a claim to be called the capital of the region, but today there are only a few population centres. Apart from St-Christophe itself, Marcigny or La Clayette are the towns to choose as your base if you are not just making a short foray from Paray or Charlieu.

The Romanesque churches are the main reason for lingering. The Brionnais has no cathedrals and only a fragment remains of its great monastery at Charlieu, though admittedly a magnificent fragment. Otherwise, its Romanesque buildings are all parish churches or churches that, despite their monastic origin, fit comfortably into the scale of its small villages. Yet together they form a distinctive local group, finer than any you will find within such a small compass even in a region as well blessed as Burgundy. The most obvious cause for this flowering lay at Cluny, where the third great church that rose to completion between about 1088 and about 1130 not only expressed the abbey's ecclesiastical power but also spread its architectural ideas to Autun, to Vézelay and beyond Burgundy. It was inevitable that the Brionnais, on the other side of the hills less than 50km W of Cluny, should feel the breath of this invigorating wind. The monasteries at Paray and Charlieu were both subject to Cluny, while Marcigny possessed the first Cluniac nunnery in France. Informal bonds strengthened these official connections. Hugues, the abbot who began Cluny III, came from Semur—where, fittingly, the church faithfully echoed the design of its great parent. Odilon, Hugues' predecessor as abbot of Cluny, encouraged veneration of the shrine at Anzy-le-Duc to one of its former priors. The church here, the most beautiful of all Brionnais churches, varied the Cluniac model to become the prototype for Vézelay.

For both imitation and experiment the Brionnais was fertile ground in a literal sense. Sandstone and granite outcrop in the E of the region, intractable stones that limit ornament to bold and simple forms. But elsewhere the building material is a warm, honey-coloured limestone—as beautiful as Ham stone from Somerset—that goes ideally with the red pantiles used for the roofs. It is also so responsive to the chisel that it would tempt any workman into richly detailed carving; to Burgundian masons it offered an ideal invitation. The distinctive strength of Brionnais churches is the sculpture on the windows and arches of their towers, on the capitals of their naves and choirs, but above all on their doorways, where the Ascension makes a favourite subject for the tympana. Architectural historians have organised this great outburst of activity, extending from the 11C to the end of the 12C, into four phases: youth, maturity, decline and exhaustion. For all its pat oversimplification, this scheme offers a useful introductory framework for more detailed study. The first stage, in the late 11C, is represented by the relatively simple nave doorways at Anzy-le-Duc and Charlieu. The doorways of Montceaux-l'Étoile, St-Julien-de-Jonzy and the Charlieu narthex, as well as the tympanum from Anzy-le-Duc preserved in the Musée du Hiéron at Paray-le-Monial, show Brionnais sculpture in the full tide of its confident vigour during the opening decades of the next century. The mid 12C tympana at Fleury-la-Montagne and on the priory's outer wall at Anzy-le-Duc and the late 12C one at Semur mark the final phases of what Raymond Oursel has condemned, with unnecessary severity, as the triumph of anecdote over significance and clarity of design.

Paray-le-Monial (Route 19), where Sacré-Coeur and the tympanum in the Musée du Hiéron provide an ideal foretaste of Brionnais art, also makes the obvious place to start and finish a tour, though you can just as easily end E of Paray at **Charolles** (Route 22). In either case the simple circuit of main roads S from Paray to Charlieu and back N again via La Clayette is about 100km (62 miles), but the detours and backtracking required to see the villages and churches that give point to the journey can almost double the distance. Although there is no logical order by which to make your way through the network of country roads, the Circuit Roman marked on local signposts and sketched in tourist brochures makes it difficult to get really lost. The description below does not try to enforce a hard and fast itinerary by detailed directions but lists the major landmarks in the order you are most likely to encounter them.

Montceaux-l'Étoile, off D982 14km SW of Paray-le-Monial. The early 12C *W doorway is one of the great achievements of Brionnais sculpture. Tympanum and lintel are carved from a single block of rich honey-coloured limestone and united in a single design. Its subject is the Ascension. Holding the Cross, Christ stands inside a mandorla which angels do not just support but visibly lift above the heads of the Virgin Mary and the Apostles (who include St Peter brandishing his huge key). Note that the figures on the capitals of the arch are also excited spectators. The battles with monsters on the capitals of the lintels may echo the victory over death announced in Christ's triumphant gesture. The 18C extension to the E end makes the inside of the church a horrible botch, though a couple of foliage capitals survive.

Anzy-le-Duc, on D10 4km S of Montceaux-l'Étoile. The *church is the pearl of the Brionnais. It belonged to a Benedictine priory founded about 876, dependent on St-Martin at Autun but closely connected with Cluny and its abbots. Though building work spread over two campaigns—the first beginning at the E end around the mid 11C, the second completing the nave and W end in the late 11C or early 12C—the result is a satisfying ensemble of mellow stone and red pantiled roofs dominated by the octagonal, three-storeyed crossing tower in the Lombardic style. The grass courtyard on the S side gives the best view of it. The tympanum from the priory's main gateway is now in the Musée du Hiéron at Paray-le-Monial. The two that survive on site belong to very different styles and periods. The late 11C Ascension over the W doorway is serene and restrained in comparison to the flowing confidence of the Ascension at Montceaux-l'Étoile. The doorway on the outside priory wall to the S is mid 12C work, usually cited as an example of Brionnais carving in decay but in fact still daring and robust. The tympanum juxtaposes the Fall with the Adoration of the Magi and the lintel Heaven with Hell: note the writhing patterns which connect the serpent in Eden and the monster in Hell.

The elevation of the nave has special importance for students of Burgundian Romanesque. It abandons the example of Cluny III for a design that anticipates, in miniature, the great church at Vézelay: groined vaults separated by round transverse arches replace pointed barrel vaulting and engaged columns replace fluted pilasters. The carved capitals of the nave show a special interest in animals. On the S side they include a curious orgy (second column, W face). On the N side they include: Daniel being licked by friendly lions (first column, E face), a design that also appears at Charlieu; Samson fighting the lion (second column, W face); an acrobat being attacked by monsters (second column, E face); St Michael and the Devil (third column, W face); and old men pulling each other's beards (fifth column, W face).

Baugy, off D982 5km SW of Anzy-le-Duc. The village has a minor Romanesque church, much altered and now decaying, which has lost its tympanum but not all its capitals. Note the animals playing musical instruments, on the right of the W door.

Marcigny (2260 Marcignots; Tourist Information), off D982 2km beyond Baugy and 8km S of Montceaux-l'Étoile. A little town near the Loire, it holds a Monday market (dating back to 1226) at which poultry makes a special feature. A turkey and goose fair takes place every December. There are half-timbered houses on and near the Place des Halles. The 15C Tour du Moulin, near the adjoining Place du Prieuré, is an interesting fragment of the fortifications which defended Marcigny and its Cluniac nunnery (the first in France, founded in 1054). It now houses a local museum with a *collection of French and Italian *faïence*, including dishes attributed to Bernard Palissy.

Semur-en-Brionnais (640 people), on D989 5km E of Marcigny. Now an attractive village, it was once a little fortified town. The castle, former law courts and relics of its priory buildings make a pleasant group around the church of *St-Hilaire. Begun in about 1100–1130 but not finished until the last quarter of the 12C, it is in many respects the latest of the region's Romanesque churches. Externally, the most satisfying features are the chevet and the octagonal tower, a close relative of the tower at Anzy-le-Duc. The W doorway has a tympanum with Christ in a mandorla surrounded by angels and emblems of the four Evangelists, a disappointingly crude piece of work. The lintel depicts St Hilary (whose feast day gives its name to the legal and Oxford terms) opposing the Arian bishops at the council of Seleucia in 359: on the left they exclude him from the council table, on the right an angel helps him to a seat. The influence of Cluny III is particularly marked inside the church, in the fluted pilasters, the triforium and the corbelled tribune at the W end, a direct echo of the St-Michel chapel above Cluny's own W doorway. Note, among the carvings, the cheerful atlantes in the apsidal chapels.

The castle (open) was first built in the 9C by the family whose most famous son was Hugues, the great abbot of Cluny (1024–1109). It still has its large rectangular keep, altered in later centuries, and two small round towers which served as a prison in the 18C.

St-Christophe-en-Brionnais, 8km NE of Semur-en-Brionnais by D989, a route with some lovely views. Though the town has only about 800 people, its wide main street announces that it is the market centre of the Brionnais. Perhaps dating back to the 10C and first licensed in 1488, the market is nowadays devoted to the Charolais which are the backbone of the region's economy; 100,000 animals pass through its pens every year, making it the fifth largest cattle market in France. It takes place every Thursday morning, the animals arriving for sale by 06.30 and being loaded up into lorries again by 09.00.

Varenne-l'Arconce, 8km N of St-Christophe on the wooded D34. The late 11C church, built of sandstone and granite, has an imposing tower and chevet and, over the S doorway, a simply carved Paschal Lamb. A few capitals survive in the badly treated and badly decaying interior: note the two cheerful lions (third column on N side of nave) and the centaur (NE corner of crossing).

St-Julien-de-Jonzy, on D8 8km SE of Semur. Though the rest of the church has been greatly altered, its early 12C *W doorway survives as one of the masterpieces of Brionnais art. Its richness betrays the same hand that carved the Charlieu narthex: note the ornate, swirling robes and wings of the angels who support Christ sitting in the mandorla and, on the lintel below, the folds of the tablecloth from which Christ and the Apostles eat the Last Supper. There is a fine view of the surrounding countryside from the E end.

Iguerande (920 people), on D982 9km S of Marcigny. The village derives its curious name from the Celtic settlement, Evoranda. Its Romanesque church stands on a hill overlooking the Loire valley, a dramatic site that make the strong harmony of its proportions all the more impressive. The interior has a barrel-vaulted nave, dome over the crossing and simple chevet. Note the bases of the columns and, among the capitals, the monsters playing musical instruments (N side of the nave, first column, E face).

Fleury-la-Montagne (590 people), 4km E of Iguerande and D982. The church has a rich but now mutilated late 12C W doorway with Christ in Majesty above a charming, detailed Adoration of Magi and two interesting capitals. The interior is heartbreaking.

Charlieu (4380 Charliandins; Tourist Information), 11km SE of Iguerande by D982/D482 to Pouilly-sous-Charlieu and then D487, or 9km S of Fleury-la-Montagne by back-roads. A pleasant little town by the Sornin river, just outside modern Burgundy in the department of Loire, it marks the southern tip of the Brionnais. Charlieu grew up around the Benedictine abbey founded in 872, later attached to Cluny and still prospering after it was reduced to a priory in about 1040. Even in their present ruined state, the ˙abbey buildings are among the great works of the Brionnais. Little survives of the three churches built successively in the 9C, 10C and 11C, each larger than the last, but their ground-plans can clearly be understood from the upper storey of the 12C narthex which overlooks their W end. Among the capitals up here are a charming sun and moon. Below, the surviving fragment of the 11C W end has capitals which include a centaur and a Daniel in the lions' den of the same design found at Anzy-le-Duc. The doorway leading from the narthex to the nave bears a late 11C tympanum showing the Ascension: the same period, the same subject and almost the same style as the doorway in the equivalent position at Anzy-le-Duc. Nothing could contrast more sharply with its stiff restraint than Charlieu's masterpiece, the two doorways on the N side of the narthex. In the wedding feast at Cana, on the tympanum of the smaller doorway, the folds of the tablecloth are the most obvious detail to identify the same master who carved the Last Supper at St-Julien-de-Jonzy. The characters from the Transfiguration who appear on the arch above help to suggest a date, for the Feast of the Transfiguration formally entered the Cluniac calendar in 1132. The lintel below has scenes of ancient sacrifice, presumably seen as prefiguring Christ's passion. The great doorway has the Ascension at its centre, a rich but beautifully compact design almost overwhelmed by the quite astonishing profusion of carving that covers every available surface around it: a heightened, virtuoso display of Romanesque ornament that seems almost to anticipate the Renaissance and the Baroque. Note, for example, the fleece of the Agnus Dei on the keystone of the arch and the female figure, representing Lust, on the inner face of the left-hand column. The late 15C cloister incorporates a row of double-columned arches with capitals from the 10C church. Near by, the chapter house has a lectern built into its central column and the monks' parlour contains an interesting collection of religious sculpture.

The Franciscan convent at **St-Nizier-sous-Charlieu**, 4km SW, is one of several religious houses that sprang up in the shadow of the great abbey at Charlieu. It was founded at the end of the 13C but rebuilt in the late 14C and early 15C after an army of mercenaries demolished it during the Hundred Years War. The big church, bare except for successive layers of wall paintings and two mutilated tomb effigies, is less interesting than the cloisters. They are trapezoidal rather than square in their plan, and the capitals in the N walk have a good series of carved animals. Rescued and rebuilt after they had already been dismantled for sale to the USA in 1910, the cloisters have recently been restored with considerable tact.

Châteauneuf, 10km NE of Charlieu on D987. (Do not confuse it with Châteauneuf-en-Auxois.) The tall, late Romanesque church stands on the hill near the castle from which the village originally took its name. Its S doorway has a row of Apostles on the lintel below the blank tympanum, and the interior has a clerestory high above the pointed arches of the arcade.

La Clayette (2310 Clayettois; Tourist Information), on D985 11km NE of Charlieu. Its name is pronounced 'La Clette'. The moated 14C castle, altered in the 18C and 19C, has battlements and round towers with pointed roofs that give it a pure Walt Disney look. A *spectacle* is staged here in July and August and, though the castle itself is not otherwise open, there is a museum of vintage cars, motorbikes and bikes in its outbuildings. The 16C château of **Chevannes** (open), 5km SE, has a half-timbered gallery; it houses exhibitions of contemporary arts and crafts. The **Montagne de Dun** (721m), an outlier of the Beaujolais mountains 8km SE of La Clayette, has the restored fragment of a Romanesque church.

Vareilles, 5km W of La Clayette on D989 (which continues to St-Christophe). The church keeps its Romanesque tower, with engaged columns, and choir. At **St-Laurent-en-Brionnais**, 4km S of Vareilles and 5.5.km SW of La Clayette, the transept and tower of the late 12C Romanesque church survive with some capitals and column bases in the choir.

Bois-Ste-Marie, near the Beaujolais mountains 7km NE of La Clayette on D79 (a pleasant road that continues via Beaubery and the Mont des Carges, in Route 22, to join N79 between Charolles and Mâcon). The decayed little town has a late 11C and early 12C church. The tympanum of the Flight into Egypt on the S doorway apparently dates from 19C restoration. The interior has good capitals (note the devils) and a groined vault oddly connected to the choir. **Drée**, in wooded country W of Bois-Ste-Marie and 4km NE of La Clayette, has a 17C château (not open).

St-Germain-en-Brionnais, 8km N of La Clayette on D985 (which continues N to Charolles). The village stands on a hill with a wide view. Its sandstone and granite church, late 11C, has large aisles, some primitive capitals and a little Lombardic gallery in the apse. **Marcilly-la-Guerce**, 6km NE of St-Germain and 4km S of Charolles, has a Romanesque church with Lombardic work on the outside of the nave, not helped by the pink cement rendering.

21   The Canal du Centre: Paray to Le Creusot and Chalon

Directions and distances. Total distance 113km (70 miles). From **Paray-le-Monial** N70 and (4km) D974 to (37km) **Montceau-les-Mines**. D974 to (40km) Blanzy. D980 to (53km) Montcenis. D984 to (58km) **Le Creusot**. D28, (62km) N80, (66km) D974 to (90km) Santenay and (96km) **Chagny**. N6 to (113km) **Chalon-sur-Saône**.

Connections with other routes. Route 19 describes Paray, Route 6 Santenay and the way to Chagny, Route 7 Chagny and Chalon.

The Charolais and its adjunct, the Brionnais, make one of Burgundy's largest *pays*, filling the whole SW corner of the department of Saône-et-Loire. The previous route explored the Brionnais, and the next route runs via Charolles through the combination of gentle pastureland and granite hills that characterises the region. The present route takes in both these aspects of the Charolais but the area it explores has a special identity as Burgundy's industrial heartland. Its commercial lifeline is the **Canal du Centre**, built by the engineer Emiland Gauthey in 1783–1791 and running from the Loire at Digoin to Paray-le-Monial and then N through the gap in the Côte at Chagny to join the Saône at Chalon. For most of its course (112km, 70 miles) it follows the valleys of the Bourbince and the Dheune, rivers which flow in opposite directions, so that 61 locks are needed to link what nature had deliberately put asunder. At its centre lies the Blanzy basin, whose coal deposits have been exploited since the Middle Ages. By the 18C the industry that filled the basin already demanded its own transport canal and, with the arrival of the Schneider brothers in the 19C, Le Creusot grew into a major centre of iron and steel industries, while the mining villages collected into the town of Montceau-les-Mines. The 20C has not been kind to such places and, though industry survives and the canal is still in commercial use, the Blanzy basin shows all the expected signs of post-industrial decline. Such decline commonly brings a new awareness of industrial heritage, so it is no surprise to find a good introduction to the history of the region in the Écomusée at Le Creusot and its various branches in the smaller surrounding communities. Several detours from the main route explore the rich countryside which the growth of industry never destroyed.

Disused colliery near Ciry-le-Noble

N70, the fast road from Paray to Montceau-les-Mines, does not run close enough to the water to be very interesting. The little D974 follows a better route, branching from N79 4km E of Paray and running alongside the canal as its flows through the quiet countryside. At (16km) **Génelard** (1870 people) D985 leads NW to (4km) **Perrecy-les-Forges** (2020 people). Its Romanesque church, once part of a priory attached to St-Benoît-sur-Loire, has a splendid *narthex (c 1130). Clearly the work of Brionnais masons, with its two storeys, tower and rich sculpture, it anticipates the narthex at Vézelay in grandeur and so helps confirm the link between the Brionnais and La Madeleine. The vigorous capitals include Lust, elephants and the cockleshell emblem of the Compostela pilgrimage, apparently making its earliest recorded appearance in French sculpture. The tympanum has Christ in Majesty supported by angels with delicate wings, and the crowded scenes from the Passion on the lintel include a vignette of Judas kissing Christ. Fighting angels appear on the corbels and the hermit saints Antony and Paul (favourite subjects in La Madeleine) on the left-hand capital. The upper storey houses a local museum, a branch of the Écomusée at Le Creusot. D985 continues beyond Perrecy to (13km) **Toulon-sur-Arroux** (1870 people), a pleasant old town with a Romanesque church in the little square near the 19C church that superseded it.

In the little industrial town of **Ciry-le-Noble** (2800 people), 6km beyond Génelard on D974, the old photographer's studio is preserved as a branch of the Écomusée at Le Creusot. Its collection of old photos makes a touching record of local history.

D974 continues to (11km) **Montceau-les-Mines** (23,000 Montcelliens; Tourist Information), born from the agglomeration of mining villages which filled the Blanzy basin and systematically developed by the Chagot family in the 19C to serve the Schneider factories at Le Creusot. The mining community was swelled by the arrival of Polish refugees from the Soviet–Polish war in the 1920s. Most of its collieries have closed in recent years—though the route into the town still passes pitheads and open-cast mines—and the town now cultivates a hygienically modern look. There is a museum of fossils from the Blanzy basin on the Quai Jules-Chagot, and the old school on the Rue Jean-Jaurès, a branch of the Écomusée at Le Creusot, has reconstructed 19C and 20C classrooms. **Blanzy** (7640 people), 3km N, has the most interesting monument to the region's mining history in the St-Claude pit, closed in 1882 but now an industrial museum with its pithead machinery restored to working order, reconstructed galleries and a good collection of miners' lamps.

It is well worth following D980, the Cluny road, SE from Blanzy into the Charolais hills. The village of **Gourdon** (800 people), perched on a hill at 10km, has a granite-built Romanesque *church which combines the Cluniac and Brionnais styles. There are good capitals (note the animals) in the tall nave and the choir, which also has a 12C wall painting of Christ in Majesty. The 'Treasure of Gourdon' is a Merovingian gold chalice and oblong paten, discovered in 1845 and now in the Musée du Cabinet et des Médailles et Antiques at the Bibliothèque Nationale. At ***Mont-St-Vincent**, 3km beyond, the hill commands an even wider view, so good that even the wretched radio masts do not spoil it. The Romanesque church has an eroded tympanum, a few primitive capitals and transverse barrel vaulting over its nave, an arrangement otherwise unique to St-Philibert in Tournus. The 16C salt warehouse, one of several picturesque buildings in the village, shelters a little archaeological museum with local finds and a display about the region's Romanesque churches.

The best route from Blanzy to Le Creusot avoids the dull industrial town of **Montchanin** (5960 people) and instead follows D980 NW past ponds to (13km) **Montcenis** (2340 people), which manages to keep much of its character as an old hill town despite being on the edge of Le Creusot's industry.

D984 completes the journey to (5km) Le Creusot but it is also rewarding to explore D47 and D228 running through the hilly countryside W of Montcenis. **Uchon**, on D228 at 14km, makes a good destination. With its ruined church and 16C oratory, the little village (now 67 people) once attracted pilgrims imploring relief from the plague. It stands on the flank of the boulder-strewn *Signal d'Uchon* (681m) which has a marvellous view across the Arroux valley to the Morvan. D228 can be followed N to (8.5km) **Mesvres** (840 people), from which side-roads continue along the hills bounding the Arroux valley to (14km) Autun, passing the grounds of the 17C château of **Montjeu** (not open) and the Croix de la Libération (1945).

LE CREUSOT (28,910 Creusotins; Tourist Information) developed as the industrial centre using the coal mined in the region since the Middle Ages. When Louis XVI moved the royal glass works here from Sèvres in the 1780s the town was already known for its foundries, which went on to provide cannon for the Revolutionary and Napoleonic Wars. Eugène and Adolphe Schneider, brothers from Lorraine, bought the foundries in 1836 and created an industrial empire which lasted for four generations and well over a century, producing France's earliest steam locomotives, armaments, cranes, bridges and virtually all kinds of heavy metal equipment. In the process Le Creusot developed as a classic 19C company town, its houses, schools, hospitals and churches built by the Schneiders and its squares laid out around statues of their leading representatives. After World War II, when German occupation of the factories provoked Allied bombing raids, the family yielded place to La Société des Forges et Ateliers du Creusot and its successor, Creusot-Loire, a victim of the recession in the iron and steel industry in the 1980s. During this decade the town's population shrank by more than a tenth. Le Creusot now depends on a variety of firms to adapt its traditional skills to a changed economy. Framatome, which makes reactors for nuclear power stations, has recently been joined by SNECMA, whose current projects include parts for the European Airbus.

Next to the Place Schneider, with a statue of Eugène I and the church of **St-Laurent**, stands the *Château de la Verrerie*, built as the glass works in 1787, used as the Schneider family residence, aggrandised by Eugène II in 1905 and restored after wartime bomb damage. It now makes a splendid monument to the town's industrial history. Bronze cannon manufactured in Le Creusot flank the main entrance. The two conical glass furnaces in the courtyard were converted by Eugène II into a chapel, now an exhibition hall, and a charming private theatre where Sarah Bernhardt played before members of the family and their guests. The theatre is the highlight of the guided tour which also visits the Centre des Techniques, where scale models of machinery made by the Schneiders and Creusot-Loire include the 'Gironde' (1838), the first locomotive made at Le Creusot. The main building of the château now houses the Écomusée de la Communauté Urbaine Le Creusot-Montceau-les-Mines. Its very thorough introduction to the region, ranging from geology and prehistory to industry and folk art, is notable for a collection of 18–19C glassware and for a splendid working model of the foundries and workshops. The Écomusée also has branches at Perrecy-les-Forges, Ciry-le-Noble, Montceau-les-Mines and Écuisses.

The château faces the hillside where the railway and crane workshops once stood. Their ruins, imaginatively laid out as a public park, lead down to the valley bottom with the SNECMA factory and the railway line. The Combe des Mineurs on the opposite slope is a row of workers' cottages (1826) reminiscent of a Welsh mining town. The Promenade des Crêtes and the Rue des Pyrénées, running along the heights, offer superb viewpoints over the valley.

D138 continues N from the Rue des Pyrénées to (3km) **St-Sernin-du-Bois** (1860 people), with the remains of its castle and priory near a reservoir.

The main route from Le Creusot follows D28 and N80 to rejoin (8km) D974 where it runs along the valley between the Canal du Centre and the Dheune. The lock-keeper's house near (3km) **Écuisses** (1760 people) is now a branch of the Écomusée with a display about the history of the canal. Just before **St-Léger-sur-Dheune** (1420 people), 14km beyond, the road and canal cross D978. **Couches**, 6km left, is described in Route 6. So is **Santenay**, 17km further, and the way to (6km) **Chagny**. N6 follows the canal from Chagny to (17km) **Chalon-sur-Saône**, but Route 7 suggests a more interesting way through the Chalonnais vineyards.

22 The Charolais: Paray to Charolles and Mâcon

Directions and distances. Total distance 64km (40 miles). N79 from **Paray-le-Monial** to (13km) **Charolles**. N79, (19km) D983, (21km) D17 to (42km) Mazillé. D17, (44km) N79 and Route Touristique to (64km) **Mâcon**.

Connections with other routes. Route 19 describes Paray, Route 8 the journey beyond Mazillé to Mâcon.

Route 20 explored the Brionnais and Route 21 the Canal du Centre. Both belong to the **Charolais** (or Charollais), one of the largest *pays* in Burgundy, spreading from the Loire to the Mâconnais to fill the whole SW corner of the department of Saône-et-Loire. It is also one of the most various. The present route via the centre of the region at Charolles runs through two very different but equally characteristic landscapes. Watered by the Arconce, the country to the W is gentle pastureland for the cattle that have made the Charolais famous: a breed with white or creamy hide, short necks and long curving horns, as big and as calm as monumental marble. They fill the fortnightly market in Charolles (as well as the weekly market at St-Christophe-en-Brionnais in Route 20). E of Charolles the *country grows wilder and less fertile, with dark, wooded hills of granite—broken links between the Morvan and the Mâconnais, less severe than the forested heights of the Morvan but without the smiling vineyards of the Mâconnais. They make one of the most exciting, and least visited, landscapes Burgundy has to offer.

N79 runs from **Paray-le-Monial** through the quiet, unremarkable countryside of the western Charolais to (13km) **Charolles** (3050 Charollais; Tourist Information), a town given pleasant waterside scenery—and many bridges—by the Arconce and the Senence and the little Canal du Moulin that links them near their meeting. The market takes place every Wednesday and the cattle market on the second and fourth Wednesday of the month. From the centre, near the 19C pseudo-Romanesque church, the

Rue Baudinot climbs past the Syndicat d'Initiative, in 16C convent buildings which include a handsome courtyard with a gallery. At the top of the hill stood the castle of the counts of Charolais, now marked by the Hôtel de Ville and the two 14–15C towers in the public garden, which commands a fine view of the Charolais hills. The house and studio of the academic sculptor René Davoine (1888–1962), born in Charolles, are now a museum of his work.

N79 continues directly to (53km) Mâcon, but the rolling countryside of the eastern Charolais with its dramatically outcropping hills or *buttes* is much better seen from the *Route Touristique on the little D17 to the N of the main road. D983 branches left from N79 at 6km, and D17 branches right after another 2km. D983 continues to (8km) the quiet little town of **St-Bonnet-de-Joux** (850 people), about 2km S of the château of **Chaumont** (not open), rebuilt in the 19C but keeping its magnificent 17C stables block, set among wooded hills. D17 heads E to meet (3.5km) D79, which turns S under the N79 and past the château of **Corcheval** (not open) to (5km) the village of **Beaubery**. The nearby **Mont des Carges** (561km) commands a wide view over the surrounding hills. A huge monument remembers the Maquis of Beaubery and the Charolais battalion, which together lost 95 members—not all men—between 1943 and 1945. In September 1944 the battalion became the first Resistance group to be incorporated into Lattre de Tassigny's army as a regular unit.

D17 continues E from its junction with N79 to (4km) the little side-road that leads N via the village of (3km) **Suin** and the *Butte de Suin** (593m), with an even better view than the Mont des Carges. **Mazillé**, 13.5km further along D17, has a Romanesque church with Lombardic work on its tall tower. On the other side of the valley stand the buildings of the Carmel de la Paix (1971) by Le Corbusier's follower José Luis Sert. 2km beyond Mazillé D17 joins N79, which continues another 2km to the junction with D980 S of Cluny. Route 8 describes several possible routes to **Mâcon**, of which the least interesting is the N79 itself and the simplest alternative (20km) is the Route Touristique past Berzé-le-Châtel and Berzé-la-Ville.

CHRONOLOGY OF BURGUNDIAN HISTORY

52 BC	Caesar's victory over Vercingetorix at Alesia completes Roman conquest of Gaul
AD c 413	Burgundiones on the Middle Rhine
c 436	Attila the Hun defeats the Burgundiones
c 443	Burgundiones in the Savoie and Vaud: the beginning of Burgundia, the first kingdom
448	St Germanus of Auxerre dies
534	Frankish victory at Autun ends Burgundia
843	Treaty of Verdun divides the Carolingian Empire into Western Francia (France), Eastern Francia (Germany) and Lotharingia, the Middle Kingdom
c 855–859	Girart de Roussillon founds the Vézelay community
910	Cluny founded
1031	Capetian king Henri I makes his brother Robert duke of Burgundy
c 1085	Hugues de Semur begins Cluny III
c 1096	Artaud begins La Madeleine at Vézelay
1098	St Robert of Molesmes founds Cîteaux abbey, joined in 1113 by St Bernard (1090–1153), who leaves to found Clairvaux in 1115
1118	Cistercians found Fontenay
c 1130–1140	Gislebertus at work on Autun cathedral
1164–1170	Thomas à Becket in Burgundy
1361	Philippe de Rouvres, last Capetian duke, dies
1364	Philippe le Hardi, youngest son of Jean II, becomes first Valois duke of Burgundy
1384	Philippe le Hardi inherits Nevers, Franche-Comté and territory in the Low Countries
c 1385	Claus Sluter arrives in Dijon, becomes court sculptor in 1389, dies 1406
1396	Jean sans Peur, future duke, leads crusade against the Turks to defeat at Nicopolis
1404	Jean sans Peur succeeds Philippe le Hardi
1407	Jean arranges the murder of Louis d'Orléans
1419	Jean is murdered at Montereau and succeeded by Philippe le Bon
1420	Treaty of Troyes
1425	Jan van Eyck joins Philippe's household
1429	Philippe founds l'Ordre de la Toison d'Or
1430	Burgundians capture Jeanne d'Arc
1443	Nicolas Rolin founds Hôtel-Dieu at Beaune
1467	Charles le Téméraire succeeds Philippe le Bon
1476	Burgundians defeated at Grandson and Morat
1477	Death of Charles le Téméraire at Nancy ends Valois duchy
1506–1532	Marguerite d'Autriche builds the church at Brou
1513	Swiss, German and Franc-Comtois siege of Dijon
1740	Académie de Dijon founded
1768	Buffon establishes Grande Forge near Montbard
1790	Burgundy divided into the departments of Côte d'Or, Saône-et-Loire, Yonne and Nièvre
1791	Emiland Gauthey's Canal du Centre opens

1836	Schneider brothers buy the foundries at Le Creusot
1840	Viollet-le-Duc begins restoring Vézelay
1851	Paris–Dijon railway line opens
1934	Confrérie des Chevaliers du Tastevin founded
1944	Free French armies of Leclerc and Lattre de Tassigny meet near Châtillon-sur-Seine on 12 September
1960	Général de Gaulle launches the programme of regionalisation which restores the name of Burgundy to the map

Capetian dukes

1031–1075	Robert sans Terre (Lackland) rules as Robert I
1075–1078	Hugues (Hugh) I
1078–1102	Eudes (Odo) I
1102–1142	Hugues II
1142–1162	Eudes II
1162–1192	Hugues III
1192–1218	Eudes III (married Alix de Vergy)
1218–1272	Hugues IV
1272–1306	Robert II
1306–1315	Hugues V
1315–1349	Eudes IV
1349–1361	Philippe de Rouvres

Valois dukes

1364–1404	Philippe le Hardi (the Bold) rules. Born 1342. Married Marguerite de Flandre (died 1405)
1404–1419	Jean sans Peur (the Fearless). Born 1371. Married Marguerite de Bavière (died 1423)
1419–1467	Philippe le Bon (the Good). Born 1396. Married Michèle de Valois (died 1422), Bonne d'Artois (died 1425), Isabelle de Portugal (died 1471)
1467–1477	Charles le Téméraire (the Rash, or Bold). Born 1433. Married Catherine de Valois (died 1446), Isabelle de Bourbon (died 1465), Margaret of York (died 1503)

FURTHER READING

This is not a bibliography but an informal list of suggestions which concentrates as much as possible on works in English.

History. The Valois duchy has attracted more attention than any other aspect. Jan Huizinga's 'The Waning of the Middle Ages' (first published in English in 1924 and many times reprinted by Penguin) remains a classic. Two well-focussed modern introductions are William R. Tyler's 'Dijon and the Valois Dukes of Burgundy' (University of Oklahoma Press, 1971) and Richard Vaughan's 'Valois Burgundy' (Allen Lane, 1975). The latter condenses much of the material in Vaughan's major four-volume 'History of Valois Burgundy': 'Philip the Bold: The Formation of the Burgundian State' (1962); 'John the Fearless: The Growth of Burgundian Power' (1966); 'Philip the Good: The Apogee of Burgundy' (1970); 'Charles the Bold: The Last Valois Duke of Burgundy' (1973). Jacques Darras and Daniel Snowman's 'Beyond the Tunnel of History' (Macmillan, 1990), based on Darras' BBC Reith Lectures, is less than convincing in its description of Valois Burgundy as worthy historical precedent for a multi-cultural Europe of the future. Robert Aldrich provides an informative study of later history in 'Economy and Society in Burgundy since 1850' (Croom Helm and St Martin's Press, 1984).

Architecture and Art. Kenneth John Conant's 'Carolingian and Romanesque Architecture 800 to 1200' (Pelican History of Art, third edition 1973) remains the standard work on Romanesque. Two books which combine handsome illustrations with careful scholarly analysis are Raymond Oursel's 'Bourgogne romane' (Zodiaque, eighth edition 1986), which includes an English condensation of the French text, and Denis Grivot and George Zarnecki's 'Gislebertus: Sculptor of Autun' (Trianon Press and Collins, 1961). Robert Branner's 'Burgundian Gothic Architecture' (A. Zwemmer Ltd, paperback edition 1985) brings a precise eye to a neglected subject, and Virginia Chieffo Raguin's 'Stained Glass in Thirteenth-Century Burgundy' (Princeton University Press, 1982) is a useful specialist study. Kathleen Morand's 'Claus Sluter: Artist at the Court of Burgundy' (Harvey Miller, 1991), another scholarly text enlivened by some excellent photographs, helps fill an important gap in art history.

Wine. Good recent studies include Anthony Hanson's 'Burgundy' (Faber, 1982) and Patrick Delaforce's 'The Country Wines of Burgundy and Beaujolais' (Lennard, 1987).

Travel books. Peter Gunn's 'Burgundy: Landscape with Figures' (Gollancz, 1976) and Ian Dunlop's 'Burgundy' (Hamish Hamilton, 1990) are both above the run of the mill.

Works in French include many specialised guidebooks and studies, like the relevant volumes of two informative series: 'Le Guide des châteaux de France' published by Hermé and 'L'architecture rurale française: corpus des genres, des types et des variants' published by Berger-Levrault. First-rate examples of locally published studies to look out for include 'Patrimoine sidérurgique en Bourgogne du Nord: guide de découverte', issued by the Musée de la Sidérurgie en Bourgogne du Nord and on sale at the Grande Forge, and the history of Flavigny-sur-Ozerain issued by the

Société des Amis de la Cité de Flavigny. Jules Roy makes a personal, not a scholarly, approach to his subject in 'Vézelay ou l'amour fou' (Alban Michel/Champ Vallon, 1990): one can only hope this thoughtful essay will be made available in English. The 'Guide bleu Bourgogne' (Hachette, 1987) is a mine of information.

CALENDAR OF EVENTS

Pride in tradition and delight in celebrating, sampling and selling the region's wine and food give Burgundy an unusually full calendar of events, even by the standards of a nation as sociable and festive as the French. So the list below is not complete. It ignores the weekly shopping markets that enliven many towns, and it notices only the largest of the local *fêtes*, *kermesses* and fireworks displays that punctuate the summer from the Whit Sunday weekend (Pentecôte) onwards. Tourist Information Centres will gladly supply details of these events, as well as the precise dates of the moveable festivals noted below. A useful booklet listing the season's concerts is published by ASSECARM de Bourgogne (l'Association d'Étude pour la Coordination des Activités Régionales Musicales), 41, rue Vannerie, 21000 Dijon (phone 80 67 22 33).

Throughout the year
Charolles: Cattle market on the second and fourth Wednesday of the month in addition to the weekly Wednesday market.
Corbigny: Cattle market on the second Tuesday of the month.
Louhans: Bresse chicken market every Monday morning.
Moulins-Engilbert: Cattle market every Tuesday.
St-Christophe-en-Brionnais: Charolais cattle market every Thursday.

January
La St-Vincent tournante, a festival organised by the Confrérie des Chevaliers du Tastevin and named after the patron saint of the mutual aid societies common in the wine-producing villages of the Côte; it is held in a different town or village each year on the last Saturday of the month.
Bligny-sur-Ouche: Festival of St Sebastian on the Saturday nearest 20 January.

March
Autun: Fair on 1 March.
Auxonne: Carnival procession on the first Sunday.
Chalon-sur-Saône: Carnival.
Nevers: Annual fair.
Plombières-lès-Dijon: Carnival procession in the second fortnight.

March–April
Nuits-St-Georges: Hospices wine auction on the weekend before Palm Sunday.

April
Châtillon-sur-Seine: Spring fair.

May
Mâcon: National French wine fair during the week of 20 May.
Magny-Cours (near Nevers): Motor racing on May Day weekend.
Prenois (near Dijon): Grand Prix de France and Formula One racing.
Semur-en-Auxois: Course de la Bague, traditional horse race, on 31 May.
Tournus: Antiques show in abbey buildings.

May–June
Chalon-sur-Saône: Hot-air ballooning festival at Whitsun.

June
Auxerre: Jazz festival.
Dijon: Été Musical (music festival).
Paray-le-Monial: Sacré-Coeur pilgrimage and festival on the Friday following the Feast of Corpus Christi.
St-Jean-de-Losne: Boating festival in the second fortnight.

July
Chalon-sur-Saône: National festival of street artists.
Clamecy: Water jousting tournament on 14 July.
Vézelay: Pilgrimage and festival of St Mary Magdalen on 22 July.

July–August
Musique en Morvan, choral and orchestral concerts held in Autun and elsewhere.
Ancy-le-Franc: Festival of music, opera and theatre.
Anzy-le-Duc: Music festival.
Autun: 'Il était une fois Augustodunum', historical pageant at the Roman theatre.
La Clayette: 'Le rêve de Marie Jacquet', historical pageant at the château.
Dijon: L'Estivade, summer festival of ballet, film, music and drama.
Mâcon and Flagy: three-week theatre festival.
St-Fargeau: Historical pageant at the château.
Tournus: Concerts in the Abbaye St-Philibert.
Vitteaux: Horse racing.

August
Anost: Fête de la Vielle (hurdy-gurdy) on the weekend after 15 August.
Bouhans (near St-Germain-du-Bois): La Foire de la Balme, a traditional market and fair dating back to 1645 and famous for its horse sale, on the last weekend.
Chagny: Wine fair on the weekend nearest 15 August.
Charolles: International folklore festival (alternate years).
Château-Chinon: Cycling championships on the first Monday.
Clamecy: Andouillette and white wine festival on the first Sunday.
Cluny: Grandes heures de Cluny, a series of concerts.
Pouilly-sur-Loire: Wine fair on 15 August.
St-Gengoux-le-National: Sheep fair on the first Saturday.
St-Honoré-les-Bains: Flower festival at the end of the month.

Saulieu: Charolais cattle festival and exhibition on the weekend following 15 August.
Tannay: Wine festival on 15 August.

September
Alise-Ste-Reine: Pilgrimage, procession and performance of the 'Mystère de Ste Reine' on the first or second Sunday.
Autun: St Ladre (or Lazarus) fair on 1 September.
Dijon: International folklore and wine festival.
Garchizy: Wine harvest festival on the fourth Sunday.
Mâcon: Vine and wine festival on the first Sunday.
Meursault: Banée de Meursault (official proclamation of grape harvest and wine tasting).
Nevers: Music festival at the end of the month.
La Journée des Portes Ouvertes, usually a Sunday near the middle of the month, when Monuments Historiques otherwise closed to the public are open and special events (concerts, audio-visual displays) take place at many of those that are normally open.

October
Chalon-sur-Saône: Festival of photography and film.
Châtillon-sur-Seine: Autumn fair.
Châteauneuf: Festival of St Hubert on the first Sunday.
Devay: Unfermented wine festival on the first Sunday.
Magny-Cours (near Dijon): Charolais calf auction on the fourth Friday.
Paray-le-Monial: Festival of Ste Marguerite-Marie on the Sunday nearest 16 October.
St-Léger-sous-Beuvray: Chestnut fair on the last weekend.

October–November
Dijon: International gastronomy festival.

November
Les Trois Glorieuses, three glorious days, starting on the third Saturday of the month with a gathering of the Confrérie des Chevaliers du Tastevin at Clos de Vougeot château, continuing on the Sunday with an auction of Hospices de Beaune wine near the Hôtel-Dieu in Beaune, and ending on the Monday at Meursault with La Paulée, a banquet at which a literary prize is awarded.
Chablis: Wine festival on the fourth Sunday.
Nuits-St-Georges: Unfermented wine festival near the beginning of the month.
St-Bris-la-Vineuse: Auxerrois wine festival on the Sunday nearest 1 November.

December
Brancion: Noël des Vins, midnight Mass and celebrations on Christmas Eve.
Marcigny: Turkey and goose market on the second Monday.

TOURIST INFORMATION

French Government Tourist Offices abroad
UK: 178 Piccadilly, London W1V OAL, phone 071 491 7622, telex 21902, fax 493 6594

USA, New York: 610 Fifth Avenue, Suite 222, New York, New York 10020, phone 757 1125, telex 0126765, fax 247 6468

USA, Chicago: 645 North Michigan Avenue, Chicago, Illinois 60611, phone 337 6301, telex 0206516, fax 337 6339

USA, Los Angeles: 9454 Wilshire Boulevard, Beverly Hills, Los Angeles, California 90212, phone 271 7838, telex 0194674, fax 276 2835

USA, Dallas: Cedar Maple Plaza, 2305 Cedar Springs Road, Suite 205, Dallas, Texas 75201, phone 720 4010, telex 0791704, fax 720 0250

Canada, Toronto: 1 Dundas Street West, Suite 2405, Box 8, Toronto, Ontario M5G 1Z3, phone 593 4723, telex 0623889, fax 979 7587

Canada, Montreal: 1981 McGill College Avenue, Suite 490, Montreal, Quebec H3A 2W9, phone 288 4264, telex 5267335, fax 845 4868

Australia: BNP Building, 33 Bligh Street, Sydney, New South Wales 2000, phone 2231 5244, telex 20543, fax 715 7062 or 715 7010

For Burgundy as a whole
Comité Régional du Tourisme, Conseil Régional, BP 1602, 21035 Dijon Cédex, phone 80 50 10 20, telex DRTOUR 350984F

For the departments
Côte d'Or Tourisme: Hôtel du Département, BP 1601, 21035 Dijon Cédex, phone 80 63 66 00, telex PREFBOU 350013F, fax 80 30 48 74

Nièvre Tourisme: 3, rue du Sort, 58000 Nevers, phone 86 36 39 80, telex 802 514, fax 86 36 36 63

Saône-et-Loire Tourisme: Maison de la Saône-et-Loire, 389, avenue de Lattre-de-Tassigny, 71000 Mâcon, phone 85 39 47 47, fax 85 38 94 36

Yonne Tourisme: Maison du Tourisme, 1–2, quai de la République, 89000 Auxerre, phone 86 52 26 67, telex 351 860, fax 86 51 68 47

Ain Tourisme (for the Bresse): 34, rue du Général-Delestraint, BP 78, 01002 Bourg-en-Bresse Cédex, phone 74 21 95 00, telex 340 877

Local Tourist Information Centres (Syndicats d'Initiative and Offices du Tourisme)

The first two numbers of the postal code indicate the department: Côte d'Or (21), Niévre (58), Saône-et-Loire (71), Yonne (89), Ain (01), Haute-Marne (52) and Loire (42)

Accolay 89460: Mairie, phone 86 53 56 87

Aignay-le-Duc 21510: (15 June to 15 September) Mairie, phone 80 93 85 03
Aillant-sur-Tholon 89110: Mairie, Boulevard du Levant, phone 86 63 54 17
Ancy-le-Franc 89160: Mairie, phone 86 75 13 21
Appoigny 89380: Mairie, phone 86 53 24 22
Arcy-sur-Cure 89650: Mairie, phone 86 40 91 69
Arnay-le-Duc 21230: (1 May to 15 October) 15, rue St-Jacques, phone 80 90 11 59; Maison des Arts de la Table, phone 80 90 11 59
Autun 71400: 3, avenue Charles-de-Gaulle, phone 85 52 20 34 or 85 86 30 00; (Easter to September) Point i, 5, place du Terrau, phone 85 52 56 03
Auxerre 89000: 1–2, quai de la République, phone 86 52 06 19
Auxonne 21130: Porte de Comté, phone 80 37 34 46
Avallon 89200: 6, rue Bocquillot, phone 86 34 14 19

Baigneux-les-Juifs 21450: (1 July to 30 September) Mairie, phone 80 96 51 27
Beaune 21200: Rue de l'Hôtel-Dieu, phone 80 22 24 51, fax 80 24 06 85; Aire de Beaune-Merceuil on A6, phone 80 21 46 43 or 80 21 46 78
Bléneau 89220: (summer) Mairie, phone 86 74 91 61
Bligny-sur-Ouche 21360: (1 June to 15 September) Place de l'Hôtel-de-Ville, phone 80 20 16 51 or (at Mairie out of season) 80 20 11 21
Bourbon-Lancy 71140: Place d'Aligre, phone 85 89 18 27
Bourg-en-Bresse 01005: Centre Culturel Albert Camus, 6, avenue Alsace-Lorraine, phone 74 22 49 40
Brienon-sur-Armançon 89210: Mairie, phone 86 43 00 77
Buxy 71390: (summer season) Rue des Fossés, phone 85 92 00 16

Cézy 89410: Camping, phone 86 63 17 87
Chablis 89300: 28, rue Auxerroise, phone 86 42 42 22
Chagny 71150: (May to November) 2, rue des Halles, phone 85 87 25 95
Chalon-sur-Saône 71100: Square Chabas, Boulevard de la République, phone 85 48 37 97
La Charité-sur-Loire 58400: (1 July to 30 September) Place Sainte-Croix; (out of season) Mairie, Place de Gaulle; phone 86 70 16 12
Charlieu 42190: Place St-Philibert, phone 77 60 12 42
Charny 89120: Mairie, phone 86 63 63 56
Charolles 71120: Couvent des Clarisses, Rue Baudinot, phone 85 24 05 95
Château-Chinon 58120: (15 June to 15 September) Rue Champlin, phone 86 85 06 58
Châtillon-en-Bazois 58110: Mairie, phone 86 84 14 76
Châtillon-sur-Seine 21400: Place Marmont, BP 78, 21402 Châtillon-sur-Seine Cédex, phone 80 91 13 19
Chauffailles 71170: (15 June to 15 September) Le Château, phone 85 26 07 06
Clamecy 58500: (1 June to 15 September) Rue du Grand-Marché, BP 58, phone 86 27 02 51
La Clayette 71800: (1 May to 15 September) 7, place des Fossés, phone 85 28 16 35
Cluny 71250: 6, rue Mercière, phone 85 59 05 34
Corbigny 58800: Mairie, phone 86 20 02 53; Place de l'Abbaye, phone 86 20 11 98
Cosne-sur-Loire 58200: Place de l'Hôtel-de-Ville, phone 86 28 11 85
Cravant 89460: 9, rue d'Orléans, phone 86 42 23 34

Le Creusot 71200: 1, rue Maréchal-Foch, phone 85 55 02 46; Château de la Verrerie, phone 85 80 14 15
Cuiseaux 71480: (July to September) Hôtel du Commerce, phone 85 72 71 79

Decize 58300: Mairie, phone 86 25 03 23
Digoin 71160: (1 April to 15 October) 8, rue Guilleminot, phone 85 53 00 81; (1 July to 30 September) Place de la Grève, phone 85 88 56 12
Dijon 21000: Place Darcy, BP 1298, 21022 Dijon Cédex, phone 80 43 42 12, telex 350 912, fax 80 30 90 02; Cour d'Honneur, Hôtel de Ville, Place de la Libération, phone 80 67 12 12; 34, rue des Forges, BP 1298, 21022 Dijon Cédex, phone 80 30 35 39, telex 351 444, fax 80 30 90 02; Aire de Dijon-Brognon, A31, phone 80 23 30 00
Donzy 58220: 29, faubourg de Bouhy, phone 86 39 32 49

Épinac 71360: (15 June to 30 September) 17, rue Roger-Salengro, phone 85 82 04 20
Époisses 21460: (1 July to 31 August) Mairie, phone 80 96 44 09

Fixin 21220: Mairie, phone 80 52 45 52
Fontaine-Française 21610: Mairie, phone 80 75 80 16

Gevrey-Chambertin 21220: (1 May to 30 September) Mairie, phone 80 34 30 35
Guérigny: Mairie, phone 86 68 32 91

Is-sur-Tille 21120: (1 July to 30 September) Place de la Résistance, phone 80 95 24 03

Joigny 89300: Gare Routière, Quai Ragobert, BP 52, phone 86 62 11 05

Laignes 21330: Mairie, phone 80 81 43 03
Langres 52200: Place Bel'Air, phone 25 87 67 67
Lormes 58140: Cours du 11-Novembre, phone 86 20 80 60
Louhans 71500: Avenue du 8-Mai-1945, phone 85 75 05 02
Luzy 58170: Mairie, phone 86 30 02 34

Mâcon 71000: 187, rue Carnot, phone 85 39 71 37, telex Maconot 800 762F
Marcigny 71110: 8, rue de Précy, phone 85 25 39 06
Marey-lès-Fussey 21700: (1 May to 30 November) Maison des Hautes-Côtes, phone 80 62 91 29
Matour 71520: Mairie, phone 85 59 70 20
Meursault 21190: (1 July to 31 August) Place de l'Hôtel-de-Ville, phone 80 21 25 90 or (out of season) 80 21 22 62
Migennes 89400: Place Eugène-Laporte, phone 86 80 03 70
Mirebeau-sur-Bèze 21310: Mairie, phone 80 36 71 90
Montbard 21500: Pavillon du Tourisme, Rue Carnot, phone 80 92 03 75
Montceau-les-Mines 71300: Place de l'Hôtel-de-Ville, phone 85 57 38 51
Montsauche 58520: (1 July to 31 August) Mairie, phone 86 84 51 05

Nevers 58000: 31, rue du Rempart, phone 86 59 07 03 or 86 57 35 31
Nolay 21340: (1 July to 31 August) Maison des Halles, Place des Halles, phone 80 21 70 86
Nuits-St-Georges 21700: Rue Sanoys, phone 80 61 22 47

Ouroux-en-Morvan 58230: Place J.-Gautherin, phone 86 78 21 02

Paray-le-Monial 71600: Avenue Jean-Paul II, phone 85 81 10 92
Pontailler-sur-Saône 21270: phone 80 47 80 14
Pougues-les-Eaux 58320: Route de Paris, phone 86 68 85 79
Pouilly-en-Auxois 21320: (15 June to 15 September) Mairie, phone 80 90 74 24
Pouilly-sur-Loire 58150: (10 January to 31 August) Rue Waldeck-Rousseau, phone 86 39 12 55
Prémery 58700: Mairie, phone 86 68 12 40

Quarré-les-Tombes 89160: Mairie, Rue des Écoles, phone 86 32 23 38

Recey-sur-Ource 21290: Mairie, phone 80 81 02 06
Rogny-les-Sept-Écluses (Bléneau 89220): Rue Henri-IV, phone 86 74 52 34
Rouvray 21530: Mairie, phone 80 64 72 61

St-Amand-en-Puisaye 58310: (1 July to 30 August) Square de la Poste, phone 86 39 65 70
St-Étienne-du-Bois 01370: phone 74 30 50 22
St-Fargeau 89170: Maison de la Puisaye, 3, place de la République, phone 86 74 15 72
St-Florentin 89600: 10, rue de la Terrasse, phone 86 35 11 86
St-Gengoux-le-National 71460: (1 April to 30 September) Avenue de la Promenade, phone 85 92 52 05
St-Honoré-les-Bains 58360: Place du Marché, phone 86 30 71 70
St-Jean-de-Losne 21170: (1 May to 30 September) Mairie, Avenue de la Gare-d'Eau, phone 80 29 05 48
St-Pierre-le-Moûtier 58240: (1 July to 31 August) Mairie, phone 86 68 42 09
St-Saulge 58330: Mairie, phone 86 58 30 33
St-Sauveur-en-Puisaye 89520: Mairie, phone 50 45 52 15
St-Seine-l'Abbaye 21440: (1 July to 31 August) Mairie, phone 80 35 01 38 or 80 35 01 64
Santenay-les-Bains 21590: (1 May to 31 October) Avenue des Sources, phone 80 20 63 15
Saulieu 21210: Rue d'Argentine, phone 80 64 00 21
Savigny-lès-Beaune 21420: (1 April to 31 October) Rue Vauchez-Very, phone 80 21 56 15 or 80 21 51 21
Seignelay 89250: Mairie, phone 86 47 72 83
Selongey 21260: 5, place des Halles, phone 80 75 70 41
Semur-en-Auxois 21140: 2, place Gaveau, phone 80 97 05 96
Sennecey-le-Grand 71240: Place de la Mairie, phone 85 44 82 54
Sens 89100: Place Jean-Jaurès, phone 86 65 19 49, telex 800306
Seurre 21250: (1 July to 31 August) Maison Bossuet, Rue Bossuet, phone 80 21 09 11 or (out of season) 80 21 15 92
Sombernon 21540: (1 April to 31 August) Mairie, phone 80 33 44 23

Tannay 58190: Mairie, phone 86 29 84 53
Tonnerre 89700: Place Marguerite-de-Bourgogne, phone 86 55 14 48
Toucy 89130: 20, place des Frères-Genêts, phone 86 44 15 66
Tournus 71700: (1 March to 30 October) 2, place Carnot, phone 85 51 13 10

Venarey-les-Laumes 21150: (1 April to 31 August) 6, avenue Jean-Jaurès, phone 80 96 89 13 or (out of season) 86 49 61 15
Verdun-sur-le-Doubs 71350: (1 June to 30 September) Capitainerie, Place de la Liberté, phone 85 91 87 52

Vermenton 89270: 27, rue du Général-de-Gaulle, phone 86 53 40 76
Vézelay 89450: Rue Saint-Pierre, phone 86 33 23 69
Villeneuve-sur-Yonne 89500: 4 bis, rue Carnot, phone 86 87 36 28
Vitteaux 21350: Mairie, phone 80 49 61 25

ACKNOWLEDGEMENTS

I should like to thank P & O European Ferries and the Comité Régional du Tourisme de Bourgogne for the material assistance they have given me in my travels to and around Burgundy. Mme Hannelore Durix of the Comité Régional took a personal interest in the project which proved invaluable. At every point I was helped by the staff of the Comités Départementaux du Tourisme, local Syndicats d'Initiative, museums, châteaux and archaeological sites who patiently took the time to show me around the properties in their care and answering my questions: the fact that they are too numerous to mention here does not lessen my gratitude. Annette Kelley best knows how much I owe to her support, encouragement and knowledge.

The publishers should like to thank the following for permission to reproduce photographs: James Austin, the Courtauld Institute of Art, A.F. Kersting, Ian Ousby and Caisse Nationale des Monuments Historiques et des Sites.

A NOTE ON BLUE GUIDES

The Blue Guides series began in 1915 when Muirhead Guide-Books Limited published 'Blue Guide London and its Environs'. Finlay and James Muirhead already had extensive experience of guide-book publishing: before the First World War they had been the editors of the English editions of the German Baedekers, and by 1915 they had acquired the copyright of most of the famous 'Red' handbooks from John Murray.

An agreement made with the French publishing house Hachette et Cie in 1917 led to the translation of Muirhead's London Guide, which became the first 'Guide bleu'—Hachette had previously published the blue-covered 'Guides Joanne'. Subsequently, Hachette's 'Guide bleu Paris et ses Environs' was adapted and published in London by Muirhead. The collaboration between the two publishing houses continued until 1933.

In 1931 Ernest Benn took over the Blue Guides, appointing Russell Muirhead, Finlay Muirhead's son, editor in 1934. The Muirheads' connection with Blue Guides ended in 1963 when Stuart Rossiter, who had been working on the Guides since 1954, became house editor, revising and compiling several of the books himself.

The Blue Guides are now published by A & C Black, who acquired Ernest Benn in 1984, so continuing the tradition of guide-book publishing which began in 1826 with 'Black's Economical Tourist of Scotland'. The Blue Guide series continues to grow: there are now almost 50 titles in print with revised editions appearing regularly and many new Blue Guides in preparation.

'Blue Guides' is a registered trade mark.

INDEX TO PEOPLE

INDEX TO PLACES

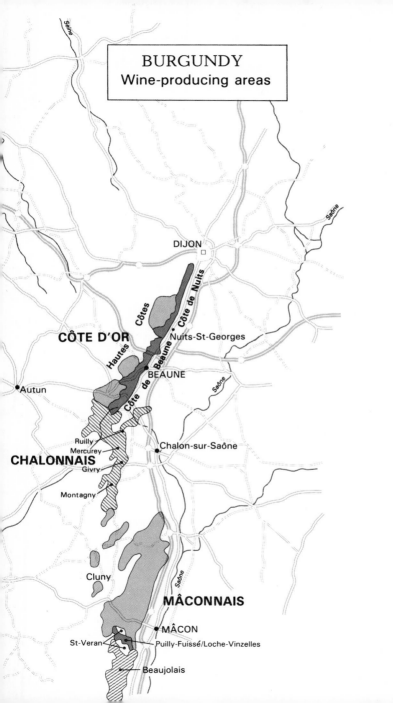

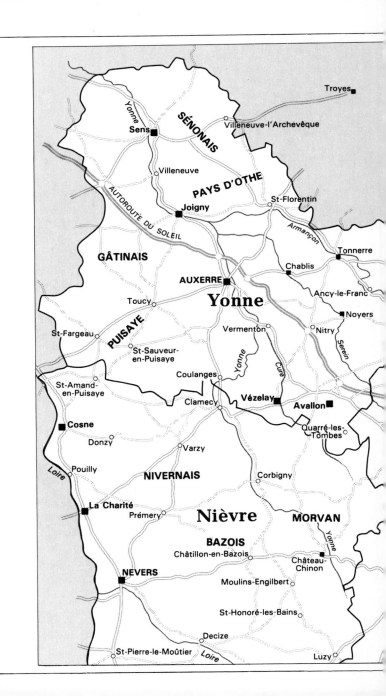

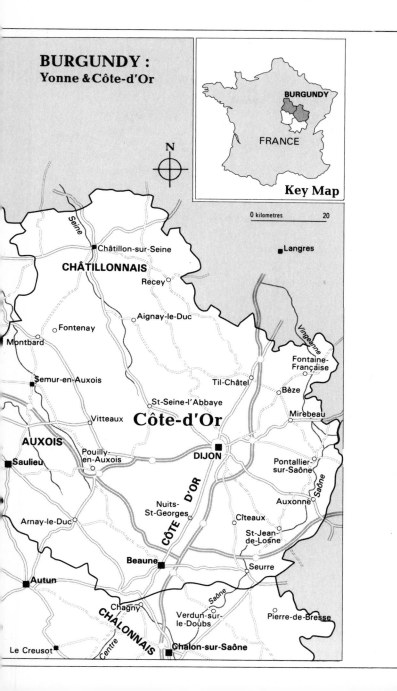

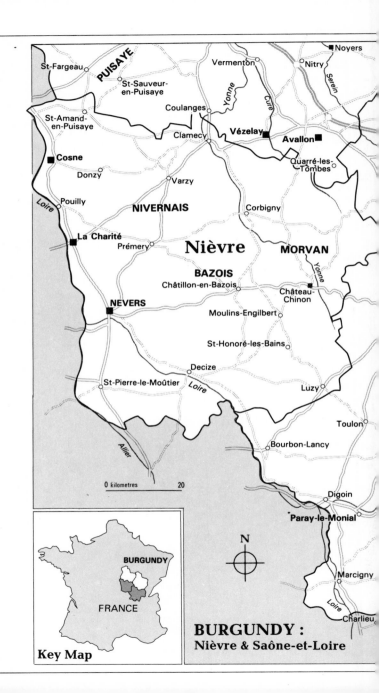

BURGUNDY:
Nièvre & Saône-et-Loire

Key Map

BURGUNDY

FRANCE

N

St-Fargeau
PUISAYE
Vermenton
Nitry
Noyers
St-Sauveur-en-Puisaye
Coulanges
St-Amand-en-Puisaye
Clamecy
Vézelay
Avallon
Cosne
Donzy
Varzy
Quarré-les-Tombes
Pouilly
NIVERNAIS
Corbigny
La Charité
Prémery
Nièvre
MORVAN
BAZOIS
Châtillon-en-Bazois
Château-Chinon
NEVERS
Moulins-Engilbert
St-Honoré-les-Bains
Decize
St-Pierre-le-Moûtier
Luzy
Toulon
Bourbon-Lancy
Digoin
Paray-le-Monial
Marcigny
Charlieu

Loire
Yonne
Cure
Serein
Allier
Yonne

0 kilometres 20

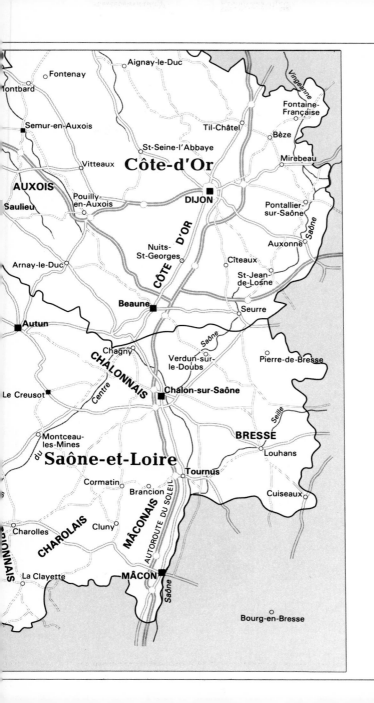